WORK INCENTIVES AND WELFARE PROVISION

For Loni, Mathilde and Albert

Work Incentives and Welfare Provision

The 'pathological' theory of unemployment

DORIS SCHROEDER

Ashgate

Aldershot • Burlington USA • Singapore • Sydney

© Doris Schroeder 2000

Published by
Ashgate Publishing Limited
Gower House
Croft Road
Aldershot
Hampshire GU11 3HR
England

Ashgate Publishing Company
131 Main Street
Burlington
Vermont 05401
USA

Ashgate website: http://www.ashgate.com

British Library Cataloguing in Publication Data
Schroeder, Doris
    Work incentives and welfare provision : the 'pathological'
    theory of unemployment. - (Avebury series in philosophy)
    1. Unemployment 2. Welfare state
    I. Title
    331.1'37

Library of Congress Catalog Card Number: 99-69529

ISBN 0 7546 1207 4

Printed and bound by Athenaeum Press, Ltd.,
Gateshead, Tyne & Wear.

Contents

List of Figures

List of Tables

Acknowledgements

My thanks go to various people in England and Germany.

Most of the research for this book was undertaken at the University of Manchester (Philosophy Department) and the University of Birmingham (Centre for Bioethics) as part of a PhD course. Dr. David Lamb, my supervisor, provided excellent support and brilliant commentary throughout. I am also grateful to Dr. Christopher Cherry whose valuable comments on an earlier draft led to important changes and to Professor David Morton whose criticism was much appreciated.

I would like to thank my husband, Dr. Armin Schmidt, for persevering through all chapters and for making excellent suggestions (never underestimate a physicist).

Alberta Nestler helped me greatly by checking references in German libraries at the last minute. Dr. Angelika Plum and I had inspiring conversations about ecological taxation.

I also acknowledge the permission of the Arts and History Picture Library, London, to include the photo 'Rickshaw Driver in Saigon' by Paul Almasy.

That my parents and my grandmother Loni are very special is already expressed in the dedication.

1 Introduction

In the 1950s and 1960s, enormous hopes were pinned on the welfare state. In Britain, William Beveridge predicted that want, idleness, ignorance, disease and squalor could be defeated forever. In Germany, the economic secretary Ludwig Erhard announced the permanent end of unemployment and related hardships. At the root of this optimism lay the Keynesian belief that governments can actively control economic cycles and thereby prevent the ills of mass unemployment. The welfare state represented an attempt to wed social well-being with economic success; to avoid the social costs of *laisser-faire* capitalism whilst simultaneously reaping its benefits (Mishra, 1984: 6). When the oil crisis of the 1970s developed into a serious recession, the faith into Keynesianism began to wither and the social and the economic started to drift apart. In the 1980s, the New Right movement established itself firmly on the political stage, especially in Britain and the United States, arguing that welfare provision has adverse effects on the economy. The Keynesian bond between economic and social welfare was separated. At the same time, in the late 1980s, another attempt to reconcile social and economic goals failed: soviet-style communism.

The rapid and unexpected demise of communism threw political analysts in the East into a moral vacuum whilst disorienting their colleagues in the West (Gellner, 1996: 7). In this climate, long-standing opponents of the Western welfare state argued that it suffered from 'guilt by association' (Lemke and Marks, 1992: 5). Social democrats were forced into defensive positions because the social market economy was regarded as a subset or soft version of communism (Hutton, 1995: 16). One proponent of this thesis was Nevil Johnson. Commenting on the collapse of communism, he (1991: 27) argued that Western social democrats should stop clinging to 'socialism dressed out as social democracy and stiffened with an egalitarian conception of the welfare state'. He went on to claim that anybody who wants to uphold the ideals of social democracy must be 'either remarkably perverse or

1

simple-minded' (ibid.). In a short period of time, in the early 1990s, all forms of socialism including Western social democracy, the social market economy and the welfare state were pronounced failing or in crisis. Famously, the end of history was announced and more moderately the 'end of the social democratic century' (Dahrendorf, 1992: 136).

The early 1990s were not only characterised by disorientation versus triumphalism in the realm of political philosophy, but also by the recurrence of serious mass unemployment, particularly in Continental Europe. In 1960, Nobel Laureate Gunnar Myrdal (1960: 50) predicted that West Europeans will never again tolerate pre-war unemployment levels. In 1929, at the time of the Great Depression, three million Germans were unemployed (Immisch, 1966: 101). In 1998, the number reached four million.

Together, the collapse of communism and the resurgence of mass unemployment had a strong impact on one particular criticism of the welfare state; the claim that welfare provision creates work disincentives. On the one hand, it was argued that 'the failure to provide incentives is ... a central reason for the failure of the Soviet System' (Stiglitz, 1994: 68). On the other hand, it was alleged that the principal cause for ever increasing social security budgets in the West were work disincentives created by the welfare system (Germanis, 1992: 384, Parker, 1982: 24). According to Yung Chul Park, there can be no doubt that high European unemployment levels are caused mainly by the social security net. He argues that 'despite good intentions, welfare provision ... is not exactly conducive to work incentives' (Park, 1997: 41 - my translation). Hence, proponents of the work incentives argument against the welfare state can point to incentives problems within the Soviet system and high unemployment levels in Europe to allege factual backing for their claim. But can their criticism stand detailed investigation?

The overall objective of this book is to refute or validate the claim that Western-style welfare provision seriously undermines work incentives. Given the findings of eminent economists and political theorists that system collapse in the East occurred partly due to a failure to provide work incentives, it is paramount to identify potential parallels in the West. The communist experiment is as close as social scientists will ever get to test tube-conditions (Novak, 1998: 1). It is therefore important to learn as many lessons as possible from its outcome and to question any elements in the Western system which might be closely related to the Eastern system. Although there are various explanations for the failure of communism (e.g.

huge bureaucracies, economic inefficiencies, epistemic impossibility of economic planning) this book will concentrate on the work incentives argument.

Investigations will be started by introducing the 'work incentives' argument against the Western welfare state in detail and by outlining why it will be referred to as the 'pathological' theory of unemployment. The third chapter will look at the history of work. Can a human universal be identified in the appreciation of work? Has work in the past been regarded as a necessary evil or a fulfilling, integral part of human lives? The fourth chapter will provide the conceptual groundwork for further discussions by defining work incentives in relation to action, intention, coercion and threats. Furthermore, it will detail the so-called narrow and broad views of work incentives. Chapter five will examine the concept of human nature which lies at the bottom of the work incentives argument, namely the depiction of human beings as *Homo economici*. Chapter six rests on relevant empirical findings and looks at benefit fraud, tax evasion and ideological elements in the 'lazy scrounger' debate. The seventh chapter will introduce an alternative to the 'pathological' theory of unemployment in the form of various 'external barrier' explanations. Finally, chapter eight will detail three visionary, but realistic, solutions to unemployment applicable in Western welfare states. To close, a résumé is being provided.

The book is situated within the field of political philosophy, the boundaries of which are briefly explained in chapter five. However, material will also be drawn from economics in line with Philippe van Parijs's (1995: 2) observation that the last two decades saw a 'cross-fertilization of economic theory and political philosophy'. The revival of this approach is seen as a return to the discipline's roots. As Anthony Skillen (1995: 1) observed: 'I can think of no British philosopher until this century... who was not deeply immersed in social and political and economic issues'. In addition, research from the fields of psychology, biological sciences and feminist studies will be brought forward to support the main line of ideas. In my opinion, Ray Monk (1998) is right when he says that philosophy becomes 'intolerably narrow, boring and useless' if it does not engage with other disciplines and this book will try to avoid the insular, the austere and the remote in favour of the relevant, the practical and the interdisciplinary.

Also, following Raymond Plant (1991: 344), questions of political philosophy will be understood as inquiries within particular societies and given sets of values. This book will be restricted to the welfare state debate at the end of the 20th century. Although the main focus will be on Britain, Germany and North-America, the book will deal with the Western welfare state as a whole rather than its particular manifestation in one individual country.

2 The 'Pathological' Theory of Unemployment

'They pretend to pay us and we pretend to work' (Fukuyama, 1992: 11). This is how Soviet workers saw their relationship with communist rulers suggesting that neither did they earn much nor did they work hard. The work incentives argument is pivotal to explanations about the collapse of communism. Economist Joseph Stiglitz (1994: 68) wrote that the 'failure to provide incentives is generally viewed as a central reason for the failure of the Soviet System'. Meinhard Miegel (1991: 17, 20), director at the Institute for Economy and Society in Bonn (*Institut für Wirtschaft und Gesellschaft*) believes that Eastern Europe under communist rule has not been able to foster well motivated and qualified workers. Michael Novak and Alan Greenspan (Novak, 1998: 1) argue that the separation and subsequent re-unification of Germany was 'as near as social scientists ever get to observing a controlled experiment' and that the socialist experiment proved devastating for human capital, including the work ethic. Harold Perkin (1996: 203) claims that Soviet workers put all their effort into 'malingering, absenteeism, alcoholism on the job, and avoiding work by whatever means they could'. According to him, 'a system that pays people to cheat and shirk rather than work constructively ... is a formula for disaster' (ibid.).

Perkin's formulation of the work incentives problem in the Soviet Union sounds reminiscent of the 1990s welfare state debate. Economist Michael Beenstock (1996: 57) argues that 'over-generous provision of unemployment benefit by the state has harmed work incentives and created an unemployment problem'. In Britain, Frank Field (1996: 11) maintains that a 'nation of cheats and liars' is being recruited by the British welfare system. Before leaving office, British Conservatives decided to employ MI5 to target benefit cheats (Norton-Taylor and Hencke, 1997: 1) and the subsequent Labour government launched the first ever anti-fraud website with tips on how to report cheats (May 1999, http://www.dss.gov.uk/hy/bfraud). The problem Frank Field (1996a: 15) sees in the system is that comprehensive welfare provision offers income independent of work which is allegedly attractive to an ever increasing number of criminal fraudsters. He (1996: 15f) states that the British social security budget is exploding at an extraordinary rate; reflected in the fact that a third of the British population relied on means-tested benefits in the mid 1990s.

All over Western Europe, social security budgets have expanded rapidly over the past two decades as has unemployment in many countries. Social protection expenditure as percentage of GDP for the EU was 18.0 in 1970, 24.4 in 1980 and 26.0 in 1991 (Taylor-Gooby, 1996: 117). Explanations are diverse, but they can be classified into two major categories: 'pathological' and 'external barrier' interpretations.

'Pathological' and 'External Barrier' Explanations of Unemployment

The term 'pathological' theory was chosen by Mary Hawkesworth (1992: 390) to characterise Lawrence Mead's explanation for poverty in the United States. Mead's theory alleges that poverty is rooted in character or behaviour problems of the poor themselves. In contrast, an 'external barrier' explanation for poverty would maintain that economic and social factors beyond individual control, such as the unavailability of jobs, cause poverty and deprivation. To clarify this point, Lawrence Mead's standpoint will be summarised briefly.

Mead (1986: ix) claims that the welfare state is in crisis not because of its size, but because of its permissiveness. Income is given as an entitlement without setting any obligations in return, such as working, keeping families together or coping with school (ibid. 9). Mead believes that an inclusive society can only be established and maintained if its citizens function well (ibid. 6). By this, he means that they have to accept a range of social obligations, namely 'the capacities to learn, work, support one's family, and respect the rights of others' (ibid.). A civic society can only be built if people are competent in all these areas. This can be achieved, according to Mead, by introducing an authoritative element into social policy, i.e. by enforcing compliance with social obligations (ibid. 12). Workfare, he believes, is the best means to produce better 'functioning' people (ibid. 1, ix) and reduce the disproportionately high numbers of family break-ups and crime amongst welfare recipients (ibid. 9).

Mead refuses poverty explanations which assume external barriers such as the unavailability of paid work or racial discrimination (ibid. 11). According to him, experts have looked long enough for these external impediments without success (Mead, 1997: 6). It is not the unavailability of jobs which accounts for unemployment but rather difficulties in keeping jobs due to individual pathologies (Mead, 1986: 24). To strengthen this claim, he argues that 10 million illegal immigrants did not have problems in finding jobs in recent years in the United States (ibid. 35). Since the late 1960s, he thinks, functioning difficulties rather than social barriers account for poverty (ibid. 13). However, he does admit that poverty and non-functioning do not always go together. There are 'needy people who function well' and better-off citizens who do not (ibid. 22). But still, in the majority of cases, he maintains, that 'low income and serious behavioral difficulties go together' (ibid.)

Charles Murray, who famously coined the phrase 'underclass' shares Mead's views. He believes that the so-called underclass is not characterised by a level of poverty but by a type of poverty. Reminiscing about his childhood in Iowa, he (1996: 23) writes:

> I was taught by my middle-class parents that there were two kinds of poor people. One class of poor people was never even called 'poor'. I came to understand that they simply lived with low incomes, as my own parents had done when they were young. Then there was another set of poor people, just a handful of them. These poor people didn't just lack money. They were defined by their behaviour. Their homes were littered and unkempt. The men in the family were unable to hold a job for more than a few weeks at a time. Drunkenness was common. The children grew up ill-schooled and ill-behaved and contributed a disproportionate share of the local juvenile delinquents.

The implications from this excerpt are clear. 'Poor' is only a term for those who have serious behavioural problems; the others will eventually work their way out of poverty. Explanations which make the poor themselves responsible for their fate were called 'pathological' theories of poverty by Mary Hawkesworth. If, however, a sufferer of advanced multiple sclerosis was poor because she had spent all her savings on treatment, one would not argue that the 'pathological' theory applies. Instead, one would maintain that the reasons for her poverty were external and beyond her control. Those explanations of poverty belong to what will be called 'external barrier' theories.

Just as explanations for poverty can be grouped into the classifications 'pathological' or 'external barrier', so can theories of unemployment.

The Work Incentives Argument

> The benefits of the welfare state are far too easy to obtain and too attractive to resist. It subsidises irresponsibility and makes a mockery of those citizens who still believe in independence, hard work and self-reliance. The welfare state corrupts us all (Novak, 1996).

> The road to a near-workerless economy is within sight. Whether that road leads to a safe haven or a terrible abyss will depend on how well civilization prepares for the post-market era ... The end of work could spell a death sentence for civilization ... [but it] could also signal the beginning of a great social transformation, a rebirth of the human spirit. The future lies in our hands (Rifkin, 1995: 292f).

The two major positions in the unemployment debate are represented by the above authors. On the one hand, unemployment is interpreted as an individual failure or the consequence of antisocial behaviour under modern welfare provision (the 'pathological' theory of unemployment). On the other hand it is attributed to problems which concern economies as a whole, which cannot be overcome by single individuals (the 'external barrier' theory of unemployment). Proponents of the work incentives argument against the welfare state represent the 'pathology' strain in the discussion. They impute work-shyness, scrounging, malingering and fraud (Cooper, 1997: 7; Sahawe, 1996) to benefit recipients and assume their underlying reasoning to be: 'if you can have the good life anyway, why bother to work and strive?' (Minford, 1992: 117). Social democrats, on the other hand, attribute the rise in social expenditure to external factors such as involuntary unemployment, ageing populations or globalisation.

Radicals in the work incentives debate advance rather extravagant theories. John Hospers (1992: 358), for example, claims that recipients of benefits, including unemployment assistance, are 'moral cannibals' who believe that they have 'a right to live off the "spirit" of other human beings' and who maintain that they have 'a moral claim on the productive capacity, time, and effort expended by others'. Similarly, it is held that the unemployed 'have slaves working for them ... able to exist on the earnings of others' (Govier, 1992: 374). In Britain, Ralph Harris (1995: 174) argues that the social security system allows citizens to 'make some kind of a living out of being poor'.

Accusations such as these are countered by, for example, Alan Deacon (1996: 61) who argues that 'If there are not enough jobs, then talk of work incentives or of the work-shy is both irrelevant and inhumane. To increase incentives while unemployment accelerates upwards is like trying to encourage someone to jump into a swimming pool while the water is drained out'. James Robertson (1986: 85) agrees when he insists that societies which promote the job ethic whilst leaving millions unemployed will 'inflict great damage on those people and themselves'.

The work incentives argument against the welfare state will be at the core of this book. We will seek to substantiate the position of external causation whilst refuting the 'pathology' claims.

3   The History of Work

Underpinning the work incentives debate is a plain and straightforward question: do human beings in general like or dislike work? Is there an anthropological constant regarding the appreciation or refusal of work; a human universal? In the course of history, two conflicting theoretical standpoints have crystallised. On the one hand, work has been seen as a necessary evil, a mere requirement to ensure survival. According to this view, paradise is a place of eternal leisure; work a punishment for the original sin. There is only one incentive to work and that is to avoid starvation and related evils. On the other hand, work has been glorified as a means of *Weltgestaltung* (world forming), a way to 'elementary sensual bliss' through creative production and a means of self-expression and self-fulfilment (Arendt, 1981: 92; 98 - my translation). Given this understanding of work, idleness is seen as creating misery, destitute boredom and the impotence of life without vitality (ibid. 98). Work incentives are abundant according to this philosophy of life (details in the next chapter). The first standpoint will be called the 'necessary evil' position on work; the second the *'Homo Faber'*[1] position.

Both standpoints find expression in the welfare state debate, namely in the dispute about work incentives. Those who regard work as an unpleasant but unavoidable necessity emphasise material incentives for work. In their opinion, incomes available independent of work, e.g. state benefits, will attract huge numbers of idlers. Those who see work as an expression of creativity and productivity regard unemployment and other factors hampering work as a major problem. Instead of condemning benefit recipients as malingerers, they concentrate on external reasons for non-work rather than an intrinsic desire for repose.

This chapter will introduce historical representations of both the 'necessary evil' and the *'Homo Faber'* position by looking at perceptions of work in the Stone Age, Ancient Greece and the Middle Ages and by

10

examining early modern utopian literature, the Protestant work ethic as well as utilitarian, romantic and Marxian positions. In addition, Hannah Arendt's evaluation of the two polarised theories of work will be introduced. Very concise descriptions are regarded as sufficient for the main purpose of this chapter, namely to see whether one of the two major standpoints can claim historical dominance. Before proceeding, the definition of work - as relevant in this book - will be outlined.

Defining Work

How can 'work' be defined? Potential answers to this question are manifold. The Oxford English Dictionary, for example, reserves eleven pages for the task and David Macarov (1982: 12) remarks that 'much hard work has gone into the effort to define ... *work*'. According to Michael Rose (1985: 22), work is understood as a synonym for employment in modern Western societies. Support for this contention can be found from Keith Grint (1991: 9) who claims that, in conventional terms, work implies being employed, i.e. paying social insurance. On the other hand, Hans-Jörg Bullinger (1995: 34 - my translation) delineates a broader definition when claiming that 'work is the conscious and purposeful employment of physical and mental powers to achieve the satisfaction of material and psychological needs and desires'. André Gorz (1983: 77) goes further by arguing that all socially useful activity must be described as work, a view which is supported by Charles Handy (1994: 185), who defines work as useful activity and divides it into four different types: 1) paid work, 2) gift work, 3) home work and 4) study work. Although Handy's definition is seen as the most acceptable of the above, for our present purposes, work will be understood as paid, legal activity.[2] The reason why this operational definition is adequate in the present context is that unpaid work is irrelevant to proponents of the work incentives debate. They see the acceptance of *paid* work to support oneself and one's family as the 'clearest social obligation' (Mead, 1986: 242). Voluntary work does not count as work because it does not enable citizens to provide for themselves, i.e. to fulfil this prime obligation. In order to examine the work incentives debate from within, the identification of work and paid work will be accepted.

The Stone Age

Historians divide the Stone Age into two main parts: the Older Stone Age and the Younger Stone Age (Voelske and Tenbrock, 1970: 1, 4). The basis upon which this distinction rests is work; more precisely, the type of activity undertaken to sustain life. In the Older Stone Age, human beings lived as hunters and gatherers; in the Younger Stone Age they settled down as farmers. Although knowledge about the Older Stone Age is scarce, the present section will concentrate on this period. Our ancestors led the lives of hunters and gatherers for more than 99 per cent of human history (O'Hara, 1993: 150), making it a very important part of human heritage.

How did hunters and gatherers live? What were their daily occupations? And how did they regard work, i.e. the activity which sustained them? The most basic facts known about early human beings are that they lived in caves, used fire for protection, cooking and warmth and believed in life after death. The latter was concluded from the fact that their dead were buried with food, jewellery and weapons, probably for the journey to come (Voelske and Tenbrock, 1970: 3). What is more interesting here, however, is what they did to ensure survival, i.e. what they did as work.

An excellent investigation into work in the Stone Age is Marshall Sahlins's (1974): *Stone Age Economics*. Sahlins not only describes Stone Age activities but also judges them in terms of modern conceptions of work. His research relies on archaeological findings as well as the study of so-called primitive societies which have survived into this century. The Stone Age occupation he sees as equivalent to modern work is the quest for food which he describes as the 'primary productive activity' (ibid. 23). He lists four major jobs connected with food: hunting, the collection of plants, the preparation of food and the repair of weapons (ibid. 15). Sahlins's research and his study of other authors shows that hunters and gatherers worked less than we do. A similar claim is found in *Sociobiology* by Edward Wilson (1975: 572). He maintains that hunter-gatherers spent less time working than modern farmers. Their days were characterised by an abundance of leisure and a considerable amount of sleep which was seen as the main alternative to work (Sahlins, 1974: 14, 19). Sahlins estimates that adults spent about four or five hours each day on the procurement and preparation of food (ibid. 17). For men the figure is estimated lower than for women who were responsible for plant collection and cooking, according to Sahlins (ibid. 35).

He concludes that 'the amount of work (per capita) increases with the evolution of culture, and the amount of leisure decreases' (ibid.). More recent research by Ferdinand Seibt (1990: 79) roughly confirms Sahlins's assessment by estimating that hunters and gatherers spent between two and four hours on activities which could be called work.

But did Stone Age people think in terms of work and leisure? According to Keith Grint (1991: 50), they did not; Stone Age time was not divided between work and recreation and consequently 'work and non-work are not so much merged together as irrelevant terms to describe the activity' of food acquisition. Similarly, David Macarov (1980: 21) and Herbert Heneman (1973: 14) ascertain that early humans made no distinction between work and non-work. Given that the concept of work was probably not known in the Stone Age, it cannot be decided whether early humans detested or appreciated it. However, Sahlins (1974: 18) claims that one group of modern hunter-gatherers, the Arnhem Landers, do 'not consider the task of subsistence onerous'. This is nevertheless too little evidence to justify a major statement about work attitudes. We will therefore proceed to Ancient Greece, a culture which is known in more detail.

Ancient Greece

Plato's position on work is reflected in the *Republic*. Three essential activities are undertaken in the ideal state, according to him. Philosopher kings govern the country; guardians protect it and workers provide for life's essentials. The latter include farmers, builders, weavers, shoemakers, traders, craftsmen etc. Although they provide all necessary goods and services for their fellow countrymen, Plato does not regard their work as honourable. Whilst reflecting on justice, he compares the three essential activities with, what he perceives, as the three elements of the soul (reason, spirit, appetite). Later, he explains that appetite represents the base side of human beings and can be identified with the working class. Thereby, he expresses his disrespect and condescension for work. This attitude is also apparent in *The Laws* where he demands that full citizens must not engage in industry, crafts or trade (847St.).

In *Politics*, Aristotle also excludes peasants, craftsmen and merchants from citizenship and thereby from political influence. He argues that they do not have the time for contemplation; a necessary prerequisite for statesmanship. In addition, he claims that earning a living precludes achieving pure virtue and leading a noble life; two further conditions for statesmanship (1328b/1329a). For him, any work which involves physical effort is slavish and graceless (1258b). Aristotle's attitude towards work within the boundaries of our definition (activity to sustain life) is hence, one of strong disapproval.

Both Plato and Aristotle regarded work as coercive, dishonourable and incompatible with a free life (Walther, 1990: 6). It was carried out by slaves, foreigners, captured enemies and servants whilst wealthy landowners relied on income from their *oikos* (estate). Only two work incentives were recognised in Athens: to avoid the despot's whip or to prevent starvation (Rose, 1985: 28). Paradise, according to Ancient Greek philosophers, implied a life without work; a belief which is reflected in Hesiod's (1978: 2) poetry. In mourning the loss of paradise, a state when mankind lived the easy, idle life of gods, he wrote: 'all goods were theirs... and the fruitful grainland yielded its harvests to them of its own accord'. It can therefore be concluded that work was not valued in Ancient Greece; rather it was straightforwardly rejected as a degrading curse.[3]

The Middle Ages

'Work' as a topic was given more thought in the Middle Ages than in Ancient Greece. Society was divided into three classes: the priests, the warriors and the workers (*oratores, bellatores, laboratores*). Whilst the first two classes were homogenous, the third lacked a clear structure. This stimulated scholastic thought to ponder about the significance of work (Walther, 1990: 11). Since Thomas Aquinas is regarded as 'the greatest Christian philosopher of the Middle Ages' (Lillie, 1955: 107) his reflections on the topic will be summarised briefly.

Following Aristotle, Aquinas devalues all physical work (Walther, 1990: 12). He distinguishes between *vita activa* and *vita contemplativa*, clearly stressing the superiority of the latter. Meditative life in the cloisters or the pious life of begging monks is seen as highly superior to the life of peasants or artisans (ibid. 13). Given the restricted definition of work used here (efforts to sustain life), it is clear that the Thomasian and the ancient Greek attitudes towards work are similar. The spiritual, contemplative life is in much higher regard than productive, working lives. However, there is one major difference between Aristotle and Aquinas. Aquinas uses the term 'work' in a much broader sense. He divides it according to a four-levelled hierarchy consisting of: 1) pure contemplation; 2) asceticism and good deeds; 3) honest work, like Jesus' work as a carpenter, and 4) work to earn a living[4] (*ad victum quaerendum*) (ibid. 12f). This hierarchical view of work broadens the meaning of the concept immensely. It is no longer possible to give a single viewpoint about the acceptance or refusal of work. Pure contemplation is highly desirable[5] and respected, whereas working to survive is still detested.

It therefore seems that Aquinas's position does not illuminate straightforwardly whether general agreement about the value of work existed in the Middle Ages. However, for the scope of this book it is reasonable to concentrate on Aquinas's devaluation of work undertaken to sustain life. This type of work is relevant in the discussion about work disincentives in welfare states. Opponents of the welfare state are concerned with the lack of people's will to earn a living, not with their inability or unwillingness to conduct pure contemplation. Hence, Aquinas's low regard for life-sustaining, non-contemplative work will be seen as relevant for the present project. It can be concluded that despite the broadened concept of work, his views are highly similar to Aristotelian thought. The Middle Ages, as represented by Aquinas, can therefore be grouped with the 'necessary evil' strain of thought.

So far, three historical periods of human life and their respective views of work were introduced. It was seen that Stone Age people most probably did not differentiate between work and non-work. The élitist views of Plato and Aristotle as well as Aquinas showed that Ancient Greece and Christian Middle Ages despised work as a necessary evil. However, at the beginning of the Modern Age, opinions about work were to divide into two main streams of thought.[6] On the one hand, the dominant refusal of work as a demeaning necessity continued. This line of thought can, for example, be observed in early utopian literature. On the other hand, the Protestant work ethic launched by Martin Luther started the glorification of work.

Utopian Literature in the Modern Age

The study of utopian literature can reveal the concept of work present in historical periods. If work is abolished or reduced in an ideal world, its author is likely to support the 'necessary evil' position. This is the case in early utopian writings, such as Thomas More's *Utopia* (1516) and Tommaso Campanella's *Civitas Solis* (1602).

More's utopian state is found by a European sailor on an island far away from the common naval routes and well-protected through a highly inaccessible haven. The state comprises 54 city states organised on a democratic basis. All citizens bear equal rights and duties. The most important duty is the duty to work. It was possible to reduce working time to six hours per day because nobody is exempt and work is shared equally. However, the most unpleasant and heavy work is carried out by slaves. These are either native criminals or people who received the death penalty abroad but accepted to continue their lives as slaves in Utopia. (More, 1981).

Tommaso Campanella's (1960) *Civitas Solis* (City of the Sun) is ruled by an elected priest who stands out because of his superior knowledge and wisdom. Citizens are obliged to work four hours a day and in addition they spend time on learning and studying. Since common ownership is practised in the city, Campanella explicitly addresses Aristotle's concern, that human beings only work for selfish reasons and not for the community.[7] He agrees with Aristotle that human beings have a desire to avoid work. This, however, can be counteracted, according to Campanella, by a strong sense of duty and patriotism, as in the City of the Sun.

Both utopian creations are built on two assumptions, as far as work is concerned. First, work cannot be avoided, it is necessary to sustain life. Second, it is unpleasant and should therefore be distributed equally amongst all citizens, so as to reduce the burden every single individual has to carry. Campanella needs to rely on a high amount of patriotism to secure the willingness to work from his utopian citizens. More's devaluation of work is especially obvious since he uses it as a penalty for criminals. Accordingly, More and Campanella represent the strain of thought at the dawn of the modern age which does not break with tradition. Work is still regarded as an unpleasant but necessary evil. However, a contemporary of More, Martin Luther, expressed a very different opinion.

The Protestant Work Ethic

Martin Luther (1483-1546) was heading towards a career in public services when he suddenly decided to join the cloister of Augustinus eremites in Erfurt. He wished to secure eternal bliss after a frightening incident during a thunderstorm (Tenbrock and Goerlitz, 1966: 142). The cloister was part of a mendicant friars movement set against the worldly, ostentatious, arrogant and indecent influences in the catholic church at the time. After quickly gaining respect amongst colleagues, Luther articulated his revolutionary ideas,[8] some of which dealt with work. In his view, every type of work is a service to God. According to David Macarov (1980: 25), Luther 'endowed work with religious dignity by defining it as a vocation, or a calling, commanded by God'. Able-bodied non-workers were sinners in Luther's eyes. Through him, work received religious and moral connotations (Walther, 1990: 14).

Luther's religious ideas generated enormous response in Europe. Less than ten years after he published his demands for change, whole countries converted to the Lutheran faith including Sweden, Denmark and Norway. Other countries, such as Prussia, Austria, Hungary, the Netherlands and Switzerland were divided on the issue. For the first time in known Western history (sporadic exceptions excluded) work was not seen as a necessary evil but as an ennobling, moral and religious duty.

Victorian Romantics and Utilitarians

The work debate was characterised by an increasing polarisation in the 19th century. In Britain, romantic thinkers such as Thomas Carlyle (1795-1881) and William Morris (1834-1896) praised work unreservedly. In sharp contrast, utilitarians like Jeremy Bentham (1748-1832) and James Mill (1773-1836) comprehended it as a burden and an unpleasant evil.

Romantics on Work

In *Past and Present* (1965), Thomas Carlyle preaches the 'Gospel of Work' without any reservations. It is work and work only which ensures human happiness, fulfilment, blessedness and sacredness, according to him. In the tradition of Luther, Carlyle gives work religious justification and meaning. The extent to which he glorifies work can best be understood by looking at the following quotes.

- The only happiness a brave man ever troubled himself with asking much about was, happiness enough to get his work done... It is, after all, the one unhappiness of a man that he cannot work; that he cannot get his destiny as a man fulfilled (Carlyle, 1965: 161).
- For there is perennial nobleness, and even sacredness in Work ... there is always hope in a man that actually and earnestly works: in Idleness alone is there perpetual despair (ibid. 202).
- Blessed is he who has found his work; let him ask no other blessedness. He has a work, a life-purpose (ibid. 203).
- All work, even cotton-spinning, is noble; work is alone noble (ibid. 158).
- All true Work is sacred; in all true Work, were it but true hand-labour, there is something of divineness. Labour, wide as the Earth, has its summit in Heaven (ibid. 208).

Carlyle's standpoint sounds eccentric and élitist. His own occupation as a poet might have filled him with feelings of pride and blessedness, but it is difficult to imagine child labourers sharing his views. However, he was not the only Victorian who glorified work. His highly romantic attitude was also reflected, for example, in the paintings of Ford Madox Brown (1821-1893), especially in *Work* displayed at Manchester City Art Galleries.

William Morris's notion of work can also be described as romantic, although not to the same extent. In contrast to Carlyle, Morris selects certain types of work and glorifies those rather than work in general. In his utopian novel *News from Nowhere* (1993), he expresses his love of artisan life in the Middle Ages and his hatred of early industrialised England. He detests the disfigurement of the formerly beautiful English countryside by smoking chimneys as well as the mass production of cheap consumer goods. He dreams about country people rediscovering arts, craftsmanship and natural farming in a pastoralised landscape. According to him, industrial production should be abolished and manual work celebrated. In his utopian land of the future, citizens are afraid that work will run out because 'happiness without happy daily work is impossible' (Morris, 1993: 123). Everybody, children included, enjoys work so deeply that the divide between leisure and work is blurred and unimportant. The inhabitants of Nowhere land ask each other: 'fancy people not liking to work! - it's too ridiculous' (ibid. 76).

Morris's utopia is very aesthetic. Work is always pleasant; poverty and ugliness are eradicated; women are beautiful and the sun shines continuously. His ideas are not as naive as they sound, though, and it is necessary to bear in mind that his writings convey a perceptive critique of the prevailing conditions of work. Although his notion of work is very romantic, he differentiates between hard, unpleasant work in a 19th-century factory and artisan work in a carefree society. He does not promote an élitist glorification of all work, as Carlyle did, but he still regards work as an important source of happiness and contentment.

Utilitarians on Work

The opposite view of Carlyle's glorification can be found in the works of utilitarian thinkers who characterise all work as unpleasant. Jeremy Bentham's (1970: 1) *An Introduction to the Principles of Morals and Legislation*, begins with the famous sentences: 'NATURE has placed mankind under the governance of two sovereign masters, *pain* and *pleasure*. It is for them alone to point out what we ought to do, as well as to determine what we shall do'.

In this book, Bentham gives expression to a doctrine of radical hedonism and lists different types of pleasures and pains in order to establish a moral arithmetic enabling people to calculate the utility of actions. What is important in the context of attitudes towards work is the fact that he groups work with pain rather than pleasure. He equates it with toil and fatigue and claims that human beings have an inborn love of ease and an aversion to labour (Bentham, 1962: 204). This attitude is also apparent in his reflections about legal punishments. After examining different possible types of punishment, he concludes that labour is best. He writes (ibid. 439): 'upon examining laborious punishment, we shall find it to possess the properties to be wished for in a ... punishment, in greater perfection ... than any other single punishment'. It is obvious that Bentham sees work as an evil to be avoided. Otherwise he would not promote it as a punishment for criminals. Under Benthamite regulations, work was not only forced upon criminals. Beggars, tramps, vagrants and other poor people could be consigned to workhouses. Workhouses, also called correction houses, were one element of the Elizabethan bills for Poor Relief passed in 1597. City and town authorities could consign the employable to work; 'women to spin, the men to weave, carpenter etc.' (Rowse, 1973: 384) whilst the aged and infirm poor were provided for in almshouses and children received apprenticeships (Himmelfarb, 1997: 5).

James Mill takes a very similar position on work. Despite differences in his expression of utilitarianism, he groups work with pain (Mill, 1975: 125). For him, those 'above solicitude for the means of subsistence ... who, having their time at their own disposal, freed from the necessity of manual labour, subject to no man's authority ... obtain, as a class the greatest sum of human enjoyment' (ibid. 101). However, he makes one reservation and argues that work can maximise pleasure and reduce pain if one thinks of it in terms of deferred gratification (Mazlish, 1975: 125). This means that work can either help to avoid greater pain in the future (e.g. starvation) or compensate for pain with greater pleasure (e.g. enabling workers to buy goods). Overall, Bentham and Mill maintain that human beings have an inborn aversion to work and a genuine and hereditary love of repose.

Marx on Work

Karl Marx (1818-1883) is an important figure in the discussion on work. His criticism of the capitalist class structure focuses on the exploitation and alienation of human labour. However, his ideas on work cannot be grouped straightforwardly into one of the two categories. He neither regards work as an unavoidable evil, nor does he necessarily see it as a source of happiness and fulfilment. To understand Marx's ideas on work it is essential to grasp his distinction between *productive activity* and *labour*.

Productive activity lies at the heart of Marx's ontology. For him, it is the essence of human beings who can both realise their potential and come to know themselves through it. In the tradition of Hegel, Marx understands the world dialectically. He postulates the opposition of *man* and *nature* and sees a mediator in productive activity. Man has no immediate unity or immediate opposition to nature, instead there is a continuing dialogue or mediation to be achieved. By transforming material existing in nature according to their own plans, human beings establish a relationship with nature and realise their potential. 'He [man] develops his productive powers and knows himself in and through his activity and its result' (Arthur, 1986: 5). Therefore productive activity is essential for human beings. It is 'man's fundamental ontological activity' (Oakley, 1984: 190). Marx perceives of productive activity as a necessary and positive good in human lives. Unfortunately specific forms of class organisation prevent people from engaging in productive activity. To contrast productive activity with work under capitalism, Marx calls the latter 'labour'.

Labour is a coerced activity, necessary to achieve material subsistence. Instead of voluntarily engaging in productive activity, the labourer is forced to offer his or her productive capacities as a commodity 'alongside horses, steam and water' (Marx, 1984: 77) to be bought by the capitalist. Labour, that is forced onto people, 'is shunned like the plague' (ibid. 64). The reason lies in the alienation that forced labour creates. Marx's theory of alienation is very complex and involves alienation of different dimensions (Oakley, 1984: 63). For the scope of this book, a simplified explanation will be sufficient. Alienation is mainly caused by the following two features that are typical of the worker / capitalist relationship:

- Modern workers are reduced to a mere attachment of machines and are left with the simplest, most boring and monotonous work. They thereby loose all contact with the products of their labour. They are only responsible for such a tiny part of the production process that they cannot identify with the final product (Marx and Engels, 1981: 53).

- Society is split into two major classes, the property owners and the workers. The material necessities to sustain life force the workers to offer their labour to property owners. As workers, they produce according to plans that are not their own. They create commodities but do not follow their own ideas and inspirations. Instead, they execute the plans of the property owners (Arthur, 1986: 7). Under these circumstances they cannot realise their own potential because a large part of their activities - their labour - is not self-determined. In addition, the end product of their labour is taken away from them, enriching property owners and leaving themselves with a bare minimum to sustain existence.

To paraphrase: work, according to Marx, is the main ontological activity of human beings. It is fulfilling and even essential to human beings' understanding of themselves and nature. Marx calls this type of work 'productive activity'. However, in all known history, mankind has never experienced the benefits of productive activity. The organisation of work in class systems has prevented this from happening. Productive activity must be self-determined. So far, workers have always been exploited by the owners of the means of production and work has been an alienating experience. Marx calls this type of work *labour*. Hence, he takes a third standpoint in the evaluation of work. He falls in line with Bentham and Mill saying that work is a coerced evil, but for him this is not a principal and unavoidable problem. After the abolition of private property, work - as productive activity - could be a source of fulfilment and happiness.

Hannah Arendt on the Two Theories of Work

Historical analysis revealed two main theories of work: the 'necessary evil' approach and what we called the '*Homo Faber*' position. According to Hannah Arendt, attitudes towards work will always be ambiguous because the concept embraces different activities. For her (1981: 17), the active life (*Vita Activa*) comprises three elements: labour, work and action.[9] Labour is the work of our bodies fuelled by the necessity of subsistence. To maintain body and world, daily, repetitive efforts are necessary. By providing the means for consumption, labour has a strong destructive aspect: food, for example, is harvested, prepared and consumed (ibid. 91). The person who undertakes labour is called *Animal laborans* by Arendt; a being driven by its biological life cycle over which it has no control (ibid. 107). In contrast, *Homo Faber*, the workers, are characterised by having control over their actions. Work, according to Arendt (ibid. 127) is creation; it gives humans the power to become nature's masters by transforming natural processes and natural materials according to their wishes. *Homo Faber*'s activities produce goods with endurance which can be shown with pride rather than being consumed immediately, as the products of *Animal laborans* are. Arendt claims that *Homo Faber* is the 'master of his hands' whilst *Animal laborans* is 'not the master of his body' (ibid. 107 - my translation).[10]

Arendt makes use of a distinction which is not only reflected in English ('labour' and 'work') but also in other European languages. Latin differentiates between *laborare* and *facere* or *fabricari*. French distinguishes *travailler* and *ouvrer*, German uses *arbeiten* and *werken*, and Greek πονειν and εργαζεσθαι (Riedel, 1973: 126). Often, the former is being associated with pain, drudgery and misery; the latter with achievement and production.

It would be appealing to conclude that the 'necessary evil' position on work refers to '*laborare*' whilst the glorification of work refers to '*fabricari*'. That way, Arendt's distinction would explain the polarisation in the work debate. However, this would be untenable. Although Arendt's position on *Homo Faber* is indeed positive, she does not equate labour with evil either. She maintains that lasting human happiness can be achieved within the natural cycle of labouring, i.e. exhaustion and regeneration. Once this cycle is broken, either because severe poverty prevents regeneration or wealth obstructs exhaustion, the blessedness of life and vitality is lost (Arendt, 1981: 98). Hence, Arendt not only regards the activities of *Homo Faber* as positive and vital to human life, but also the efforts of *Animal laborans*. Thereby her view, conceptually clarifies a distinction between work as necessity and work as fulfilling creation but also merges both approaches by claiming that together they are indispensable elements of a vital human life.

Whilst various concepts of work can be delineated, none have achieved universal consensus and it is therefore not possible to reveal an anthropological constant in human attitudes towards work by studying historical thought. Both the 'necessary evil' and the '*Homo Faber*' position have enjoyed widespread support in the past. Today, both strains of thought are apparent in the work incentives debate. Those who maintain that humans are characterised by an innate aversion to work, criticise the welfare state for promoting malingering. They explain unemployment in terms of individual pathologies such as idleness and fraud. Opponents of this position insist that unemployment is not caused by weakened work incentives but rather by external barriers to work, like structural unemployment or full-time care commitments. Since the historical analysis could not determine an anthropological constant regarding work, the next chapter will ask: what are human motivations for work? Are pecuniary incentives predominant as the 'necessary evil' view would predict or can other important incentives be revealed?

Notes

[1] The expression was chosen on the model of Hannah Arendt's distinction between *Animal laborans* and *Homo Faber* (more in the last section of this chapter). However, it will neither be used in Arendt's restricted sense nor in the sense Henri Bergson uses it (the making and using of tools as the one differentiating feature

between humans and animals). It will stand for a positive attitude towards work in the broadest possible sense.

2 For the early historic section, work will be defined as an activity which sustains life. This second formulation is necessary to cover societies before the introduction of money or before the abolition of slaves.

3 It has to be born in mind that Plato's and Aristotle's views represent an élitist perspective. As Keith Grint (1991: 16) remarks, we do not know what the great majority of Greeks; the slaves, farmers, traders etc. thought about work.

4 Aquinas's hierarchy of occupations was more intricate than just described. He also subdivided levels. Merchants and shopkeepers were, for example, valued less than farmers, peasants and artisans (Rose, 1985: 28). For the scope of this section, the subdivisions are irrelevant.

5 Pure contemplation was highly desirable in Ancient Greece, but it was not called 'work'.

6 Divisions about the topic were present throughout history. For example, Phokylides from Milet condemned idleness and claimed that only work can give life true meaning (Apelt, 1993: 459). During the Middle Ages a reform movement among monks raised the acceptance of physical work (Walther, 1990: 12). However, these were minority positions that did not dominate contemporary thought. It is therefore considered permissible to locate the ultimate division on the subject at the beginning of the Modern Age.

7 Campanella refers to Aristotle's critique of Plato's advocacy of common ownership in the *Republic*. In *Politics* (1261b), Aristotle claims that common ownership leads inevitably to neglect of property.

8 His main statements were: 1. letters of indulgence do not release people from their sins and do not offer redemption; 2. the pope is not infallible and 3. the catholic councils (documents with instructions and interpretations of the Bible) are not infallible (Tenbrock and Goerlitz, 1966: 145f).

9 The third element from the *vita activa*, action, is not relevant in the present context. It describes political actions as understood within the Greek *polis*; dedicating your life to the *res publica*, the public space.

10 Feminist interpreters of Arendt's work claim that women have traditionally been shut away in the sphere of *Animal laborans* as reproducers whilst men traditionally occupied the realm of *Homo Faber* as fabricators (Dietz, 1991: 241).

4 Action, Intention and Work Incentives

> Few people, in the long run, are likely to work and contrive their utmost if they are to be in no better position ... than the helpless, the lazy or the unlucky (Acton, 1971: 48f).

Work disincentives allegedly caused by welfare policies are at the root of H. B. Acton's predictions about human behaviour. He warns that few people will work in earnest if alternative incomes, such as benefits, are readily available. To fully understand this type of criticism, it is necessary to clarify the concept of incentives. The first section of this chapter will therefore analyse the meanings and relationships of action, intention and incentives. It thereby prepares the conceptual groundwork for the present discussion. The next two sections will contrast opposing understandings of work incentives, the so-called narrow and broad views. It will be seen in the second section that proponents of the work incentives argument against the welfare state accept only one type of incentive: a pecuniary one. They completely disregard other incentives. If indeed income was the only work incentive available, a substitute income from welfare institutions independent of work would be highly desirable for everybody. That this is doubtful will be shown by presenting a broad range of other work incentives in the third section.

The aim of this chapter is threefold. First, to clarify the meaning of incentives. Second, to show that proponents of the work incentives argument have too narrow a view of the topic. Third, to underline this claim by compiling a comprehensive list of non-pecuniary work incentives. It will be seen that the narrow view on work incentives coincides with the 'necessary evil' strain of thought as introduced in the previous chapter. The broad view, on the other hand, carries further the contrasting belief that work is a potential source of happiness and fulfilment rather than an unpleasant necessity.

Action - Intention - Incentives

Incentives are usually understood as stimulants, motivations or impulses for *actions* which might otherwise not take place. According to the Oxford English Dictionary (1989) an incentive is something which has the 'quality of inciting, or arousing to feeling or action'. To fully comprehend the concept, it is useful to proceed from a basic understanding of the term 'action' and then go on to the meanings of intention and incentives.

It is possible to distinguish at least two elements in actions. First, the person who is involved (agent) and second the activity which is undertaken (act). This distinction between agent and act is reflected in linguistic terminology. In traditional syntactical terms, for example, the agent is the subject and the act the predicate of the sentence. Or according to Dionysios Thrax's (200 BC) categorisation of word groups, the agent is represented by a noun and the act by a verb (Digel *et al.*, 1987, Vol. 24: 199).

It is worth staying within linguistic terminology to further clarify the concept 'action'. It was just said that verbs describe acts. However, there are two reservations regarding this rule both of which imply that not all verbal structures express actions. First, the word 'act' is restricted to activities undertaken by human beings or other biological organisms (Kwiatkowski *et al.*, 1985: 176). If a tile falls from a roof during a hurricane, this tile is not acting although its movement is expressed by a verb; to fall. Second, acts in the philosophically interesting understanding of the word require intention and hence introduce a third element into the definition of action. Now there is an *agent* with an *intention* who performs an *act*. The latter definition of action represents the narrow understanding of the word thereby reducing the number of verbs which describe actions again. This point can best be illustrated by contrasting intentional with unintentional actions.

The broad understanding of actions comprehends both intentional and unintentional activities. The latter can be subdivided into behaviour, habits, skills and movements. If somebody sneezes or stumbles, this is usually not intended, and therefore called behaviour rather than action in the narrow sense of the word. Uncontrolled automatic repetitions of actions which are undertaken unconsciously, such as chain smoking, are called habits. Similarly, actions can be described as skills if they have a high element of unconsciousness coupled with an ability evolved from training, such as piano playing. Lastly, movements can be unintentional such as a fall from the top of the stairs (ibid.). The following table summarises the division of actions into intentional and unintentional ones.

Table 4.1   Actions

Intentional actions	**Unintentional actions**
(not classified)	Behaviour
	Habits
	Skills
	Movements

In philosophy, particularly moral philosophy, intentional actions are significant. It makes a major difference in moral ponderings whether somebody knocks over a ladder in order to injure the person standing on it or whether he slipped on a banana skin and tried to grab hold of the nearest object available, the ladder. That is why Bela von Brandenstein (1973: 678), a Neo-Aristotelian, claims that action is characterised by consciousness and willingness. Behaviour, habits, skills and movement are either unconsciously or unwillingly undertaken. Hence Brandenstein's definition equals what was hitherto called the narrow meaning of action. This understanding will be relevant for the remainder of this section. It is now essential to clarify 'intention' which distinguishes between actions in the broad and the narrow sense of the word.

'Intention' derives from Latin *intendere*, meaning to direct mental powers at a specific target (Digel *et al.*, 1987, Vol. 10: 267). It describes the 'action of straining or directing the mind or attention to something' (*Oxford English Dictionary*, 1989). Roget's *Thesaurus* (Kirkpatrick, 1987: 369, 922) groups intention as prospective volition with expectation, will, predetermination, motive, plan and aspiration. If an action is targeted to achieve a certain aim or purpose, this action is said to be intentional, i.e. to have stemmed from an idea or plan developed by a human mind. Imagine a group of people sitting in a room, perhaps an evening class. A man secretly observes a fellow student to whom he is attracted when she suddenly winks with one eye whilst looking in his direction. It will make a major difference to him whether this was an intentional wink or whether she simply blinked because the sun suddenly came through the blinds. Intentional behaviour has a preconceived purpose which might be to signal interest in a person with a wink. Hence, the meaning of intention will be defined as 'having a preconceived idea or plan for action'.

The last step in this section is the addition of 'incentives' to the discussion. So far, the meanings of action and intention were briefly explored leading to the following definition: actions in the narrow sense of the word are consciously and willingly performed acts of human agents with preconceived plans, i.e. intentions, directed to achieve specific goals. At the outset of this section, incentives have been described as stimulants for actions. They are a mental propeller or a driving force to do something (Hügli *et al.*, 1991: 400); in plain words: a potential reason for action or non-action. To illustrate the meaning of incentives, it will be contrasted with threats and coercion.

If incentives are used to promote actions, threats and coercion would be possible alternatives. The Chinese government, for example, wants to dampen further population growth. The 1990 population count revealed that including Tibet but excluding Taiwan, Hongkong and Macao the Chinese population amounted to 1,130,510,638 people; an average of 121 inhabitants per square kilometre[1] (Baratta *et al.*, 1993: 282). The most severe measures that could be taken by the government would be involuntary sterilisations and enforced abortions. This type of action, i.e. coercion, would infringe upon citizen's negative rights. Another set of action could be described as inhibiting positive liberty. This might include threats such as: only the first child will have access to schooling and health care. In contrast to coercion and threats, incentives can achieve a desired result without violating either negative or positive rights. An example would be to grant childless couples the highest possible pensions.

As can be seen from these thoughts about China, coercion, threats and incentives represent three ways to achieve certain goals. The common denominator is that the goal is not intrinsically valued. People, on average, do not want to stop having children. All above measures only come into play because natural motivation is lacking. If 'not having children' was a motive as strong as the urge for water after a long walk through the desert, neither coercion nor threats nor incentives would be necessary. Hence, incentives enter the stage as an alternative to coercion and threats to achieve actions which contravene natural inclinations. However, in contrast to coercion and threats, incentives preserve individual liberty.

How does this view of incentives fit into the previously defined concept of intentional action? A quick reminder of the definition: actions in the narrow sense of the word are consciously and willingly performed acts of human agents with preconceived plans, i.e. intentions, directed to achieve specific goals. Hence, intentional action is directed at a target and undertaken consciously and willingly. It was just seen that external stimulants to trigger action can be coercion, threats and incentives. Since the above definition presupposes willingness, threats and coercion are incompatible with intentional action. This leaves incentives as the only external stimulant to incite a wanted action in a person. If, for example, somebody wanted to stop a friend from smoking, she could promise her a trip to Greenland after three smoke-free months. The friend might have the natural inclination to smoke, but she also wants to see Eskimos on husky sledges rushing over icy hills. The choice is hers, there is no coercion involved. She does not have to give up smoking but there will be a reward if she tries and succeeds. Incentives can therefore be understood as the only external stimulant which can trigger intentional action, i.e. willingly and consciously planned acts.

Before proceeding to two different views on work incentives, one final point must be made. The concept of incentives as uncoerced external stimuli for action implies that the required action contravenes natural motivations. Incentives can be seen as a bribe to achieve goals where natural inclinations are lacking. The mere addition of the word 'incentives' to an activity therefore indicates that the action is unpleasant and does not come naturally. Hence, 'work incentives' declares that work is an activity without intrinsic value which requires external stimulants to be carried out. The following two sections will look at the type of stimulants needed to encourage work from two different perspectives: the narrow and the broad view of work incentives.

Work Incentives - The Narrow View

One basic principle has been implemented in welfare states throughout the West: 'nobody should get from welfare that which he or she could get from working' (Macarov, 1980: 38). This rule has been advocated both in Anglo-Saxon and Continental European countries (Macarov, 1970: 15; Kühl, 1996: 37). According to former German Chancellor Kohl, for example, the application of the above principle is essential for the functioning of society. 'Who works must get more than those who don't', was one of his frequently voiced messages to parliament in 1996 (Kohl, 1996: 2 - my translation). The principle is taken so seriously in Germany that a name was created for it: *Lohnabstandsgebot* (literally: a command to keep a distance to wages). Even the *Deutsche Bundesbank* (1996: 13) is interested in compliance with the rule. They regularly collect income data from low-paid employees and conduct comparisons with the financial situation of benefit claimants. In 1994, one of these surveys found that in rare cases, benefits could exceed earnings but only in families with no income and three children between the age of fourteen and seventeen. Members of the conservative coalition immediately demanded to increase the gap between lower earnings and benefits. Allegedly, the work ethic was at stake (Brower-Rabinowitsch, 1994: 19).

Similar concerns have been voiced in Anglo-Saxon countries. S. Dex (1989: 15) believes that rational individuals cannot be expected to work unless their earnings exceed benefit levels. Support for this claim can be found in Jane Millar's book on the economics of labour supply. According to her (1994: 77), economic theory alleges that individuals will choose not to work if income levels from earnings and benefits were similar. The obvious worry underlying these statements is that people only work if they cannot obtain income from other sources, for example, the benefit system or earn above benefit levels. As soon as benefit levels approach earnings, it is argued that deliberate idleness can be expected (Galbraith, 1962: 241).

At the core of this argument lies the 'necessary evil' assumption regarding work which was introduced in the previous chapter. Work is seen as an 'essentially unpleasant activity' (Fukuyama, 1992: xix) which, alas, is often unavoidable to obtain income. Francis Fukuyama thinks that this approach to work is deeply embedded in Western liberal economics. The individual is seen as a consumer who is not interested in work but highly attracted to spending power. The next chapter will examine the anthropological foundations of this view crystallised in the concept of *Homo economicus*. Currently, however, we are interested in explaining the narrow view of work incentives.

The narrow view of work incentives coincides with the necessary evil strain in the work debate. Demands to maintain or possibly maximise the gap between benefits and earnings rely on the following reasonings. In human history work has been undertaken as a necessity to avoid starvation, finance shelter, pay for clothes etc. This rather obvious assertion aligns with older philosophical thought, such as James Mill's belief that the pain of work is acceptable because it helps to avoid greater pain in the future (e.g. starvation). The modern welfare state, however, provides for basic needs such as food, clothes and shelter, rendering work for subsistence obsolete. The most basic incentive to work has therefore been removed by welfare provision through the state. On the other hand, human beings might wish to obtain income to satisfy desires beyond subsistence. Hence, they work to maximise earnings and thereby spending power. A problem occurs, according to proponents of the work incentives argument, when benefit levels come close to earnings. Then, they argue, it does not make a difference in terms of spending power whether somebody is in or out of work. Since work is a necessary evil and the welfare state removes the 'necessary' from the equation, non-work will be chosen over work. 'If you can have the good life anyway, why bother to work and strive?' (Minford, 1992: 117).

According to this argument, there is only one incentive which can tempt human beings from repose to work: money used either to provide for basic needs or to satisfy desires beyond subsistence. Since basic need provision has already been taken over by the state, money to finance non-subsistence wants is the only work incentive left. It will, however, be removed when benefit levels approach earnings. It is therefore crucial, according to proponents of the work incentives argument, to maintain a significant gap between income from work and income from social services. If not, income available through the state would present too pleasant an alternative to work. Or in the jargon of welfare state critics: the state would provide a 'social hammock' for 'work shy individuals' and 'shirkers' (Muhr, 1994: 57 - my translation). The position which has just been explained will be called 'the narrow view' on work incentives because it acknowledges only one incentive: money.

Work Incentives - The Broad View

This section will introduce the so-called broad view on work incentives which accepts non-pecuniary reasons for work. The presentation will be made under three headings: 1) extrinsic incentives to work; 2) intrinsic incentives to work and 3) general characteristics of work. This division of incentives into three main groups has been made for two reasons. First, it facilitates presenting numerous individual points by arranging them in a certain order. But more importantly, the categorisation is necessary because not all incentives apply to all types of work. Those belonging to the first group are restricted to work that carries a certain regard. This also applies with reservations to the second group, but not at all to the third group.

The presentation will be brief because the main purpose of this section is to show that research exists which validates non-pecuniary work incentives. To this end, a table was compiled mainly by surveying studies on the effects of unemployment and by examining relevant literature from the field of psychology. As psychology lies outside the current field of expertise, research results will be presented rather than advocated. However, even without the relevant technical knowledge in psychology, most of the findings are intuitively accessible.

Table 4.2   Incentives to work

Extrinsic incentives	Intrinsic incentives	General characteristics of work
Prestige, status	Pride of accomplishment	Time-structure
Respect, acceptance	Happiness	Social contact
Power	Self-respect	Purpose
Income	Identity	

Extrinsic Incentives to Work

Extrinsic incentives to work will be understood as reasons for work based on positive external events or reactions. A money transfer from employer to employee at the end of the month is such an external, positive event for the employee. It is also the only work incentive accepted by the narrow view, thereby carrying heavy weight. However, there are other motivations for work than obtaining money, the most important extrinsic of which are: prestige (status), respect (acceptance) and power.

Prestige was singled out by John Kenneth Galbraith (1962: 274) as a highly motivating factor for work. He argues that one offends the advertising man, the business executive, the professor, the poet, the tycoon and the scientist by alleging that their prime motivation for work was pay. Although pay is 'not unimportant... prestige - the respect, regard, and esteem of others - is ... one of the more important sources of satisfaction' (ibid.).

In a psychological study on the motivation to work, Lutz von Rosenstiel (1996: 51f) found three motives which can be categorised as extrinsic: money, prestige and enhanced attractiveness leading to better chances in the 'marriage market'.[2] In *Incentives to Work*, David Macarov (1970: 82f) lists acceptance and recognition by fellow workers as well as attaining a sense of power, both of which can be called extrinsic. The so-called field of occupational psychology which mainly deals with work incentives has established that status is a powerful force behind the decision to work (McLaughlin and Millar and Cooke, 1989: 122). Based on these three studies, prestige (status), respect (acceptance) and power were listed in the above table as non-pecuniary extrinsic incentives. The group was completed by adding income, which is recognised as a work incentive by both the narrow and the broad view.

As was noted earlier, this first group of work incentives, which has been classified as 'extrinsic' does not apply to all types of jobs. Prestige is not associated with plumbing; power is alien to newspaper delivery. It could be claimed by welfare state opponents that the existence of non-pecuniary extrinsic work incentives does not effect their argument. Those who demand a significant gap between earnings and benefit levels, are not suggesting that barristers, professors, consultants, scientists or surgeons will stop to work when benefits reach earnings. Not only do their jobs carry prestige, respect and power but they are also highly paid and income could never be satisfactorily substituted by benefits.

This point will not be refuted here. Extrinsic work incentives have indeed no bearing on the discussion regarding the benefit-earnings gap because prestige, power and respect are not associated with low-paid jobs. And it is the exchange of low-paid jobs for benefits which causes concern to welfare state critics, not the possibility that brain surgeons might decide to try life 'on the dole'. However, the discussion about the benefit-earnings gap does not capture the whole point. It is the underlying reasoning, that work is an essentially unpleasant activity, not just at the borders of poverty, which is of interest to us.

Given the above list of extrinsic work incentives, the general denotation of work as an evil undertaken solely for financial reasons cannot be upheld as universal. For a limited group of employees and employers, work means power, respect and prestige, i.e. providing amenities other than money. The existence of strong non-pecuniary incentives to work also explains why inheritors of wealth or self-made millionaires in the West rarely choose to live idly as David Macarov (1970: 86) pointed out. And similarly it helps to understand the results of a study by Nosow and Form (1970: 145). They found that 80 per cent of interviewed Americans would continue to work if they inherited or won money. It must therefore be concluded that work offers non-pecuniary benefits, even if this claim must, for now, be restricted to specific types of jobs. The next section will introduce work incentives which have a broader scope than those referred to as 'extrinsic'.

Intrinsic Incentives to Work

Extrinsic incentives are characterised by the fact that they cannot be achieved in Robinson Crusoe situations. Lookers-on and team or opposition players are fundamental to the concepts of power, respect and prestige. It would be perfectly reasonable for Robinson Crusoe to feel pride of accomplishment after having built a fishing boat. However, his prestige would not be enhanced even if he had managed to rebuilt the *Titanic*. Pride of accomplishment is an example for an incentive felt from within rather than being acknowledged from outside, which is why these types of incentives will be called 'intrinsic'. The most important intrinsic incentives are happiness, self-respect, identity and the above mentioned pride of accomplishment.

It would be possible to categorise these four incentives into even smaller boxes. Happiness and pride of accomplishment could be called positive side-effects of work whereas *lack* of identity and self-respect could be called negative side-effects of unemployment. This distinction does not further the line of thought in this section but it points out where to look for research findings. Psychological studies on work will be helpful to expand on happiness and pride of accomplishment but it is studies on unemployment that will give crucial information about identity and self-respect.

Let us first consider pride of accomplishment. It is named as a highly enduring work incentive by A. J. Speakman in *Work Study and Incentives* (1951: 12). He claims that every human being possesses instincts of craftsmanship and ambition which lead to initiative and enthusiasm for work and the feeling of satisfaction and pride of accomplishment. It is this sense of pride which runs through William Morris's utopia *News from Nowhere* which was briefly introduced in the previous chapter. In Nowhere Land, citizens only produce superior goods (Morris, 1993: 127); industrial machines are abolished in favour of handicrafts (ibid. 201) and work has become ever more pleasant because people constantly seek to raise the standard of excellence (ibid. 128). It is the aim of every citizen to produce work which is a credit to them and this desire is fuelled by a craving for beauty and a craving for art (ibid. 160). The perception of work as pleasure which is built on pride is one reason why people in Nowhere Land are living in bliss and harmony. According to one of Morris's fictitious characters, 'happiness without happy daily work is impossible' (ibid. 123).

Sigmund Freud (1970: 89; Mazlish, 1975: 62) also connects happiness with work, he even propounds that 'work is indispensable for human happiness', bringing him close to Morris's fiction. More than half a century after Freud's death Mihaly Csikszentmihalyi (1996: 14) draws the same conclusion. The American psychologist from the University of Chicago has been examining the requirements of happiness for over twenty years. In meticulous empirical research he found that work contributes greatly to happiness; not monotonous labouring, but highly concentrated work which ends in, what he calls 'flows', euphoric streams of creative activity. According to Csikszentmihalyi, 'flows' are experienced not only by obsessed scientists and heart surgeons but also by welders, farmers, joiners etc. The flow-like feeling of satisfaction depends on reaching the personal ability limit and not on the regard a job carries in a community. The important factor is to be neither over- nor underchallenged.[3]

A third intrinsic incentive from the above list is self-respect whose meaning is frequently discussed in philosophical literature. John Rawls (1995: 125), for example, suggests that self-respect has two aspects. First, self-respecting people believe that their concept of the good and their plan of life is worth putting into practice. Second, they expect that it lies within their power to execute these plans.[4] Elizabeth Telfer (1995: 107ff) distinguishes estimative self-respect, a favourable and positive opinion of oneself, from conative self-respect which merely expresses the belief that one 'comes up to scratch', i.e. that one attains a minimum standard. What is important in our present discussion of work incentives is the relationship between self-respect and independence. Telfer claims that 'a man with self-respect ... will have the quality of independence' (ibid. 111). The second aspect of Rawls's definition also suggests that independence is an important prerequisite for self-respect. Being dependent often means to be drawn into the life plans of others and having to fit theirs rather than carrying out one's own.

How do self-respect and independence link into the work incentives debate? According to research into unemployment carried out by Graeme Shankland (1980: 29), most able-bodied people without paid work would like to have a job in order to improve upon or 'maintain their independence and self-respect'. Receiving unemployment benefits robs claimants of self-respect, dignity and confidence, according to Paddy Ashdown (Ashdown and Rogers, 1997: 16). A similar view is taken by McLaughlin, Millar and Cooke (1989: 122) whose study of welfare benefits showed that unemployment is not only tedious and boring but also highly stigmatised. This stigmatisation has a demoralising effect upon those who are out of work (Govier, 1992: 375) and leads to a feeling of dependence and loss of self-respect. Employment is associated with independence, the receipt of benefits with dependence; a feeling which is overwhelmingly negative for the majority of unemployed, according to Paul R. Jackson (1994: 115f). In modern-day Western societies, jobs do not only bring income but also self-respect, pride and confidence (Showstack Sassoon, 1987: 169). Hence, self-respect can be categorised as an intrinsic work incentive although only its loss or diminution in periods of unemployment might point to its link with work.

Identity, the last intrinsic work incentive from our above table, is characterised by the same feature as self-respect. It is often taken for granted when present but its lack can be connected with unemployment. In psychology, identity is understood as the establishment and maintenance of a balance between personal individuality and the entirety of role expectations in any given social setting (Kwiatkowski *et al.*, 1985: 195). One of the major social expectations in the post-war West is to hold a job in order to provide for oneself (Mead, 1986: 242). This expectation explains why unemployment can interfere unfavourably with the sense of identity.

Elizabeth Wilson (1977: 177) claims that the ability to provide for a family is seen as an essential part of manhood and thereby a proof of virility. Once a man loses his job he is often confronted with a feeling of lost identity both in his eyes and in the view of his wife. However, lack of identity in periods of non-employment is not an essentially male problem. Studies about women who care for young children or look after dependants show that staying exclusively at home is often associated with low morale and poor mental health (Pascall, 1986: 57). Gillian Pascall tries to explain this by suggesting that the wife / mother / carer identity on its own is not rewarding but often demoralising and stigmatised in our society. Women appreciate having an identity separate from the household and an identity derived from work gives them self-confidence, a feeling of being in touch with the world and a better relationship with their family, according to Sue Sharpe (1986: 57). That work presents people with an identity irrespective of their gender is confirmed by Paul Jackson. He claims that work in general is 'a crucial component of personal identity' (Jackson, 1994: 119).

The establishment and maintenance of personal identity must be counted as a non-pecuniary work incentive. Although balancing social, i.e. external, expectations is a major part of identity, it was grouped with intrinsic rather than extrinsic incentives. Extrinsic incentives can never be present in Robinson Crusoe settings and it is possible to assume that Crusoe had a strong sense of identity despite being stranded on a deserted island.

Since we are interested in identifying non-financial reasons for work, it is worth asking whether our four intrinsic incentives apply to paid work in general. It was argued earlier that extrinsic incentives are only relevant to the upper echelon of highly regarded jobs. This restriction must not be made as strongly for intrinsic incentives. As was just described, 'flows' of happiness linked with work are experienced without reference to social regard. Instead, they occur when the personal ability or performance limit is reached. Similarly, loss or lack of identity and self-respect are related to unemployment in general rather than not being an architect or computer consultant. However, monotonous labouring does not lead to flows of happiness or pride of accomplishment as the above studies claimed. Hence, intrinsic work incentives will be seen as non-pecuniary reasons for work applicable to a large group of jobs and occupations without suggesting that they apply to work in general. The next and final section in this chapter lists work incentives which apply to work in general without reservations.

General Characteristics of Work

One of the most influential studies of unemployment in the post-war period was carried out by Maria Jahoda *et al.* She meticulously researched the impact of job losses on people's lives over a long period of time. The essence of her studies are mirrored in the following extract (Jahoda, 1975: 83 - my translation):

> Whoever observed the tenacity of the working classes to fight for more leisure ... could come to the conclusion that there is at least one gain in the misery of unemployment: unlimited free time. But a closer look shows that this free time is a tragic gift. Dissociated from their work and without contact with the outer world, workers have lost the material and moral possibilities to make use of their time. They, who do not have to hurry anymore, do not make any new beginnings and gradually decline from a regulated existence into unbounded emptiness. When they run back over a section of their free time, nothing comes into their mind which would warrant the effort to talk about it.

This excerpt from Jahoda's research confirms a statement cited earlier which claimed that unemployment is an overwhelmingly negative experience for the majority of those concerned (Jackson, 1994: 115). According to William Robson (1977: 121), unemployment means misery and hardship for individuals and a waste of human resources for society. It even has medical implications. Studies showed a straightforward correlation between rising unemployment and higher levels of mental health problems such as depression and psychotic morbidity (Rifkin, 1995: 195). The majority of those concerned view unemployment as an act of violence, according to Oskar Negt (1995: 7). They feel that it is an attack on their physical and mental integrity; a robbery and expropriation of their abilities which are no longer in demand. They feel as though they are rotting away in a society which stopped them from acting productively. These experiences can lead to severe personality disorders (ibid.). In the long-term unemployed, doctors even observed symptoms similar to those of dying patients (Rifkin, 1995: 195). Since life is strongly associated with work for many people, those who are cut off from employment can manifest clear symptoms of dying. Even the short- and medium-term unemployed experience symptoms that are normally only correlated with the loss of a friend or a relative, namely ill health, chronic lethargy and feelings of despair (Grint, 1991: 41). A study in

West-Yorkshire undertaken in 1983 also revealed a rise in male impotence (Franks, 1999: 139). In a nutshell and with the words of Dennis J. Snower (1994: 41): 'For most people the state of unemployment is far from agreeable; it commonly brings with it illness, family problems, and loss of self-esteem'.

Why does unemployment cause such an amount of misery? Apart from the previously mentioned positive side-effects of employment such as money, prestige, identity etc. it is the more mundane features of work which are missed strongly by unemployed people from all strata of life, namely: time structure, social contact and purpose. The latter will be referred to as general characteristics of work because they do apply to nearly all types of jobs.

Let us first consider time structure. According to Keith Grint (1991: 45), the experience of unemployment usually follows a well-established pattern. After the initial shock has subsided, unemployment is taken as a temporary rest period which enables individuals to reduce stockpiled jobs in the household and other areas. This is followed by an optimistic phase when employment is looked for actively. Optimism, however, is gradually eroded and after approximately six months, fatalism sets in. Unemployment is then seen as a forced way of life rather than a transient stage between jobs. What do people do when they are not looking for employment? Research showed that men do not usually start to share domestic responsibilities with their female partners, neither do they begin moon-lighting or charitable work. One study showed that unemployed of both sexes spend much more time watching television and sleeping compared to previously (Warr, 1985: 165). In general, observations suggest that unemployment robs people of the will to begin any kind of constructive activity (Grint, 1991: 45). Instead, some try to keep up appearances by leaving the house during what they perceive as working hours.[5] This indicates that they cling to out-dated time structures instead of establishing new ones. Others lose all sense of time and despite abundant leisure are often unpunctual for job interviews. The above findings show that structures taken for granted by those in work are destroyed through unemployment: 'structures of time, routine ... and social networks' (ibid.).

This leads to the second general characteristic of work which might be lost due to non-work: social contact. Peter Warr (1985: 165) sees two reasons why interpersonal contacts are significantly reduced in periods of unemployment. First, if there is no work place to go to, there are no colleagues to meet during working hours. Second, unemployment often leads to lack of money and a need to reduce social events (pub, tennis, parties etc.) for financial reasons. The decrease of social contacts is not only experienced by individuals who are made redundant during their working lives. Studies about compulsory retirement also showed that those concerned regard it as a form of 'social banishment' (Shankland, 1980: 48), excluding them from highly appreciated socialising at work. The previously mentioned field of occupational psychology identified four major non-financial incentives to work: social contact, purpose, status and the satisfying deployment of skills (McLaughlin and Millar and Cooke, 1989: 122). Status has been categorised as an extrinsic incentive. The satisfying deployment of skills can be strongly associated with pride of accomplishment, an intrinsic incentive. This leaves social contact, which has just been described and purpose as general characteristics of work.

We will now turn to 'purpose' as an incentive to work and the last in our category 'general characteristics of work'. A very strong proponent of the claim that work and purpose are linked was Thomas Carlyle. He (1965: 203) believed that people who found work found blessedness and a life-purpose. It has to be said, though, that Carlyle tended to exaggerate the blessings of work. It is therefore necessary to look at contemporary authors who express a similar opinion. Charles Handy (1985: xii), for example, sees a strong link between purpose and work. However, he does not believe that this link is embedded in human nature, rather it stems from the fact that modern Western societies are employment societies, i.e. wealth is generated and distributed through jobs. He describes work in employment societies as the 'financial and the social lynchpin of most people's lives and ... the source of much of the meaning of their existence' (ibid.). If individuals are made redundant in this type of society their purpose of life is being called into question, according to Handy.

The best source for studies on the relationship between work and life-purpose are feminist publications. According to Daniel Rogers (1978: 209), the feminist movements of the 19th and 20th century equated idleness with constriction, work with purpose and paid work with freedom. They demanded engagement in work to escape suffocation, play a part in society and give purpose to life (ibid. 196). A feminist case study unfolded when Eastern Germany was united with the Federal Republic in 1990. In 1989, 90 per cent of East German women were in paid work. Four years later, nearly a third had lost their jobs. By imposing the West German system onto the East, most mothers found it impossible to juggle careers and children. Part-time work is not freely available, schools finish at 1pm and most nurseries do not accept children under three. Although some mothers were pleased to stay at home, most 'were embittered by the loss of purpose and income' (Fisher, 1995: 160).

The above studies on unemployment established a link between work on the one hand and purpose, time structure and social contact on the other hand. None of the studies made reservations about the types of jobs which have been lost. It will therefore be suggested that redundancy in general can lead to loss of purpose, time structure and socialising. This is why the present section was called 'general characteristics of work'. Although it might be very hard to believe that mundane, boring or dirty jobs have any sort of attraction, research did indeed show that they are often preferred to unemployment. The majority of unemployed feel that stigma, purposeless-ness and boredom outweigh any gain in leisure, according to a study by McLaughlin, Millar and Cooke (1989: 122). 50 per cent of those questioned by McLaughlin and his colleagues said that they would even prefer employment if they could secure a higher income from social security. This is an extraordinary finding given that more money from the state would normally imply a higher standard of living and possibly a quicker recovery from debt. Similarly, Paul Jackson's (1994: 115) research shows that employment in general not only in specific jobs represents an important part of adult life in our society.

The previous three sub-sections described the broad view of work incentives to illustrate that benefits are not compensating for everything which is missing from a life without employment. The good life in modern employment society cannot be equated with subsistence on state benefits. Apart from income, employment provides contact, purpose, and time-structure. Often, it is the basis for self-respect, pride of accomplishment, happiness, and identity and in some cases ensures prestige, respect, and power. In contrast to the 'lazy scrounger' typology which paints the picture of a carefree malingerer with plenty of agreeable leisure pursuits, studies on the effects of unemployment reveal a disquieting intensity of misery, hardship, illness, boredom, and unhappiness.

Accordingly, the claim that work will be replaced by benefits at every opportunity must be considered doubtful.

Notes

[1]   In comparison, Russia counted 9 inhabitants per km^2, Great Britain 238, India 263, Japan 329 and the Netherlands 359 in the early 1990s (Baratta *et al.*, 1993: 575; 426; 442; 459; 535).

[2]   Some of the work incentives found in the surveyed literature were not listed in the table. It was considered sensible to include only those which were mentioned in several studies to avoid the inclusion of obscurities or minor points.

[3]   Although happiness is a very general term under which the other identified incentives (identity, self-respect, pride of accomplishment) could be subsumed, it was listed separately; mostly because Freud and Csikszentmihaly used it rather than one of the others and because its connotations are more extensive than those associated with identity, self-respect and pride.

[4]   The concept of self-respect is disputed in philosophy. In contrast to Rawls, Michele M. Moody-Adams (1995: 275) defines self-respect more generally as a sense of one's own worth whilst subsuming those aspects which Rawls concentrated on, in her words 'confidence in one's life plan', as self-esteem. A detailed investigation of the term can be found in Robin S. Dillon (1995) (ed.); *Dignity, Character and Self-Respect*, Routledge, London. I prefer Moody-Adams's distinction because it allows for self-respect in situations of total dependency (e.g. advanced old age) where the belief in one's abilities to carry out life plans might be completely lost. According to her definition, self-esteem not self-respect would be at risk.

[5]   This act of despair was well presented in the most successful British film to date: *The Full Monty* (1997). Gerard, who formerly worked as a supervisor in a Sheffield steel company could not bear to tell his wife about his redundancy. Instead, he set off every morning with his briefcase as though nothing had happened and spent the day sitting on various park benches distributed all over picturesque Sheffield. Only when bailiffs moved in on his house to the utter astonishment of his wife, did he tell her the truth ... She left him.

5   *Homo Economicus*

Proponents of the narrow view of work incentives who criticise the welfare state for allegedly supporting malingering and scrounging often rest their case on a particular concept of human nature, namely *Homo economicus*. They argue that one feature derived from this concept is an innate aversion to work (Macarov, 1970: 88). This chapter will investigate the relevance of human nature studies for political philosophy and then introduce the mainstream economists' view of human nature (*Homo economicus*). It will be examined what exactly are the main features of *Homo economicus* and whether they are acceptable as a general depiction of human beings. In the course of this analysis research from the areas of feminist economics and sociobiology as well as earlier philosophy will be brought forward to question the concept. The aim of this chapter is to criticise the work incentives argument by showing that it is not built on solid foundations.

Political Philosophy and the Study of Human Nature

Homo economicus is a concept relevant to different fields in the arts and social sciences. In order to uncover its basic assumptions it is useful to examine the relationship between political philosophy and the study of human nature first. Political philosophy is a subdiscipline of philosophy which centres around three major questions: 1) the authority question: why should one have a government rather than anarchy? 2) the design question: which type of government should one have? and 3) the legitimacy question: which policies should the government pursue? (Kwiatkowski *et al.*, 1985: 399). To clarify the idea behind each question, they will be illustrated with an example.

Authority: how can the establishment of a government be justified at all? Why not have anarchy? Where do governments get their authority from?

Jean-Jacques Rousseau (1712-1778) outlined a theory of human nature proceeding from a so-called natural state (*état de nature*) to life in a society. According to him, human beings are intrinsically good whilst they are in the natural state. They do not exhibit any feeling of selfishness (*l'amour-propre*) and peace and innocence reign (Rousseau, 1983: 167, 169, 287). However, there comes a time when the first person encloses a piece of land and says: '*Ceci est à moi*', and thereby founds civil society (ibid. 190). Selfishness starts to grow, building the foundation stone of the new order and rendering human evil possible. Once civil society has been established a return to the natural state and its peace is not possible (ibid. 287). Instead, it is necessary to find a way of organising society so that individuals can live in freedom and harmony with each other. The way forward is the creation of a state that is built on the basis of a social contract (*contrat social*). Citizens declare freely that they want to join this state and thereby subordinate their individual wills under a common will (*volonté général*). Rousseau believes that a state formed according to this principle can guarantee freedom and harmony for its citizen, the next best solution to the natural state that is irrevocably lost. Hence, according to Rousseau, the existence of a state as opposed to anarchy can be justified by the irrevocable loss of the natural state which leaves only one alternative to re-establish freedom and harmony: a created state.

Design: which types of governments should be chosen? In the *Republic*, Plato names six possibilities: democracy, tyranny, oligarchy and three varieties of aristocracy, the Cretan, the Laconian and the philosopher king's. To find arguments for and against individual types of governments is the task of the design side of political philosophy. Plato chose the philosopher king's aristocracy as the most merited form of government. He claims that the only way to preclude harm and reach happiness ($\varepsilon\upsilon\delta\alpha\iota\mu o\nu\iota\alpha$) for human kind is to entrust government to philosopher kings. Because of their wisdom and their ability to see the truth, they were the only people to whom governing was due. The philosopher king's aristocracy is therefore the best possible type of government, according to Plato.

Legitimacy: 20th-century political philosophy has mainly concentrated on the legitimacy question: Which policies should governments pursue? Robert Nozick and John Rawls, for example, take two different standpoints on the policy of redistribution. Nozick argues that only the minimal state restricted to the 'functions of protection against force, theft, fraud, enforcement of contracts' etc. (1974: ix) is legitimate. Any more extensive state, which, for example, includes redistributive welfare measures, violates citizen's rights (ibid. 149). In contrast, Rawls supports redistribution to satisfy his second principle of justice, namely that income, wealth and opportunities must be distributed equally unless deviations from equality benefit the least advantaged group in society (1972: 11).

These three traditional questions from the field of political philosophy were in the past intimately connected with the study of human nature. Aristotelian philosophy, for example, is characterised by attempts to uncover not only the nature of human beings but the nature of all things. He equated the essence of objects with their purpose, their *telos*. The *telos* of a knife, to give an example, is that it cuts, not that it can also be used to measure baking powder. The *telos* of human beings, their essence, is to live in the polis, since humans are essentially political animals (Aristotle, 1981: 4).[1] As can be seen from this example the study of human nature led Aristotle to answer the first of the three major questions in political philosophy: why not have anarchy? How can the authority of governments be justified? If, as Aristotle believes, it is the essence of human beings to be political, the establishment of a *polis*, a state, a government, is unavoidable. It would not make sense to have knifes which are not allowed to cut. In the same way it does not make sense to deprive human beings of political activity, which is their *telos*, according to Aristotle.

A second example of how the study of human nature is intimately intertwined with political philosophy comes from Thomas Hobbes's *Leviathan* (1588-1679). Hobbes's ambition as a political philosopher was to arrive at a scientific account of human nature in order to design the most appropriate political system (Plant, 1991: 38). He concluded that human beings are driven by two forces: the instinct for self-preservation (*conservatio sui*) and the desire for power (*potentia*). Given these natural tendencies, a war of all against all comes to pass. The only way to come to terms with those aggressively self-seeking creatures, called humans, is to rule them by force. Since the instinct for self-preservation in humans supersedes all other drives, including the desire for power, they are prepared to relinquish individual powers to a central government (sovereign) which they all fear and which protects them from each other. This is the basic idea behind Hobbes's political philosophy and it is also his answer to the authority question in political philosophy. Government is justified to prevent a war of all against all. As Aristotle's answer to the authority question, Hobbes's conclusions in the field of political philosophy are based on his account of human nature.

The above two examples show that the study of human nature was of great importance in philosophical thought in the past. But is this still the case? Yes it is, according to Christopher Berry and Isaiah Berlin. Berry claims that it is possible to find an account of human nature at the bottom of *all* political arguments. He (1986: 28) writes: 'if political disputes and arguments are analysed then certain assumptions about human nature will be uncovered'. Berlin (1986: 39) supports this claim by arguing: 'the ideas of every philosopher concerned with human affairs in the end rests on his conception of what man is and can be'. If Berry and Berlin are right, then it should be possible to unveil and analyse assumptions about human nature that are made by libertarians and conservatives in the welfare state discussion.

However, not all modern philosophers agree with Berlin and Berry on the relevance of human nature studies to political philosophy. Although Aristotle and Hobbes relied heavily on their perceptions of human nature when dealing with problems of political philosophy, this approach can be very contentious. Although it is beyond the scope of this book to explore the relevant criticism in depth, two major objections will be summarised, namely 'Hume's fork' and Sartre's existentialist thought. 'Hume's fork' is topical because it allows the study of human nature but prohibits moral conclusions for the field of political philosophy. Sartre's approach is important because he denies the study of human nature any relevance at all.

'Hume's Fork'

David Hume (1711-76) was the first philosopher who explained what became known as the principle of 'why *ought* cannot be derived from *is*' also called 'Hume's fork'. What does this principle entail? Hume made a clear distinction between empirical facts and normative statements and postulated that the latter can never be derived from the former. It is not possible to analyse empirical facts and come to moral conclusions, according to him (1978: 469).

> In every system of morality, which I have hitherto met with, I have always remark'd, that the author proceeds for some time in the ordinary way of reasoning, and establishes the being of a God or makes observations concerning human affairs; when of a sudden I am surpriz'd to find, that instead of the usual copulations of propositions, *is*, and *is not*, I meet with no proposition that is not connected with an *ought*, or an *ought not*. This change is imperceptible; but is, however, of the last consequence.

It is this unexplained, imperceptible change from 'is' to 'ought' which Hume deplores in moral systems. To say what *is* the case and to say what *ought to be* the case are two unrelated things. On the one hand, empirical facts do not contain normative statements, otherwise they would not be purely empirical. On the other hand, if there are no normative elements in the facts, they cannot suddenly surface in the conclusions because a conclusion is only valid if all necessary information is present in the premises. Raymond Plant (1991: 11) explains 'Hume's fork' as follows:

> ['Hume's fork' is] the principle that 'ought' cannot be derived from an 'is'. That is to say it articulates the principle that there can be nothing in the conclusion of a valid argument which is not already present in the premises. If we draw an evaluative conclusion then either the premises contain evaluative elements, in which case they are not verifiable, or the inference cannot go through if the premises do not contain normative elements.

To see why 'Hume's fork' presents a very serious problem for traditional political philosophy, the following syllogism is useful:

Premise 1: Self-preservation (sp) and the desire for power (dp) are basic human drives.

Premise 2: Humans whose basic drives are sp and dp will cause a war of all against all.

Premise 3: Governments can suppress sp and dp to enforce peace.

Conclusion: Governments should establish peace.

This is basically the Hobbesian justification for government which was introduced at the outset of this chapter. If put into a classical syllogism (admittedly a rather awkward one), it is apparent that it neither meets the requirement for validity, i.e. the conclusion must only include information present in the premises, nor for tenability, i.e. the premises must be proven to be true. The jump from 'governments *can* establish peace' to 'governments *should* establish peace' happens in between the premises and the conclusion, i.e. the syllogism is not valid. In addition, the contents of the premises are contentious and not open to empirical verification. Whether human beings are only, or even uppermost, driven by just two forces has not been proven and might never be. It is equally impossible to prove empirically that a war of all against all is the natural state of human kind, as it is impossible to prove that governments can always prevent this war. This means that the syllogism is also untenable. Hobbes's approach to combine the study of human nature with political philosophy must therefore be rejected if one accepts 'Hume's fork'.

What can be gained from Hume's thoughts? According to him, normative conclusions can never be drawn from empirical premises. This means that the empirical study of human nature (given it were uncontentiously possible) could still not lead to prescriptions for government. All three cornerstones of political philosophy are suspended in the normative realm and they must be held separate from empirical findings. If, for example, medical scientists came up with a drug that removed all war-creating aggression from human beings and if at the same time a survey established that no human being *wanted* war, this find would still not justify the drug's application, according to 'Hume's fork'. That it *is* possible to avoid war does not conclusively imply that war *should* be avoided. Hence, if one fully supports 'Hume's fork' and its implications, one cannot use the study of human nature to arrive at political prescriptions.

Sartre: Existence Precedes Essence

A second, very different, argument against the study of human nature to facilitate political philosophy is developed by Sartre. He supports the 'Blank Paper view' as far as human nature is concerned. He claims that human beings are born without any predetermined nature. Firstly they exist and only later do they acquire characteristics on an individual and subjective basis. As he (1991: 34) puts it:

> Man first of all exists, encounters himself, surges up in the world - and defines himself afterwards. If man as the existentialist sees him is not definable, it is because to begin with he is nothing. He will not be anything until later, and then he will be what he makes of himself ... Man simply is.

Sartre's 'Blank Paper view' towards human nature rests on his radical concept of freedom. For him, human beings are condemned to freedom. He rejects any determinism and claims that traditions, norms, human nature or society cannot be held responsible for individual choices and the outcome of individual lives. Rather than being determined by their past, circumstances or biological heritage, humans are under constant pressure to choose who they want to be in the future. Choices are made with reference to an open future, not a closed past. His (1978: 15 - my translation) comments on Charles Baudelaire (1821-1867), the author of *Les fleurs du mal*, show his strict and pitiless rejection of determinism:

> 'He did not have the life he deserved'. This comforting dictum seems to illustrate Baudelaire's life excellently. Of course, he did not deserve this mother,[2] these constant financial worries, this family council[3] this greedy lover and this syphilis. And what is unfairer than his early death? On reflection, however, doubts surface: Baudelaire, the human being, is not without faults and neither without contradictions, or so it seems. This pervert adopted the most banal and strict moral beliefs; this refined hedonist associated with the most wretched prostitutes ... Is he so different from the existence he led? What if, in contrast to popular belief, humans never had a life they didn't deserve?

According to Sartre, there is no precious substance within human beings which can be forced into a life they do not deserve. People are what they make of themselves. In a 1967 interview with *Playboy* magazine, he (1985: 133) conceded that fate gives humans a predictable future. The son of a farmer, for example, is forced by society to leave his home and earn his living in a factory in the city. This is the future others have carved out for him; a future which seems to be predestined. However, it is possible to escape this future, to fight against it and to change it, according to Sartre (ibid. 134). This claim and Sartre's reasonings on Baudelaire illustrate his belief that human nature (amongst others) is no deterministic factor in human lives. If one takes this existentialist view of life, human beings are solely the result of their choices, they do not have any instincts. The study of human nature is therefore a waste of time; there is nothing to be studied.[4]

The approach to human nature studies taken in this book 'Hume's fork' and Sartre's existentialist position were introduced because they are the two major criticisms against linking human nature studies with political philosophy. The difficulties raised are acknowledged but a different position will be taken here. The aim of this book is to analyse the concern that welfare provision causes major work disincentives. Proponents of this argument base their claims on assertions about human nature, especially an allegedly inborn desire for repose. Thereby, they observe neither Hume's nor Sartre's prescriptions. First, they make essentialist statements about human nature and hence do not support the 'Blank Paper view'. Second, they draw normative conclusions (stop welfare payments) from allegedly empirical evidence (human instinct to avoid work). It is therefore necessary to look into human nature studies to meet proponents of the work incentives argument on their own ground. However, the approach to draw normative conclusions from empirical evidence will not be endorsed here. Instead, a more modest approach supported by Christopher Berry will be taken.

Berry (1986: 49, 132) postulates the following: politics (including the study of the welfare state) cannot be treated as a pure and descriptive science. Even if one only compares government systems or studies technical administrative issues, there always lurks the question: which ends should be attained with which administration or which policy? Ends imply values and these in turn are based on human aims and purposes (ibid. 132), whether they only apply in a cultural setting or whether they are claimed to be essentialist. Berry does not assert that the study of human nature can find the essence of humankind and end political dispute. That would be expecting too much from human nature studies. However, he argues that it can be 'used with profit diagnostically to see what makes a political theory 'tick' (ibid. 140). This is exactly what it will be used for here. What makes the theory of *Homo economicus* tick? This question will be examined in the main part of this chapter. The study of human nature will not be used to design the perfect government, as Hobbes set out to do, but to analyse and potentially criticise political philosophy which is based on human nature studies, namely political claims which are based on the concept of *Homo economicus*.

Homo economicus - A Profile

Homo economicus is the abstraction of human nature devised by mainstream economics to assist in theory formation. To identify his[5] individual features, it is helpful to examine basic assumptions built into the definition of economics first. The following three are amongst the most popular definitions of economics in modern textbooks.

- Economics is 'the science which studies human behaviour as a relationship between ends and scarce means which have alternative uses', (Lionel Robbins, 1993: 25).
- 'Economics is the study of how men and society end up choosing ... to employ scarce productive resources which could have alternative uses, to produce various commodities and distribute them for consumption, now or in the future, among various people and groups in society', (P. A. Samuelson (1987: 3)
- 'Economics is a study of mankind in the ordinary business of life', (Alfred Marshall, 1987: 3).

Which information relevant to *Homo economicus* can be derived from these definitions? First, human beings do not live in a world of abundance. Instead they are faced with scarce resources, as both Robbins and Samuelson point out. Second, because of this scarcity, it is human choices between alternatives which are the linchpin of economics. Both Robbins and Samuelson emphasise that the field deals with decisions about resources which can be put to alternative uses. Economics is thus defined as the study of choices made by human beings regarding the production and distribution of commodities in a world of scarcity. So far, two features about *Homo economicus* have been learned. First, he lives in a world which does not offer plenty and second, he is forced into constant decision-making regarding the use of resources. This observation sets the general framework for his character. It describes the external circumstances he finds himself in; in other words: the human condition. In addition, economists are interested in human nature, i.e. the 'internal' characteristics of human beings. This is reflected in the above definitions by Marshall and Robbins who claim that economics *is* the study of humankind and human behaviour in the everyday pursuit of life. Which conclusions have economists drawn about humankind? What are the essential features of *Homo economicus*?

According to Herman Daly (1995), the most important of the canonical assumptions of economics is the belief that human beings act as isolated individuals. Economists, he asserts, remove all notions of community before setting out their theories. The subjects of economics are individual, autonomous actors independent of social ties. Charles and Linda Whalen

(1994: 20) agree. They claim that mainstream economics is based on one fundamental unit, the isolated, atomistic individual who is prior to his or her society. Norman Barry draws a connection between atomistic individualism in economics and the above feature of constant decision-making, i.e. choice between alternatives. He argues that the entirely individualist orientation of neo-classical economics rests on a 'concept of man as an autonomous individual whose actions are the product of choice' (Barry, 1986: 4). Constant individual decision-making presupposes atomistic decision-makers. The first character trait of *Homo economicus* can thus be described as being individualistic. He is an isolated, autonomous agent with no social ties.

The second element in the economists' model of human behaviour is the assertion that humans in the marketplace act primarily out of self-interest (Trumbore, 1995). One of the earliest but still the most famous formulation of this claim was written by Adam Smith (1986: 119) in the 18th century: 'It is not from the benevolence of the butcher, the brewer, or the baker that we expect our dinner, but from their regard to their own interest'. Classical and neo-classical economics are built on the assumption that individuals are by nature highly self-interested. Although self-interest is seen as a private vice, its pursuit leads to public virtues. The idea of the 'invisible hand' which transforms individual egoism into national wealth was devised by Smith and Mandeville. They claim that the atomistic pursuit of self-interest will inevitably lead to the general good of all in the long run (Hickey, 1993: 76). The great advantage of the promotion of private vices, according to classical and neo-classical economics, is that they are 'a far more reliable way to ensure that the public interest will be served than any alternative' (Stiglitz, 1994: 7). Taken to an extreme, the invisible-hand-idea suggests that 'the individual pursuit of private vices, motivated by greed, smallmindedness and childish vanity, would lead to public virtues' (Hickey, 1993: 76). The spirit of Scrooge infused into the market will start the workings of the invisible hand leading to general economic well-being (Baumol and Blackman, 1991: 13). The second feature of *Homo economicus* can therefore be identified as being highly self-interested.

The third and final core feature of *Homo economicus* is rationality. Here again, a connection can be made with economics as 'choice theory'. According to Chandran Kukathas (1992: 108), rationality is the ability to reflect and deliberate in order to make *choices*. Raymond Plant (1991: 263) defines rationality similarly. For him, it is a distinctive human feature which enables individuals to order their lives and actions according to principles which have been deliberated upon. Hence rationality is the faculty of humans to reflect in order to make choices. It is a tool to facilitate decision-making. However, the usage of 'rationality' in economics does not just describe it as a generic tool but as a tool with specific purposes and targets, namely the maximisation of profits, utilities and advantages for the self (Homann, 1997: 19). The problem is that tools do not normally come with restrictions as to their usage. As a tool, rationality could be used to further own interests, utilities of others, or those of specifically defined individuals (the King of Denmark) or entities (the environment, God). In mainstream economics, however, the maximisation of self-interest is the only goal which is furthered by rationality. This has to be born in mind, when rationality is listed as the third core feature of *Homo economicus*. It is rationality directed at the maximisation of self-utilities which characterises *Homo economicus* (Lohmann, 1997: 33). The following table summarises our findings about *Homo economicus*:

Table 5.1   *Homo economicus*

Human nature	Isolated, autonomous individual without social ties
	Self-interested being
	Rationality used to achieve utility maximisation
Human condition	Scarcity of resources necessitates constant decision-making

Based on these findings, the previous definition of economics will be extended as follows: 'Economics is the study of choices made by atomistic, self-interested rational human beings regarding the production and distribution of commodities in a world of scarcity'. This definition includes mainstream economists' thoughts on both human nature and the human condition.

It was claimed at the outset of this chapter that proponents of the work incentives argument against the welfare state often rest their case on the concept of *Homo economicus*. They argue that one feature of human nature is an innate aversion to work. The three core features of *Homo economicus* have just been described and none of them deals with an inborn dislike of work. This is true. However, from the basis of atomism, self-interest and rationality other characteristics are derived, one of them being an alleged aversion to work. It is the field of labour supply within economics that deals with human attitudes towards work. Just as mainstream economics builds its findings on *Homo economicus*, so does labour supply theory. It is argued that rational self-interest precludes work unless relinquishing leisure is compensated for by increased income. As McLaughlin, Millar and Cooke (1989: 7) put it:

> Economic theories of labour supply ... state that a 'rational individual' would not choose work over 'leisure' unless this means an increase in income. It thus becomes a taken-for granted fact that state provision for unemployment is a disincentive to work.

Homo economicus' aversion to work does not belong to the canonical assumptions in economics. It is only necessary for certain studies within the field. The remainder of this chapter will deal with the pillars of *Homo economicus* only, namely atomism, self-interest and rationality. *Homo economicus* is the undermost foundation stone upon which derivations, such as the inborn aversion to work, are built. It is therefore necessary to confirm or refute its assumptions before proceeding with the work incentives debate. It is *Homo economicus* which makes welfare criticism tick and which must therefore be analysed in addition to specific claims regarding work incentives.

Homo Economicus - A Realistic Depiction of Humankind?

For thousands of years, philosophers have tried to reduce human nature to a few essential overriding characteristics. The essence of humankind was seen in rationality, religion, work, language and many other features. The following table shows only a few attempts to trace the innermost secret of humans.

Table 5.2   The essence of human beings

Origin	Concept	Distinguishing aspect
Aristotle	*Zoon logon*	Reason and language
Burke	Religious animal	Ability to be religious
Bergson	*Homo Faber*	Ability to make and use tools
Hobbes	*Homo homini lupus*	Desire for power
Smith	*Homo economicus*	Self-interest
Cassirer	*Animal symbolicum*	Ability to create language, myths & art
Gould	Storytelling animals	Ability to invent and tell stories
Huizinga	*Homo ludens*	Playfulness
Jonas	*Homo pictor*	Ability to make pictures
La Mettrie	*L'homme machine*	Humans are mechanical machines
Arendt	*Vita activa*	Social, earthly, time-bound
Sartre	Man simply is	Humans do not have an inborn nature
Dawkins	The selfish gene	Humans are shells of reproducing genes

If one compares these varied assumptions about the essence of human beings, one has to draw the conclusion that the quest to find a single distinguishing aspect has not been greatly successful. Some definitions overlap, but others are highly incompatible. A creature that is mainly self-interested seems to be very different from a being that is mainly religious. The above characteristics are obviously too varied to be summarised under one meaningful heading. Hence, there are four possibilities. 1) Human nature is unintelligible to human beings and all attempts of philosophers are in vain. 2) There is no such thing as human nature, which would validate Sartre's position. 3) Human nature is reducible to a few distinguishing features and human beings can determine what these are. Hence, some or one of the above philosophers might be right. 4) Human nature consists of diverse characteristics, which are intelligible but not reducible to one or a few single features, i.e. all of the above philosophers might be right but their reductionist approach is misguided.

What can be said about the four above listed possibilities for the analysis of *Homo economicus*? 1) If human nature was unintelligible to human beings, *Homo economicus* would be a highly unreliable foundation stone for the field of economics. However, neither could it be replaced by an alternative. It would imply that all sciences or studies involving ponderings on human nature would be futile. 2) The same would hold if human nature did not exist, as Sartre maintains. Again, mainstream economics would be robbed of its foundation stone without being offered a new one. The question whether human universals exist or not and whether they are intelligible or not is unlikely to be settled soon.[6] For the purpose of this book it is therefore regarded as more promising and constructive to concentrate on the latter two possibilities. 3) *Homo economicus* might indeed be the right way to sketch human nature or 4) be at least an important part of the human essence.

The following section will examine whether *Homo economicus* stands up to criticism. Is it a fair depiction of human beings? In recent decades the study of human nature has become an interdisciplinary field that is researched from a variety of angles. Relevant for our project are sociobiology and feminist economics, which offer new insights into human behaviour. However, before we proceed with this 20th-century research, we will go back in time to see what schoolmen and Plato might have thought about *Homo economicus*.

Homo economicus *and Earlier Philosophy*

The depiction of humankind as *Homo economicus* has only surfaced in modernity alongside the development of economics as a social science. Although economic questions were asked in earlier times, answers were far removed from modern theory. For example, price theory can be traced back to the 13th century when schoolmen asked what constitutes just prices. It was argued that a just price needs to guarantee the 'continued reproduction of the social order' (Wusfeld, 1994: 9). Hence, it had to allow producers, merchants and buyers to provide for their families whilst also enabling merchants and producers to stay in their trade. A famous parable elucidates medieval thought on prices (ibid. 10):

> A monk on a pilgrimage to Rome purchased a silver chalice for his cathedral. Travelling back to Germany with a band of merchants, he showed them the vessel and told what he had paid for it. The merchants congratulated him on his purchase, telling him that he had bought it for far less than its true value, and laughed that an unworldly monk could drive a better bargain than any of them. Horrified, the monk left immediately, made his way back to Rome, and paid the seller of the chalice enough to make up the fair price.

It seems that self-interested, maximising *Homo economicus* is already glimpsing from the merchants' eyes but the overwhelming medieval attitude towards personal gain is best represented by the monk. Rather than 'driving a good bargain' it is important to pay a fair price, i.e. a price which does not disrupt the social order by shifting the balance of wealth without justification. A more profit-orientated outlook on economic life only emerged with the Reformation in the 15th century. The new morality was based on the belief that every human being could find a God-given place in society. This 'calling' had to be identified by intent soul-searching. Once found, it had to be pursued with hard work. But how were people to know that they had found their calling? The place God had intended for them? Theologists drew the conclusion that success measured in wealth was the right indicator (ibid. 11). Those who had discovered their calling would be rewarded with prosperity. These ideas were later described as the 'Protestant Work Ethic' which was briefly introduced in Chapter 3.

The Protestant Work Ethic led to the belief that the rich were hard-working and thrifty whilst the poor were idle, lazy and undeserving. As R. H. Tawney (1990: 1) puts it: 'Baptised in the icy waters of Calvinist theology, the business of life, once regarded as perilous to the soul, acquired a new sanctity'. When this world-view first established itself, religious beliefs equating luxury with vice, counterbalanced the new search for profit and wealth. But from the 18th century onwards, religion and the new 'ethics of economics' went separate ways. The break-through for *Homo economicus* came with the publication of *The Fable of the Bees* (1704). Its author, a Dutch doctor named Bernard de Mandeville (1670-1733) proclaimed that advances in society came about by selfish behaviour of individuals rather than their concern for others or their inclination to work (Wusfeld, 1994: 20). At the time, Mandeville was regarded as a 'moral monster by whose ideas one must not be infected' (Hayek, 1966: 127). But his theory and later Adam Smith's 'invisible hand' justified profit-seeking behaviour which was utterly detested during the Middle Ages by equating it with the public good.

The origin of *Homo economicus* as the self-interested utility maximiser can, hence, be traced back to Mandeville's publication (1704), which means that the concept's 300th birthday is approaching. In this sense, he is only an infant compared to other depictions of humankind. For example, Ancient Greek concepts of a rational essence have persisted for 2,000 years and it is the Greek concept of rationality which will be introduced now to see what

Plato would have thought about *Homo economicus*.

In the *Republic*, Plato explains his concept of justice regarding both persons and states. He begins with reflections on states arguing that scale facilitates insight. Later, he hopes to transfer his interpretations to persons. In order to appreciate his ideas on rationality, it is necessary to follow his chain of thought starting with the origin of states. In his view, states form because individual human beings cannot efficiently provide for themselves. They need help from each other and are therefore drawn together in settlements. The uppermost necessity facing human beings is the acquisition of food followed by the need for homes and clothes. A basic city will consist of a peasant, a builder, a weaver and a shoemaker. This type of settlement which only provides for basic economic needs will soon start to grow to include merchants, prostitutes, actors, musicians, doctors, servants and many others. Once this growth has been unleashed, war is unavoidable since land must be appropriated to allow for expansion. War will add another group to the city, namely warriors or guardians. Finally, a city of that size needs rulers and according to Plato they will be chosen amongst the guardians. Plato's state by then has three classes: workers, guardians and selected guardians who will later be called philosopher kings. To avoid potential unrest amongst citizens who might not accept a three-tier state, the selected guardians will spread a myth. They will explain that God added gold when he created the philosopher kings, silver when he created the guardians and iron or bronze when he created the workers. When every citizen in the state concentrates on his own task, a just state has been formed. This is Plato's reasoning on justice in states. Every citizen has to fulfil their jobs, stay in their trade and do their best in the place meant for them. Workers provide for economic needs, guardians defend the city and philosopher kings rule.

In the second part of the *Republic*, he transfers his ideas to individuals. He argues that the three social classes can also be represented as the three elements of the soul: reason, spirit and appetite. Both reason and philosopher kings are characterised by wisdom; spirit and guardians by the desire to win and appetite and workers by the urge for profit and pleasure. As within states, it is the highest goal to establish harmony within the soul. A just person has focused reason, spirit and appetite on their appropriate tasks with reason in control.

Given these ideas from the *Republic*, what can be said about Plato's concept of rationality? For Plato, reason or rationality, is the most worthy and noblest of human faculties which is why he wants to see it reign in both states and individuals. According to him, it enables human beings to see the light of truth and to contemplate ideas. Plato compares those who do not share the benefits of rational insight to prisoners in a dark cave surrounded by grey shadows. Those who are freed from the cave and see the sun, see the truth and share the gift of reason.

How does this concept of reason compare with rationality as present in *Homo economicus*? *Homo economicus* uses rationality as a tool to achieve the maximisation of profits, utilities and advantages for the self. He is not intent on contemplating but rather on creating personal wealth. For Plato those who primarily live to increase their prosperity are evil or at most weak. Their only goals in life are the satisfaction of primitive desires, namely eating, drinking and love-making. According to Plato, this life-style will lead to decline, both of states and individuals. Reason, however, can intervene and prevent regression. It enables human beings to differentiate between bad and good desires and to suppress the former. The desire for honour and glory, for example, is a good desire. The desire for profit, wealth and money is not and must be held in check by rationality. Hence, there is one very crucial and fundamental difference between Plato's concept of rationality and rationality as mirrored in *Homo economicus*. Both see it as a tool or a faculty which can achieve certain goals. The achievement for Plato is to suppress bad desires such as lust for profit, greed, vanity, debauchery, shamelessness etc. and move on to nobler pursuits such as contemplation. *Homo economicus* does quite the opposite. He uses rationality to support and further what Plato calls bad desires or appetites and claims in addition, that the pursuit of private vices such as greed will lead to public virtues. It must therefore be concluded that Plato's idea of rationality and the modern concept derived from mainstream economics are highly incompatible. Although they are both seen as a tool, this tool is used for exactly opposite aims; on the one hand to suppress and on the other hand to support what Plato sees as the base side of humans.

As can be seen from the above, both Plato and medieval schoolmen would despise *Homo economicus*, particularly his self-interest and his employment of rationality to achieve utility maximisation. In defence of *Homo economicus*, one could argue: 'It is most unfortunate that Plato was deluded about the nature of mankind. His romantic vision of human beings is highly appealing but far from the truth'. Bob Goudzwaard and Harry de Lange, two Dutch economists, who argue for a fundamental renewal of economic practices to mitigate poverty, environmental degradation and unemployment are often faced with arguments of this type. In *Beyond Poverty and Affluence - Toward an Economy of Care* (1995: 120), they write:

> When discussing the patterns of today's economic practice in the light of the prospects for economic renewal, we often hear the phrase 'but that's how people are,' or 'that's human nature,' or 'people are greedy by nature.' ... Perhaps the most common argument ... is that because people are greedy by nature, economic renewal is out of the question.

This reveals a clear conflict: on the one hand the features of *Homo economicus* are disapproved of. On the other hand those who believe in their validity assert that 'Alas, this is the essence of mankind'. The following section will examine research from more recently developed disciplines, namely sociobiology and feminist economics to enlighten this conflict.

Homo economicus *and Sociobiology*

Sociobiology is a field which can provide support and new data for human nature studies. This section will briefly introduce the discipline and explain why it can be relevant for the study of human nature. The aim of this section is to determine whether non-cultural features of human beings are in line with the depiction of humans as *Homo economici*.

In 1948, at a conference in New York, scientists decided to initiate new interdisciplinary research between zoologists and sociologists. 'Sociobiology' was the name given to the new discipline aiming to find universally valid regularities in the social behaviour of animals and humans (Wuketits, 1984: 112). Emphasis was put on the study of biological, i.e. non-cultural, behaviour. The field did, however, not get off the ground until Edward Wilson published his groundbreaking book *Sociobiology - The New Synthesis* in 1975. According to Wilson (1975: 4), 'sociobiology is defined as the systematic study of the biological basis of all social behaviour'.

Sociobiological research results are highly contentious when claims are being made about human beings. An example will be given to see why and to explain which reservations have to be made before biological behaviour studies can be used to further knowledge about human nature.

Long-term observations of mammals have revealed a treatment of offspring which, at first, astonished and puzzled biologists. If a lion 'acquires' a new female, his first reaction is to kill all her offspring (Wuketits, 1984: 124). Similarly, a female mammal kills, eats or leaves her own brood if it is very small, particularly if there is only one individual. Female pigs are even in the position to chemically establish the number of fertilised eggs and if it is lower than five they spontaneously abort all embryos twelve days after conception (Wickler, 1990: 181). This behaviour is explained by sociobiologists in terms of maximisation of individual gene survival. The male lion who kills his new partner's brood shortens the time it will take her to conceive his offspring and thereby carry on his genes. The same is true for animal mothers who kill their 'unproductive single child' (ibid. - my translation). Instead of investing valuable time in breeding a single individual they abandon or eat it to conceive a bigger brood more quickly. Animal behaviour such as the one described, maximises the quantity of offspring and the passing on of own genes. It is therefore adaptive,[7] according to sociobiologists.

Authors of the above research did not draw conclusions for humankind. However, research such as this one could be misused or abused by drawing indirect conclusions. It could be argued that it is natural and important for the group to ensure its continued existence as well as the survival of its genetic material. In a further step it could be maintained that humans with certain genetic conditions which significantly reduce the chance of parenting such as Down's syndrome, Fanconi anaemia, Klinefelter syndrome[8] etc. cannot efficiently contribute to the long-term survival of genes. Hence, embryos with these chromosomal abnormalities, it might be suggested, could be aborted for the sake of the group. This leads us to two reservations which have to be made when using research from sociobiology to further knowledge about human nature.

Why research from sociobiology cannot be used unreservedly for human nature studies Sociobiology is in constant danger of providing material for ideologists. To observe nature, to state what is natural and what is unnatural can be the first step towards eugenics. Even Darwin, in his *The Descent of Man and Selection in Relation to Sex* (1871) wrote that modern medicine can keep the weak and ill in a state that enables them to reproduce. This, he continued, is undoubtedly a disadvantage for the race as anybody who breeds animals would immediately concede. No breeder would allow weak animals to procreate. Only in the case of human beings is an exception being made, according to Darwin (1990: 123).[9] As this example shows, proponents of eugenics are likely to find material in biological sciences.

It is here that 'Hume's fork' is very helpful. If an *ought* can never be derived from an *is*, i.e. normative conclusions never be drawn from empirical premises, eugenic practices cannot be based on sociobiological research. What lions or pigs do to their offspring has no relevance for human norms. This opens the question why sociobiology was introduced into the field of human nature studies at all? It is not the 'ought-situation' we are interested in but rather the 'is'. Mainstream economists do not maintain that humans *should* be like *Homo economicus* but that they *are*. It is the 'is-situation' which can be enlightened by research from the above field. Sociobiology will be used to examine and question the validity of *Homo economicus* as a depiction of humankind without drawing any normative conclusions.

The second reservation returns to Sartre's claim that human beings are born without a nature. Similarly, it could be argued that human nature can be fully overridden by education, i.e. nurture is significantly stronger than nature. In both cases the study of biological, instinct-based, non-cultural behaviour might not further the *Homo economicus* debate. In the former instance ('Blank Paper view') the whole discussion is misled. If there is no human nature, *Homo economicus* is as wrong a depiction of humankind as any other, a point made earlier. The second case (human nature can be overridden by education) implies that inborn tendencies, the research area of sociobiology, are irrelevant for human beings. It could be argued that humans can and do distance themselves completely from their biological heritage by superimposing cultural choices. Neither of these views will be supported in this book. For explanations why the two above positions seem unlikely, philosopher Mary Midgley's *Beast & Man - The Roots of Human Nature* (1980) is recommended. Midgley gives numerous examples showing that the 'Blank Paper view' and the 'nurture view' do not square with observations of biologists who found abundant evidence of human instincts which are not suppressed by culture.

Findings from sociobiology on the validity of Homo economicus This section will use research from sociobiology to examine the traits of individualism and egoism or self-interest, two of the characteristics of *Homo economicus*, in both early humans and animals. These characteristics will not be dealt with separately. Altruism (non-egoism) presupposes sociability (non-individualism); they are entwined. Solitary species have no opportunity to show altruism. The implications of biological research on rationality will not be examined since there are none. Rationality is considered to be a trait restricted to human beings; hence there is no room for comparative behaviour studies.

One aim of sociobiology is to uncover biological roots of human social behaviour. Relevant research concentrates on comparing pongides (anthropoid apes) with hominids and on finding differences between various types of hominids. In a second step these differences are judged on their adaptive qualities. Are they aiding the long-term survival of the species or not? Important for our project are differences between various types of hominids. Simplified, the two major groups distinguished by anthropologists are *Australopithecus* and *Homo*, the latter having emerged 1.5 million years ago and the former around 3-4 million years ago (Wuketits, 1984: 119; Digel *et al.*, 1987, Vol. 14: 181). Presumably the following differences set the two types of hominids apart (Wuketits, 1984: 120):

- *Australopithecus* was an individual hunter and gatherer, whilst *Homo* preferred common, cooperative forms of hunting and food collection.
- As an individual, *Australopithecus* was restricted to chasing, attacking and killing small animals. In contrast, *Homo* was able to capture and kill all range of animals because he hunted in formation.
- *Australopithecus* distributed food only to offspring. *Homo* shared killed animals and collected foods with the group or tribe.

From the point of view of sociobiology, it is interesting to see what happened to both *Australopithecus* and *Homo*. *Australopithecus* is extinct, *Homo* has survived (Digel *et al.*, 1987, Vol. 14: 181). Why? According to Franz Wuketits (1984: 120), because the significant adaptive quality of *Homo* was the cooperation in large groups which represented a major competitive advantage over the individualism of *Australopithecus*. It can therefore be said that present-day human beings descended from a socially inclined being rather than the lone, individualist hunter.

Sociability is a very old innate drive in many species. Its phylogenetic origins are traced back to the time when birds 'invented' brooding, hatching and caring for young offspring (Eibl-Eibesfeldt, 1984: 270). To render beings able to fulfil parental responsibilities required social mechanisms unnecessary at earlier stages of evolutionary history. Amoebae, for example, which reproduce by division or frogs which leave their tadpole-offspring to fend for themselves do not need the social instincts present in birds. The parent-offspring relationship laid the foundation for altruistic communities that grew from nuclear families, to family-groups, herds, packs, clans, tribes etc. (ibid. 271). At the same time as facilitating the raising of offspring, social instincts counterbalanced innate aggression. It became possible to distinguish between 'them' and 'us' and aim aggression towards individuals that did not belong to one's group (ibid. 270). This behaviour is clearly adaptive in the sense of ensuring the survival of one's family or one's family's genes. First, by putting effort into raising offspring and second by discriminating between family and non-family members during fights. The fact that human beings descended from a sociable, rather than an individualist hominid, can also be supported with observations from anthropologists. As George Murdock (1978: 22) summarises, every culture in known history shared a huge list of characteristics, amongst them: community organisation, cooperative labour, games, gift giving, hospitality, postnatal care, visiting, funeral rites, government, kin groups and personal names. All these features presuppose sociability.

To go one step further than sociability, we will now look at social behaviour that presents a serious puzzle to sociobiologists and that is interesting in the *Homo economicus* debate: altruism to the point of getting killed for the sake of others. As Wilson (1975: 3) puts it: 'The central theoretical problem of sociobiology [is]: how can altruism, which by definition reduces personal fitness, possibly evolve by natural selection?' And altruism is not a rare event. Evolutionists from Darwin onwards have been observing that it is a widespread phenomenon in the animal kingdom (Ruse, 1985: 43) and according to R. L. Trivers (1985: 69) also in human societies. The answer to the perplexing question how altruism can be explained on the basis of individual selection is kinship, according to Wilson (1975: 3f).[10]

> If the genes causing the altruism are shared by two organisms because of common descent, and if the altruistic act by one organism increases the

joint contribution of these genes to the next generation, the propensity to altruism will spread through the gene pool.

Altruism could evolve genetically because it enabled kin survival, albeit by requiring individual sacrifices. It is interesting and supportive of Wilson's thesis that altruism is found more often the closer the kinship is (Wuketits, 1984: 124). Still, Wilson's theory on altruism has faced criticism. According to Stephen Jay Gould (1990: 138), it is conceivable that altruism is no genetically steered phenomenon but possibly learned. Both authors agree, on the other hand, that altruism appears widely in higher animals and also in humans. One example that Gould gives for altruism in humans deals with the behaviour of old Eskimos. Eskimos live in family-groups and do not have permanent homes. When food supplies dwindle and the family has to move to a new area, some grandparents decide to stay behind so that they do not delay family travels. It was found that Eskimo families without altruistically inclined grandparents often died as a group, whereas those groups whose grandparents stayed behind survived. Although this chapter focuses on human nature rather than nurture, it is not essential to know the steering mechanisms (genes or learning) behind altruism; it is sufficient to bear in mind that is a widely recognised phenomenon.

Another finding from sociobiology regarding altruism is that communities in which the relationship between altruism and selfishness is unbalanced in favour of selfishness run a high risk of becoming extinct. Wilson (1975: 562) argues that the prevalence of egoistic individuals will make a community vulnerable and ultimately lead to the extinction of the whole group. Egoism pays very badly in genetical terms and a 'consistently egoistic species would be either solitary or extinct' (Midgley, 1980: 94). Mary Midgley's conclusion is: 'Since ... we [human beings] are social and not extinct, we cannot sensibly view ourselves as natural egoists' (ibid.).

Hence, according to Midgley, human beings are neither natural egoists nor a solitary species. (In the section on feminist economics it will be seen how mainstream economists try to square altruistic behaviour with their picture of *Homo economicus* by claiming that altruistic behaviour dominates the private and selfish behaviour the public sphere.) John Kingdom's (1992: 87) evaluation of research from sociobiology summarises the above findings:

> Our wode-daubed forebearers of the Upper Palaeolithic became the dominant human type because they were socially solid with an intense sense of community. Living in bands or hordes they were able to defend themselves and develop life-sustaining hunting and agricultural practices ... In this environment, *Homo economicus*, engaged in the lunatic war of all against all, would have scant record in the history texts of the dolphins or apes who would have inherited the earth.

As this quote eloquently expresses, sociability was an important feature of early hominids. In addition, it was shown that altruism is a widespread phenomenon both in animal and human societies. That means that two of the three characteristics that constitute *Homo economicus* can be seriously questioned with findings from sociobiology.[11]

Potential defence of Homo economicus The claim that humans are primarily autonomous, individual beings will also be dealt with in the next section on feminist economics as will be the phenomenon of altruism. Before, a possible criticism other than the reservations made at the beginning of this section will be addressed. Proponents of *Homo economicus* as a depiction of human nature could make the following point: the example of early hominids who were socially inclined does not prove anything. Even in Palaeolithic times individualism could have been a major feature of human beings but self-interest was even stronger. Only in groups was it possible to successfully hunt big game and to defend the community. Self-interest demanded cooperation, i.e. the natural tendency towards individualism was repressed in order to satisfy the appetite for big game and to provide security. In our times, it could be argued that cooperation is not required any more and that the type of help that is provided by the welfare state is not mutually beneficial and therefore violates self-interest. A Nozickean minimal state (Nozick, 1974: ix) where everybody lived autonomously with no cooperation other than organising police, courts and the army would be the only acceptable state of true individualists. This state would correspond to the life of hunters and gatherers whose cooperation was also kept at the minimum that best served egoistic aims. Nowadays, Western welfare states enforce a one-sided, unwanted altruism that violates individualism and goes against natural inclinations of self-interest. Hence, a major change has occurred: cooperation during the hunt was beneficial to every individual, but only because every individual contributed. Today, it could be argued, the benefits are all drawn from one group which is frequently called the underclass (Murray, 1996: 23) and the burden is carried by another group, the so-called honest taxpayer (Houghton, 1989: 58).

Libertarians could conclude as follows: human beings value autonomous individuality in line with their natural dispositions. Sometimes, however, self-interest (another feature of human nature) requires them to cooperate. This cooperation must involve both contributions and benefits, otherwise the self-interest of the contributing group would be violated. The latter happens in Western welfare states, where contributions and benefits are unbalanced. Since there is no social bond between autonomous individuals and no inborn altruism this imbalance goes against human nature.

In order to advance on this argument, it is necessary to reflect on the meaning of self-interest. One could say that pure self-interest is 100 per cent receiving plus 0 per cent giving and pure altruism is 0 per cent receiving plus 100 per cent giving. One could include only two parties, the contributor and the receiver, or allow third parties into the equation. The latter would open the door for utilitarian calculations. In addition, the situation is made difficult by the fact that human beings think and judge. It is easier to establish egoism and altruism in animals. When male lions appropriate a female, for example, they kill all cubs from the previous 'owner', as was seen earlier. From a human perspective, this obviously looks like a 100 per cent egoistic act. Examples with human beings are more difficult to categorise. Consider this: X murders Y in order to inherit his money. This looks like an act of 100 per cent egoism on X's part, just like the lion's murdering of cubs. However, the example could be changed as follows: X murders Y in order to inherit his money. X has two children who suffer from a rare genetic disease which is fatal unless a bone marrow transplant is carried out. Unfortunately no donor is available for his two children but scientists in the US offer places on a gene therapy trial. To be included, X has to cover all costs himself. Y is X's brother and he asked him for a loan but Y said: 'What do I care about your children? Do you expect me to forego my thrice yearly holidays to Bali just to save your children?' X becomes beside himself with disappointment, rage and grief, grabs a table lamp and hits his brother once. In despair he realises that he killed him. He takes an oath that he will give himself up to the police as soon as his two children's health is secured, takes his inheritance and registers the children in the trial. If one only allows the contributor and the receiver, in this case the murderer and the murderee, into the equation, this is still an example of 100 per cent egoism. However, if one allows the two children in, a certain amount of altruism could be detected. X will give himself up to the police once his children are safe and accept a court's judgement. In addition, the murder was not premeditated which makes it manslaughter, a difference that is not applicable in the lion's case. Given the above, it seems reasonable to assume a long road between 100 per cent altruism and 100 per cent egoism on which many mixed cases can be found. There will be more impure cases if one allows third parties into the equation and if one does not treat humans as black boxes whose thoughts are irrelevant for the establishment of altruistic versus egoistic behaviour. It is, in fact, difficult to find examples of people who are consistent in either being purely altruistic or purely egoistic all their lives.

Not only are acts mostly a mixture of self-interest and altruism but self-interest can also be perceived differently. As mainstream economists have conceded, humans do not live in a world of abundance but in a world of scarcity. It is impossible for every human being on earth today to have all their material wishes fulfilled. This is why the field of economics has developed in the first place and why it puts high emphasis on choice. One could argue that there are two major choices in today's Western world and it is useful to go back to our characters X and Y. They might be asked how they would define their self-interests. Y could say the following: 'My self-interest is best served living in luxury in a gated community, heavily guarded by private police and I am prepared to pay a high amount of money to keep the underclass out'. (Scarcity does not allow Y to live in luxury without possible intervention from others.) X might argue: 'I want to live comfortably with my family but I do not want to be shut out from the world in a guarded cage. I also cannot bear to see people suffer. I do not want to see a shivering beggar in heavy rain or an unemployed youth with nothing to do and no hope of 'a life'. I am ready to part with a percentage of my earnings in order to live in a community of cooperation even if it looks as though I am only a benefactor and not a beneficiary'. Y is a prototypical *Homo economicus*, in the sense that is relevant in this section, i.e. excluding rationality for the moment. He is 100 per cent individualist (private police could be replaced by electric fences and a field of mines) and 100 per cent self-interested ('keep all these beggars out'). X's self-interest rests on his sociability and is mixed with what Schopenhauer (1979: 110) calls empathy or sympathy.[12] He cannot ignore the people around him and is prepared to make a contribution to their well-being.

If one accepts that both X and Y represent plausible pictures of human beings, one has to ask, why are they so different? Assuming for a moment that there is a universalist human nature, one of them has to be closer to it whilst the other has been changed during his upbringing and life. What is nature and what is nurture? This brings us back to the beginning. Is a human being properly characterised by the concept of *Homo economicus*, i.e. is he Y? Or put differently: where does evil come from? (100 per cent egoism will be taken as part of evil.) That's an age-old question. Rousseau assumed that humans are naturally good and evil comes with civilisation. Hobbes believed that humans are naturally evil and only civilisation in the form of an absolute sovereign could save them from each other. Since human beings cannot be put into test tubes and shaken, this question is difficult to answer. Hence, the few hints from sociobiology are welcome. Mary Midgley has studied results from these fields in great detail and she draws the following conclusion: if one wants to reduce human beings to one driving force, it would be innate sociability. She (1980: 130) writes:

> Why affection? Why time-consuming greeting procedures, mutual grooming, dominance and submission displays, territorial boasting, and ritual conflict? Why play? Why (on the human scene) so much time spent in nonproductive communication of every kind - idle chatter, lovemaking, sport, laughter, song, dance, and storytelling, quarrels, ceremonial, mourning and weeping? ... Insofar as there is one 'impelling force,' it is sociability.

For her, humans who only see their own advantage and do not care about others, i.e. *Homo economici* outside the family, are disappointed psychopaths (ibid. 355). Overall, it has to be concluded that sociability (non-individualism) and altruism (non-egoism) can be strongly associated with the biological heritage of *Homo sapiens* which means that *Homo economicus* is not a reliable and true depiction of humankind. The next section will support this claim with findings from feminist economists and feminist theory in general.

Feminist Economics and Homo economicus

Feminism is not one homogeneous theory which could be employed straightforwardly to support or criticise the concept of *Homo economicus*. Instead it subsumes a multiplicity of theories and methods under its wings which can even be incompatible with each other. If one tried to identify the main directions in feminist thought, one could name the following: liberal, Marxist, radical, psychoanalytic, socialist, existentialist, and postmodern (Tong, 1989: 1). If one wanted to find a minimal denominator amongst these various forms of feminism, Janet Radcliffe Richard's (1983: 21) definition might be suitable. She uses the word 'feminism' for all theories whose purpose is to show that 'women suffer systematic injustice because of their sex'. However, to complicate things, postmodern feminists regard any attempt to find *the* one and only feminist viewpoint or theory as just another instantiation of androcentric thought (Tong, 1989: 7). As Rosemarie Tong (ibid.) puts it:

> A synthesis [of feminist theory] is neither feasible nor desirable. It is not feasible because women's experiences differ across class, racial and cultural lines. It is not desirable because the One and the True are philosophical myths that have been used to club into submission the differences that ... best describe the human condition. That feminism is many and not one is to be expected because women are many and not one.

Postmodern feminism This leads to the first viewpoint that could be taken on *Homo economicus* from a feminist angle: if one cannot even define or describe the concept 'woman' homogeneously across race, class and culture, how far removed is the possibility of a universal concept of human nature? (Alcoff and Potter, 1993: 4). According to Sandra Harding (1993: 60) any attempt to find *one* universally valid description of human nature is to be discredited as an ethnocentric undertaking by the domineering group to impose their standards and ideas on the powerless and marginalised. Knowledge is always limited by social context and the status of the knower (Alcoff and Potter, 1993: 1). It is necessary to dispense with the belief that knowledge can be universal and accept that it will always be context-dependent. Context-dependent, however, does not mean relative.[13] It is possible to obtain more objective knowledge about the human condition (without ever claiming universality) by including the ostracised, the marginalised and the so-called abnormal in the knowledge process (Tong, 1989: 233). To challenge knowledge that was created by the dominant social group in Western societies, i.e. 'propertied, educated, white men' (Code, 1993: 23) other groups must be heard. If one started the knowledge process from the lives of women

> who are holocaust survivors, Chicana cannery workers, older lesbians, African-American women in slavery, Japanese-American concentration camp survivors, and others who have had [different] lives, [this would] increase our ability to understand a great deal about the distorted way the dominant groups conceptualize politics (Harding, 1993: 58).

This way, one would arrive at what Harding calls 'socially situated knowledge' (ibid. 50), which is the only knowledge that will ever deserve the name. The belief of the dominant group that it is possible to transcend historical and social boundaries in order to arrive at objective value-free knowledge only makes their research androcentric as well as biased and not, as they claim, objective. According to Harding, research can only gain in objectivity from feminist scepticism. Current practices are not 'too rigorous or too "objectifying", [but] not rigorous or objectifying enough' (ibid. 50f).

As this brief and simplified description of postmodern feminist epistemology indicates, any group that claims to have found *the* universally valid description of human nature is mistaken. It is impossible to abstract from social ties and draw an ahistorical and acultural picture of human beings. In this respect, the outcome of feminist research can be compared to Sartre's belief that there is no such thing as human nature, the 'Blank Paper view'. If there is no human nature, *Homo economicus* is just as unreliable a guess as any other. In this case, the whole enterprise of sketching human nature would be futile. Postmodernist feminism, however, could be interpreted as slightly more tolerant on this issue. If one arrives at knowledge in 'collaborative, democratic, community enterprises with marginal peoples' (ibid. 68) and if one does not sell this knowledge as resistant to time and space, one could claim a certain objectivity. Hence, one might argue that reflections on human nature and the human condition are permissible (in contrast to Sartre's viewpoint) if one does not fall into androcentric traps. This allows for a more substantial, less general occupation with *Homo economicus*, trying to figure out whether the concept is riddled with androcentric beliefs or not.

Androcentric biases in Homo economicus Marianne Ferber and Julie Nelson (1993: 1) observe that mainstream economics behaves as though its ideals and definitions had come to earth by 'divine intervention' or as though they were dropped from a 'Friedmanesque helicopter'. But this is not the case; they were made by human beings. Therefore they are prone to the limitations of human cognition and must be open to constant observation and criticism. The areas of interest in this section are the characteristics of *Homo economicus*, namely: individualism, self-interest and rationality.

To illuminate their theories, economists frequently use Robinson Crusoe as a good model of quintessential economic man (Grapard, 1995: 33). With his help they show how the maximisation of utility and minimisation of cost works, how a general equilibrium model could work, what comparative advantage means in economics etc. (ibid. 36f). It seems that Robinson Crusoe indeed fits the role of *Homo economicus* very well. He lives autonomously and individually (until Friday arrives) on a deserted island; has nobody to be interested in other than himself; seems to be a picture of rationality with his obsession to enter accounting details into his journal and his choices are limited by the scarcity of natural resources.

But what does Robinson Crusoe say about the world? In Grapard's (ibid. 37f) words: '[What does] the story of a single, white, colonial, male - shipwrecked and living alone on an island in the Caribbean for twenty-six years before he is joined by a "savage"' has to say about economics? The popularity of Robinson Crusoe reveals a lot about the discipline which might be more difficult to extract from its otherwise mostly mathematical approach.[14] To put it crudely: 1) women are superfluous in economics; 2) Blacks (Friday) are there to serve Whites (Crusoe). 3) men spring from the earth 'like a Hobbesian mushroom' (ibid. 38), fully self-sufficient and independent (or alternatively the process of gaining independence is irrelevant to economics).

In response to this analysis, a neo-classical polemic could say: 'You don't have to take this story too literally. Other than that, there is nothing wrong with it. Economics deals with the public not the private sphere. Children have nothing to do in the market-place. They might induce their parents into acquiring the newest 'all-singing-and-dancing' Barbie, but it is only adults who hold the money and are faced with choices. Children are irrelevant from an economist's point of view. The same goes for people outside the 'employment club'. Women are very welcome to join and if they do, they become economically active and interesting. Changing nappies, however, has no room in the discipline. There is no reason why Robinson Crusoe could not be female, if she decided to step out of her kitchen. As to Blacks, if they were more successful in the market-place in greater numbers, they might have the money to employ Whites in their services. There is no principal reason why Friday could not be white and Crusoe black. As I said, economists deal with the marketplace and who isn't in it cannot be dealt with'.

What are the positions? On the one hand there is the charge of racism and sexism being levelled against mainstream economics and its image of human beings as Robinson Crusoes alias *Homo economicus*. On the other hand, mainstream economists could take the view that it is their strength to limit research to the market place and it is not their fault that women and Blacks are often marginalised. They could say pragmatically that attempts to combine economics, social justice, politics, gender issues etc. have failed in the communist utopia, partly because this attempt disregarded human nature (Ash, 1990: 132). Hence, the *laisser-faire* market system, they could argue, proved its superiority in terms of goods supply, freedom, democracy etc. beyond doubt in 1989 (Crouch and Marquand, 1993: 3). To date, no better system has been devised or has evolved. It is unfortunate that there are nevertheless injustices to be suffered. However, humans are not infallible and the perfectly just system is beyond reach (Goudzwaard and de Lange, 1995: 120; Seldon, 1982: 7). The *laisser-faire* market system is the best of all possibilities. Besides, its framework is the same for everybody giving equal opportunities to all. In contrast, feminists would argue that white, propertied men devised the system. Economics did not fall off a Friedmanesque helicopter, it was created by a social group and now both the field and the system are defended to maintain the status of domination for this group. As Marilyn Waring (1990: 45) puts it:

> The profession of economics is that of a limited social group - economically privileged, university-educated, white men. It serves neither the majority of humankind nor our fragile planet. Its structure and content have a design and a beguiling propaganda.

Arguments have arrived at a stalemate. On the one hand are self-proclaimed realists who are in no doubt about the unfavourable basic character traits of human beings and the limited choice of workable societies. From their point of view there will always be opponents (be it communists, women, Blacks) who worry about injustices and envision beautiful and impressive utopias which, alas, are completely unattainable. On the other hand, are feminists who claim that societies do not evolve on single-track roads but are steered by a domineering group. In their opinion patterns of domination can be recognised and adjusted leading not to a utopia but to a more equal and just society. It all boils down to the previous question: is *Homo economicus* a fair picture of human beings or is the field of economics a portrayal and creation of white, propertied males? The following section shall examine the *single* attributes of *Homo economicus* from a feminist point of view.

Feminism on individualism and self-interest Individualism takes the autonomous and free individual as the starting point to reason about laws, morality and action (Digel *et al.*, 1987, Vol. 10: 215). It is the fundamental belief of individualists that people are autonomous actors who are faced with choices and have a purpose in life (Barry, 1986: 4). They also maintain that individuals are 'logically and ethically prior to society' (Cramp, 1991: 53). These assumptions have been running like a thread through Western thought since the 16th century (Bell, 1976: 16) and they played a major role in the formation of *Homo economicus*.

Feminists attack this philosophy as androcentrically biased. Men are only able to feel and act as independent individuals because women do not. The independence that characterises autonomous actors represents only a transient and ephemeral period between childhood and senility (Pascall, 1986: 7). Selma Sevenhuijsen (1998: 28) even argues that vulnerability and dependency are an element of the human condition *per se* rather than a characterisation of childhood, old age, illness and disability only. Hence, individualism disregards major stages in human lives and the social work of women which enables persons to feel autonomous and atomistic in the first place. Without traditional self-sacrifices of women, men would not have had the possibility to concentrate on their individual self-fulfilment (Midgley and Hughes, 1983: 11). Individualism has only ever worked for males, who were freed by women's social labour from all concerns which require a non-atomistic standpoint in life (Harding, 1993: 55). Midgley and Hughes (1983: 222) write:

> [Individualism] has always relied on an inconsistency - on assuming that, while men regard themselves as isolated, competitive individuals, each hell-bent on his own interest, women will continue to see themselves as social beings, organically linked with those around them.

The connection between individualism and egoism is very close. Only if one assumes separate, atomistic selves is it plausible to claim that human beings are primarily selfish. As soon as one allows connection and relationships into the equation, egoism becomes contentious as a prime mover of human beings. According to Paula England (1993: 45) the experience of looking after a child or the experience of teaching makes people care about others. She maintains that 'emotional connection often creates empathy, altruism, and a subjective sense of social solidarity' (ibid.). Since this creation of empathy is a common observation, it is difficult to argue that human beings are primarily separate, egoist selves. Those isolated selves would 'have little basis on which to develop the necessary empathy to practice altruism' (ibid.).

Heidi Hartmann (1993: 62) argues that the male bias in mainstream economics can be revealed by looking at descriptions of human nature. According to her, economists describe human nature (*Homo economicus*) with reference to market exchange *only*. In her view, the mother-infant relationship could also be seen as *the* prototypical human interaction. That this relationship and others are completely ignored in the model of *Homo economicus* shows, she claims, that neo-classical economics would better be termed 'male individualism' (ibid.).

Individualism, as well as egoism, are major problems for feminists. As early modern feminists did (Midgley and Hughes, 1983: 222), one could demand gender equality by extending individualistic philosophy to both sexes. Women should have a right to individual self-fulfilment and egoistic behaviour as men have had for centuries.[15] This approach could validate the underlying assumptions of *Homo economicus*. Human beings might then indeed be proven to be primarily egoistic and atomistic. However, what makes individualism so attractive for men, is that whilst they are looking out for themselves, there is a woman that stands 'staunchly and obediently behind him' (ibid.), raises his children, cares for his well-being and possibly for elderly relatives. Assuming gender equality, this aspect would be lost. Women would not have a supportive self-denying partner at their side whilst they ventured out to fulfil their aspirations. Hence, activities which are incompatible with atomistic egoism such as raising children and caring for elderly people would have to be given up.

In order to evaluate *Homo economicus'* atomism and self-interest further, it is useful to distinguish three plausible positions based on gender specific assumptions. 1) Both men and women are by nature individualistic and heavily self-interested, but men's dominance over women secured suppression of female egoism. A society made up of atomistic, purely egoistic individuals is not tenable in the long run. In order to get altruistic work done, men forced women into the role of carers. To achieve equal rights for the sexes, women should be allowed to release their individualistic and egoistic selves. 2) Neither men nor women are intrinsically atomistic and fixated to self-interested behaviour. This is a misconception that originated from taking a minority of modern, white, middle-class, property owning men as prototypical human beings. As Marx (1986: 73) puts it: '[It needs] a genius in the way of bourgeois stupidity [to] take the modern shopkeeper, especially the English shopkeeper, as the normal man [so that] whatever is useful to this queer normal man, and to his world, is absolutely useful'. 3) Women are naturally social and altruistic, whilst men are naturally selfish and individualistic. As child-bearers, women are closer to nature and thus predestined for everyday caring, emotional and domestic work (Harding, 1993: 55). This is why self-fulfilment has a different meaning for the sexes. Women's individual self-fulfilment lies in altruistic social labour whilst men's fulfilment lies in a career in the so-called public sphere.

What could be said about these three positions? First, men and women are both atomistic egoists. This contention fits the *Homo economicus* depiction best but it has to meet one major objection: 'Instances of apparent altruism (voluntary giving, helping behaviour, etc.)' are so widespread (Collard, 1991: 17) that this claim would contradict empirical facts. In addition, the dependent-carer relationship is unworkable on the assumption of pure egoism. To circumvent empirically proven altruism, some economists have moved towards a theory of 'family greed' (Cramp, 1991: 59) or 'named benevolence' (Hahn, 1991: 9). People are seen as selfish beings in the market and altruistic beings in the family, an understanding akin to the sociobiological concept of kinship altruism. A rather gendered example for family greed is given by Tony Cramp. He (1991: 59) argues that mothers with little children in supermarkets and fathers who stick at hated jobs are making sacrifices for their families. Thus, selfishness only begins beyond the family within which altruism is dominant. The concept of named benevolence is slightly broader in that it allows more than family members into the equation. As Frank Hahn (1991: 9) sees it, named benevolence includes people in the domain of one's preferences. As examples for his concept he names nepotism, gifts to children and 'friends before country'.

By allowing altruism to pay a significant role in defined areas (mainly the family) some economists have moved away from *Homo economicus* while at the same time trying to rescue the basic concept. They have moved away from 'him' by allowing for altruism which runs counter to his basic characteristics. On the other hand, they have re-established the concept by adding a little 'but' at the end. *Homo economicus* describes human beings in the market place *but* not in the family. Paula England (1993: 48) describes the feminist standpoint on family greed very persuasively, which is why it will be quoted in full:

> My disagreement is not with the notion that altruism exists in the family... It is rather with the extreme bifurcation of the assumptions about the two spheres. If economic man or woman is so altruistic in the family, might not some altruism be present in market behavior as well? ... Doesn't the susceptibility of an altruist to being influenced by another's joy or pain suggest that s/he also might modify certain tastes through the process of interaction with others? If the answers to these questions are yes ... then the altruistic self assumed for the household is inconsistent with the separative self assumed for market behavior. It is simply not plausible that the altruist who displays an emotionally connective self in the family is the same person who marches out into the market selfish, unable to empathize with others, with utterly rigid tastes.

Hence, by allowing for family greed and named benevolence, economists[16] opened the door for altruism as a major characteristic of human beings. It is implausible that the ability to empathise and to behave unselfishly can be restricted to the family unless one assumes schizophrenia. This applies to most, probably all, human characteristics. If, for example, a professional football player is highly competitive in his job, he will also try to win a card game with friends in a pub. His competitiveness will not suddenly vanish in the private sphere. Besides, if named benevolence and even more obviously family greed could exclusively explain altruism, most charities would be out of work. Sponsor-a-child, for example, is incompatible with family greed and until a relationship is established it cannot grow out of named benevolence. It has to be concluded, therefore, that altruism cannot be disregarded in market situations since it presupposes a connected self able to feel empathy; a feature which cannot be switched on and off depending on the situation. The foundation of *Homo economicus* as predominantly selfish is, hence, not tenable.

This leads to the second possibility. Neither men nor women are purely selfish, unconnected beings; reflecting the view previously supported. Accordingly, no further evidence for this view must be brought forward. However, this leads immediately to the following question: how did the image of *Homo economicus* develop in the first place and why is it so acceptable in economics and right-wing politics? The answer of feminists could be: because it mirrors beliefs of the dominating group of white, middle-class males in positions of power. The attributes of marginalised groups (which can easily be in the majority but splintered) are not reflected in the picture. The following discussion will highlight the relativity of thoughts that led to the concept of *Homo economicus*. The discussion will begin with a quote from Marilyn Waring (1990: 22f) who argued that Adam Smith developed

> an image of humans as materialistic, egoistic, selfish, and primarily motivated by pursuit of their own self-interest. [For Waring] this is ... not a 'scientific opinion,' ... but a created, and moral, judgment ... If Adam Smith was fed daily by Mrs. Smith, he omitted to notice or to mention it. He did not, of course, pay her. What *her* interest was in feeding him we can only guess, for Adam Smith saw no 'value' in what she did.

With this example Waring makes two points. 1) Concepts of human nature are not scientifically discovered but created inside a moral, social and political framework.[17] 2) Those who create the concept can be - as in the case of Adam Smith - biased, i.e. they might not take all possible standpoints into account and instead only proceed from their own experiences. By basing insights exclusively on own experiences, a restricted world-view is likely to be created. For centuries, up until the 20th, discourse in both the sciences and the arts was the domain of men. Female voices were either not present (e.g. Mrs. Adam Smith) or ignored (e.g. Mary Wollstonecraft). One need not be a committed postmodernist to accept that knowledge creation can only gain from discourses which are fuelled by different experiences.

Homo economicus, however, is not a concept that arose out of diverse discussions that included minority and marginalised groups. From the humble beginnings with Mandeville and Smith[18] in the 18th century, until today economics has always been dominated by a certain group of males. As seen earlier, 'the profession of economics is that of a limited social group - economically privileged, university-educated, white men' (ibid. 45). This limited social group has established their depiction of human nature in the form of *Homo economicus*. It is very possible that they believe to have hit the target of describing human beings admirably. However, many of their assumptions and theories completely disregard female experiences.

'Disregard female experiences?', they could argue, 'where is the problem? Newton did not need female experiences to formulate the law of gravity. Economics is a science. Discourses with the marginalised are unasked for'. Without venturing into the dispute about the objectivity of science, there is a major difference between natural and social sciences and economics does belong to the latter. Unless one takes a highly postmodernist standpoint, one must admit that many findings from the natural sciences can be proven to be universally valid and independent of researchers' background. Down's-Syndrome in males, females, Blacks, Whites, children, adults around the world and through the centuries is caused by trisomy of chromosome 21. No 'finding' from economics can make a similar claim to universality and independence. The new neo-classical macroeconomics shall be used to substantiate this point. Its fundamentals are as follows (Wusfeld, 1994: 170):

> There is a 'natural rate of unemployment,' say 6 percent, at which the rate of inflation is zero. Efforts to reduce the actual rate of unemployment to a level below the natural rate, say 4 percent, by using fiscal and monetary policy to increase aggregate demand [post-Keynesian approach], can be successful in the short run, but will set inflationary pressures in motion.

Regarding universality over time, one has to say that this 'finding' is invalid or meaningless in all barter economies. Regarding universality in space, one only has to look at Post-Keynesians, who do not accept 'natural' unemployment. To put it simply: it is highly capricious to reject or challenge the insight that trisomy of chromosome 21 causes Down's-Syndrome. This has been shown beyond reasonable doubt. In economics, on the other hand, it makes perfect sense to even attack 'fundamentals', such as the above. 'The great charm of economic theory ... is that, if you stand in one place long enough, discarded ideas come round again' (Cramp, 1991: 50). There are no universally accepted, non-tautological findings; a fact which also explains the endless number of jokes about economics and economists. (There is, for example, the old professor who year after year puts the same questions to his students ... but each year changes the answers. Or the belief that you can get five different opinions on any subject from any four economists. Or why did God create economists? So that long-term weather forecasters look good.) Robert M. Solow (1993: 155) writes:

> It seems obvious that economics is at least a little different from biology and chemistry, partly because there is no poking or prodding, just passive observing, and partly because the economist, in thinking about the economy, is inevitably thinking about herself or himself. Introspection plays no part in the framing of hypotheses about chemistry or molecular biology, but I do not see how it can be wholly avoided in framing hypotheses about economic behavior. It would be crazy not to ask: what would I do in those circumstances?

Hence, economics is open for discourse and it does matter who undertakes research. If it is only one social group (white, privileged, educated men) findings will be biased. Since *Homo economicus* was designed by a restricted group of researchers, its underlying ideas need to be challenged by other groups in order to arrive at a less biased result. Female experiences need to be built into the canonical assumptions of mainstream economics.

Where does this leave the discussion? It was shown earlier that the field of economics does not cope well with apparent wide-spread altruism. By introducing the concept of family greed the challenge to *Homo economicus* was allegedly warded off. However, the strict bifurcation between public and private seems to transform *Homo economicus* into a schizophrenic. It was therefore concluded that the concept is disputable. This, however, left the question unanswered why it is so successful and resistant to criticism in both economics and politics? A feminist answer could be that *Homo economicus* mirrors the experience of a small group in a dominant position. If experiences of marginalised groups had a bearing on mainstream economics, *Homo economicus* would prove to be inadequate and deficient as a depiction of human beings in general. Indeed, this is what has been shown above. Traditional female experiences, such as child-rearing, contradict the contention that human beings are atomistic, selfish beings. Instead, the experience of raising children creates a sense of connection, a feeling of empathy that is incompatible with *Homo economicus*. Hence, if women's experiences would be implemented into the basic assumptions in economics, a different *Homo* would appear, a less selfish, more connected one.

There is still one narrow expedient left for proponents of *Homo economicus* which leads to point three. Considering the above mentioned two points, the claim that 'he' represents a universal picture of human beings cannot be upheld. First, this depiction does not account for the empirical observation of wide-spread altruism and second, it has been designed by a limited social group which drew a biased picture. However, mainstreamers who would like to uphold *Homo economicus* as a tool in economics could grant that indeed 'he' does not include female experiences and has been built on white men's world-views only. This, they could argue, does still not mean that a new all-embracing concept of human beings is required which would allow for altruism and connection in both sexes. Instead, they might claim that *Homo economicus* characterises men, whilst the altruistic *Homo* characterises women.[19] In short, the concept of family greed might be upheld if women's experiences were shown to be singular to women and male altruism was so minute that it could only be brought to light in a family and under female pressure.

To further this argument, the controversial division between the public and the private sphere is important. Defendants of *Homo economicus* could argue that men are made for the public sphere of earning money and women are best suited to the private sphere of looking after men and dependants. They might say: since economics works with a representation of humans in the public sphere, the concept of *Homo economicus* is not harmed by the arguments of female altruism and androcentrically biased knowledge creation. For the same reason, it is also misplaced to criticise the dominance of men in economic research. Since men domineer the public realm, they are also best suited to research it. In other (New Right) words: women and men were, are and will always be different. The female is the altruist who works in the private sphere; the male is the self-interested, rational choser who deals with questions in the public realm. Economics, as the science of behaviour in the public sphere, rests solidly and safely on the concept of *Homo economicus* which catches the major characteristics of males. Women's altruistic experiences and character traits are not relevant to economics, since they do not apply in the public sphere.

This looks like a very promising approach for proponents of *Homo economicus*. Feminists would have to show that their findings about altruism versus egoism are universal, i.e. applicable to both sexes. Only then would they be able to attack *Homo economicus* as a general depiction of human beings. However, this is highly unlikely since feminists usually detest claims for universality.[20] A potentially defendable New Right position on *Homo economicus* could therefore be: argue that naturally altruistic women are best off in the private sphere whilst only aggressive, 'manly' men can cope in the public sphere. Thereby the status-quo on family models might be preserved and at the same time exaggerations of the women's movement be pushed back. This is indeed the approach taken by the New Right in the eighties and nineties. Feminists refer to it as the *backlash* (Faludi, 1992). To give an insight into backlash strategies, three authors will be introduced, namely Robert Bly, George Gilder and Sylvia Ann Hewlett.

In *Iron John - A book about men* (1993), Robert Bly[21] explains how modern males can rebuild their energy, their inner and outer strength and their identity by releasing the Wild Man from within. According to him (1993: 2), the 'soft male' surfaced all over America in the seventies and characterised nearly 50 per cent of young men in the eighties and early nineties. Although Bly calls them 'lovely, valuable people' (ibid.) who do not fight wars or harm anybody, he thinks that they are not happy (ibid. 3). They have little vitality and can often be observed with strong, highly energetic women. In order to retrieve their own vigour, modern males have to make contact with the instinctive, sexual, primitive Wild Man (adapted from a fairy tale). To achieve this, they have to descend into 'the nourishing dark' (ibid. 6) of the male psyche. Although Bly affirms strongly that his book 'does not seek to turn men against women' (ibid. x), his public behaviour throws some doubt on this assertion. At a seminar, for example, he was asked: 'Robert, when we tell women our desires, they tell us we're wrong'. Upon which he answered: 'So, then you bust them in the mouth' (Faludi, 1992: 345).[22] The undercurrent tenor of the book is: let men be men again! Good-bye to Woody Allen! Hooray to John Wayne!

One man cannot be left unmentioned in a list of 'backlashers': George Gilder. In *Wealth and Poverty* (1982)[23] he simultaneously strikes out against the welfare state and women by miraculously managing to assemble an explanation for poverty which is tailor-made for white, middle-class males who want to preserve the 1950s status-quo (free housekeeper plus low taxation for redistribution). According to Gilder (ibid. 135), poverty has nothing to do with involuntary unemployment, racism and sexism, but is rather caused by the women's movement and welfare measures. Coincidentally the causes for poverty which Gilder identifies are also the two major threats to backward-looking middle-class males. With reasonable simplification, Gilder's chain of thought can be summarised as follows:

The long period of time humans spent in hunting societies accounts for the deep and instinctive feeling of men to be providers (ibid. 137). Both the feminist movement and the welfare state have challenged this male role and thereby male dominance. Working women have established their independence and the modern male has 'been cuckolded by the compassionate state' (ibid. 118), i.e. families without providers are no longer left to fend for themselves. Thus stripped of their main activity, men lose their key role and their authority in families. They 'can no longer feel manly in [their] ... own home' (ibid.). Women do not lose their sense of identity through welfare provision because their role is mainly shaped by biology (ibid. 124). Father roles, however, are shaped by society and independent women and the 'welfare culture' tell him that he and his work are no longer required. Hence, he stops to work and leaves his children (ibid. 124) thereby causing poverty for all.

Gilder's preferred solutions are: first, the welfare system must be made unattractive and demeaning (ibid. 120). Second, male superiority in the public sphere, i.e. in employment, must be re-established. In order to do that, the emphasis in the non-professional job market should be shifted to favour male aggressiveness over credentials, qualifications, academic performance and IQ, all of which put poor black women into a better position than poor black men (ibid. 136).[24] His overall conclusion is that women's financial independence, either 'self-inflicted' or 'state-inflicted' must be pushed back to revitalise the male provider role and thereby solve the problem of poverty.

Backlashers are not necessarily male as the example of Sylvia Ann Hewlett shows. Her book *A Lesser Life - The Myth of Women's Liberation* (1987) is a backlash classic. The English-born economist from New York attacks the feminist movement for three reasons. Allegedly,

- the movement's promotion of no-fault divorce regulations led to lower settlements for women who were generally the non-faulting party (ibid. 30).
- support for the Equal Rights Amendment disregarded protective unequal benefits such as extra rest periods for women and exemption from military draft and combat (ibid. 132, 134).
- the movement's contempt and hostility for motherhood[25] led to its alienation from the majority of ordinary women (ibid. 117) who want to strengthen rather than weaken the traditional family model (ibid. 143).

The last point is the most important in this context. The overall tune of the book is that the feminist movement pushed women into high-powered, time-consuming careers which were only fulfilling on the surface and in the short-term. Once these women reached their early forties, childless and unmarried, desperation set in. Only then did they realise what millions of non-feminist American women knew all along, that they 'like[d] being wives and mothers' in traditional roles' (ibid. 143, 263). Unfortunately it was too late by then as the chances of finding a husband and having a child were drastically reduced after 35 (ibid. 37). Hewlett's conclusions on the main issue in the book, the career-children question, are: career-only as male clones is not attractive for women who need children for their happiness (ibid. 266). Since 93 per cent of women do not work in top professions, government support in terms of 'generous maternity leave, subsidised child care and flexitime' (ibid. 269) would enable most women to combine family and work.[26]

Bly, Gilder and Hewlett all emphasise traditional qualities in the gender divide. Men are aggressive beings used to hunting down bread for their families whilst women's true happiness lies in child-bearing and rearing. Without explicitly calling women altruistic and connected and men egoistic and individualistic, the above authors tacitly build their demands and conclusions on these premises. The traditional family model is evoked by all three with men allegedly wanting to feel manly in their homes again and women only escaping long-term sadness and depression by marrying and having children (ibid. 266).

What feminists call the backlash, an undeclared war against women's rights (Faludi, 1992), enables *Homo economicus* to find new solid ground. As was explained earlier, 'he' might represent the basic skeleton of modern males: self-interested, individualistic and thus well suited to compete with other males in the public sphere. Erstwhile, their home-making, child-rearing, altruistic wives sit happily at home being well provided for. It is conceivable that women and men are essentially different, but is it likely, as backlash authors suggest? To answer this question would not only be an enormous scholarly task, it would also require a strong belief in universalism which is not present. However, as has been done before, it is considered reasonable and tenable to criticise a universalist position such as the backlash one without replacing it at the same time. Fortunately the criticism of major backlash positions has been done excellently elsewhere and will therefore only be summarised here.

On nearly 600 pages, American journalist Susan Faludi argued against the basic assumption of backlashers, that men and women need different things and not equality to be happy. In *Backlash - The undeclared war against women* (1992) she approaches the problem in two different ways. First, she shows that the proponents of new traditional womanhood are themselves either high-powered career women or 'new' men. Faludi reveals the hypocrisy of privately taking advantage of feminism 'while publicly deploring its influence' (ibid. 289). Second, she analyses studies, mainly from the field of psychology, to show that backlash claims are mere propaganda which cannot be corroborated. One example of each approach shall be given here.

Connaught C. Marshner, formerly Ronald Reagan's research consultant for the Heritage Foundation, is well-known in America for her promotion of traditional womanhood. She shot to fame with statements such as: 'A woman's nature is, simply, other-oriented ... Women are ordained by their nature to spend themselves in meeting the needs of others (ibid. 272)'. This, however, does not apply to Marshner herself, as Faludi shows. Although Marshner announces the age of the new traditional woman, the happy home-maker, she herself is a very busy career-woman who freely says that she is not interested in unrewarding, unfulfilling housewifely duties (ibid. 278). In contrast, she proudly calls herself a commuter mother and commuter wife (ibid. 277) who leaves her children with her husband to pursue, what she calls, a rewarding career in Washington (ibid. 278).

Faludi gives several examples of New Right women activists who 'report to their offices in their suits, issue press releases demanding that women return to the home, and never see a contradiction' (ibid. 289).[27] They 'have-it-all' by making use of the possibilities earlier feminists have given them and at the same time fight to prevent other women from sharing in. This divergence of acting and speaking makes assurances from New Right career women untrustworthy. But Faludi does not stop at disclosing this hypocrisy. In addition, she analyses studies on the subject of homemaking and female happiness. Her most important findings are:

- Considering the three important components of female lives, employment, marriage and children, employment shows the strongest and most consistent connection to female good health, mental and physical (ibid. 56).
- The strongest incidence of depression is found in women who have never worked. Mental disorders (suicide, breakdowns, insomnia, nightmares) are more frequent amongst housewives than working women (ibid. 58f).
- It is men, not women, who are adversely affected by working women with own careers. Research showed that men with working wives have greater mental problems, lower self-esteem and higher occurrence of depression than men with housewives (ibid. 60f).

Faludi's claims about women's priorities were confirmed by an ICM research survey in 1996 when young women were asked to think ahead and imagine what, lying on their deathbed, they would most likely regret not having done. Having children only came fifth after a successful career, a harmonious and enduring relationship, seeing the world and making a lot of money (Franks, 1999: 14). Similarly a survey by the National Council of Women in 1992 found that only '13 per cent of women of childbearing age think that children are necessary to being fulfilled' (ibid.).

Faludi's objective was to show that, what she calls, the backlash brains trust (Faludi, 1992: 314) have only one aim. At first sight they seem genuinely concerned about women's well-being and happiness. A second look reveals, however, that they are only interested in pushing back the women's liberation movement and trying to avoid further progress. Backlashers employ alleged insights from anthropology to corroborate their claims. Men, they argue, are hunters, women are carers. Faludi does not concern herself with the male perspective, but her research shows clearly that women want equality and that most of them 'want-it-all' (career, marriage, family) as men have done for hundreds of years.

Where does this leave the present discussion on the difficulty of reconciling *Homo economicus* with altruism? The New Right cannot go on pretending that men and women are irrefutably different and interested in contradicting things in life. The wave of new traditional womanhood in the United States was very impressive and surfaced timely when neo-classical economics came into fashion. Altruistic women ordained by nature to care would be the perfect mate for aggressive, manly *Homo economicus*. 'Unfortunately' studies showed that the majority of women in the US do not comply with the new fashion. As far as universalisations are possible, the majority want a rewarding career plus husband and children.

Backlashers tried to preserve the male 'have-it-all' status quo by claiming that equality is bad for women. Instead, vast numbers of women support the basic founding aims of the women's movement all of which serve to further women's equality: reproductive choice, equal pay, access to child-care and freedom from sexual abuse (Smith, 1992: xv). It is not possible, nor reasonable to make claims such as: all women want to work; happiness lies only in rewarding careers. At the same time, it does not make sense to claim the opposite: women's whole happiness lies in home-making for the provider husband and their joint children. Psychological studies clearly refute this affirmation. Instead, all different propositions should be accounted for.

It can be concluded that the self-denying mate for *Homo economicus* who is naturally inclined to care rather than work outside the home is a myth evoked by backlashers. It cannot be argued that women and men are fundamentally different. Psychological research showed that they want the same things; above all, women want equality. Hence, to uphold the picture of *Homo economicus* by claiming that it only refers to men and that the riddle of altruism in humankind can be explained with reference to women must be rejected.

Rationality

The main personality traits of *Homo economicus* were shown to be: individualism, self-interest and rationality. The previous section examined and questioned individualism and egoism and the discussion will now turn to rationality. Is the depiction of human beings as rational chosers a fair one?

After defining rationality, several possible critiques will be introduced briefly.[28]

The first step when dealing with the idea of rationality is to agree upon a definition. In psychology the word 'rational' is used to describe meaningful behaviour which fits a given situation and is based on understanding (Digel *et al.*, 1987, Vol. 18: 87). In philosophy the term, deriving from Latin *ratio* (reason, understanding), is used in two ways. First, 'rationalism' describes the systems of Descartes, Spinoza, Leibniz and others in the 17th and 18th century who believed that both knowledge and moral guidelines can be found by employing the rational faculties of human beings (Elser *et al.*, 1992: 274). Second, the term is used more generally to represent philosophical positions which emphasise reason in contrast to sentiment, intuition, experience and faith (Hügli *et al.*, 1991: 482). Settling on a definition for rationality is not too controversial but it is nevertheless a highly disputed concept. Questions such as the following spring to mind: what are the limits of reason? What can reason achieve? Who can distinguish between rational and irrational behaviour? Which presuppositions does rationality require? Three examples will be given to show where attacks on the concept of rationality can come from.

Friedrich von Hayek (1988: 84) opposes the modern welfare state and other interventionist systems because, he believes, that self-ordering market mechanisms will procure better and more opportunities for citizens than any rival system. One of the reasons Hayek gives for his standpoint in economic thought is the 'epistemic argument'. He claims that human knowledge (*episteme* = Greek for knowledge) can never be sophisticated enough to rationally design and implement a social order such as an economy. A human society and with it an economy is not as repetitive as an ant-hill (Barry, 1986: 69). It is therefore impossible to predict and control outcomes by rational means. Whatever action a government takes to influence economic processes, the possibility of achieving the desired result is negligible, according to Hayekians. They believe that human intervention into evolved social systems, e.g. economies, can only coincidentally bring about intended results because human rationality is not advanced enough to put deliberate social constructions into practice. Thereby, Hayek does not question the human capacity for rationality but its scope.

In a similar vein, Greens argue that many present-day problems stem from too strong a belief in rationality, i.e. in the capacity of humans to reflect, come to a decision and then rearrange the world according to their own wishes (Ehrenfeld, 1991: 45). Surfacing with the Modern Age and thinkers like Francis Bacon, the rational master set out to conquer nature and change 'her' according to 'his' plans. Unlimited faith in science and technology, which sprang from an equally unlimited belief in the rational mind, created ever more environmental problems which were then referred back to the rational scientist for new solutions.

Feminists deplore the strict dualistic world-view which divides reason from emotion, public from private, the economy from the family, mind from body, science from the humanities, men from women (Jennings, 1993: 121) 'man'kind from nature (Nelson, 1993: 25) etc. Understanding the world in a dualistic way has been described by feminists as 'peculiarly masculinist' (ibid. 33), as a way to cope with the loss of the 'medieval feeling of connection to nature' (ibid. 25) and as 'an alienated response to the social instability of the seventeenth century' (Jennings, 1993: 117). Although it is possible to define reason, emotion, experience and intuition separately, they do not present themselves purely in real life. So-called 'objective science' which claims to be 100 per cent reason and 0 per cent emotion, intuition or faith does not exist (Whalen, 1994: 21f).

The three described attacks on rationality have different aims: the feminist critique takes an epistemological angle and argues against the ideals of rationality and objectivity in the sciences. The Greens attack the philosophy of life (*Weltanschauung*) which maintains that resources can be squandered, air and water polluted and the rational scientist will still find a way out. Hayek criticises economic policies which are based on a concept of rationality that he sees as overrated. These examples show that it is not the definition of rationality but its significance for human life which is contested. Here, as well as in the above critiques, it is not maintained that reason is beyond human beings. To deliberate on a given problem, to come to a decision that is based on these deliberations and to act meaningfully upon the results is a faculty which human beings possess. In so far, *Homo economicus* is an accurate depiction of humankind in the area of rationality. However, can anything be gained from the knowledge that human beings are rational? Is human behaviour predictable because they are equipped with the faculty to reason? Economics does not make statements about human nature for their own sake. These statements are used in predicting human behaviour, for example, in maintaining that humans only work if no other source of income is available.

A glance back in times at the historical roots of the concept of rationality may prove instructive. Here is therefore a quick reminder of the essence of Plato's 'Republic'. Plato wanted rational man to rule Athens believing that only he would achieve welfare for all. For him only few humans were partaking of reason. Those who did, had their 'lower' impulses - appetite and spirit - under control. As a result, they were able to be just. Hence, for Plato, rational man was *just* man. We will now go forward in time to see whether rational behaviour is still characterised as just behaviour in Western societies at the end of the 20th century.

Dirk Meyer redefines the golden rule of reciprocity. According to him (1996: 212 - my translation), rational behaviour nowadays is not defined as it used to be: 'Act as you want others to act'. Instead the rule has been perverted to: 'Act as you fear others will act'; which he also calls the rationality trap. He believes that a rational being today is supposed to make the most of free-riding and fraud. If you have deliberately smashed an expensive Chinese vase, pretend it was an accident and claim insurance money. If you have a badly paid part-time job, pretend you have none and claim unemployment benefit. Rationality in this sense equals the maximisation of utility for the self.

This is also true for one well-known argument against welfare payments, i.e. their alleged creation of disincentives to work. Work is considered to be unpleasant, hence the maximisation of utility demands its avoidance. Rational individuals are therefore not expected to work if they can get the same amount of income from social security (Dex, 1989: 15). Accordingly, it is considered rational to be dependent on other people's income and irrational to work if this alternative presents itself.

The abyss that has opened between the understanding of rational behaviour and common-sense justice could hardly be wider as between Plato on the one hand and Meyer as well as Dex on the other hand. Plato would hardly think of an insurance cheat as an equivalent to his philosopher king, equipped with a good proportion of reason. However, both the philosopher king and the insurance fraudster share a common trait. Their rational behaviour is structured similarly. They reflect on a topic, come to a reasoned decision and act accordingly. Hence, it is not possible to call one rational and the other irrational. What, then, is the difference? Rational behaviour and rational actions have aims and it is these aims that differ. The philosopher king, at least in Plato's ideal world, will employ his reason for the good of the state, whilst the insurance cheat has only his own well-being in mind.

Present-day definitions of rationality are embedded in the New Right world-view of egoistic selves fighting exclusively for their own personal profit. To be rational does not just mean to reflect and come to sensible decisions but to reflect and come to a decision that is conducive to the egoistic, self-driven individually-minded *Homo economicus*. John Kingdom (1992: 7) writes: 'Today rational individuals poison the atmosphere, deforest the land, deplete the seas, pollute the rivers and conduce life-threatening climatic change, while countless millions die for want of food and water'. This means, that individual rational behaviour is in extreme discord with collective well-being. Not for Plato, as was briefly described. He believed that caring for ones own well-being is intimately connected to caring for the well-being of the whole (family, city, state) (Plato, 1993: 412St.). On the other hand, Aristotle disagreed on the topic and pondered about the so-called 'Tragedy of the Commons'.[29] For him individual rational behaviour leads unavoidably to a reduction of the common good if property was owned collectively (Aristotle, 1981: 38f). This leaves two possible positions on the aims of rational conduct. First, rational behaviour is self-centred and therefore always inconducive to the common good. Second, rational behaviour is orientated towards both individual and collective well-being. *Homo economicus* as a rational being could therefore be represented by both Mother Theresa and Donald Trump. Mother Theresa acted rationally for the common good, Donald Trump for his own well-being.

Where does this lead the present discussion? On two accounts we agree with the New Right's picture of *Homo economicus*. 1) It is possible to distinguish reason from intuition, experience and faith, i.e. it is possible to define the concept. In the sphere of economics, for example, it does not make sense to say: 'I've got a hunch that the plumber called Holywell is more reliable than the one called Davenport. I like the name'. This is an irrational approach to a problem that requires either experience (having employed both before) or reason (asking former customers about their experience, finding out prices and coming to a decision based on facts). 2) Humans are rational beings and they can normally distinguish between rational and irrational behaviour. If you want apples, there are numerous rational decisions available. It might be rational to buy cheap ones from Kwiksave, organic ones from the wholefood store, native ones from a local farmer, those that are sold by the shop next-door etc. There are, in fact, very few ways to acquire apples irrationally.

Disagreement only enters the discussion with the moral question: which ends are pursued by employing the faculty of reason? Merely individual, self-centred, egoistic ones or also ends which take the outcomes for the community into account? *Rationalists* such as Spinoza wanted to employ rationality to find moral guidelines, i.e. guidelines that could steer a community. *Homo economicus'* faculty of reasoning is employed solely for his own personal well-being.

It would be unreasonable to claim that people are naturally inclined to use their rationality for the common good or that they are naturally inclined to only use it for selfish purposes. There are too many examples of human beings who could be assigned to either camp. But this is not the point. By agreeing with the proposition that *Homo economicus* is rightly characterised as rational but at the same time showing that this does not give sufficient indications for actual behaviour, it was demonstrated that the mere attribute of rationality does not give substance to *Homo economicus*. To claim that people are going to stop working as soon as they found a way to claim sufficient benefits because this allegedly is the rational thing to do implies that rationality is only understood in the egoistic setting of New Right anthropology. Not only might there be rational reasons to continue work (company, routine, prestige etc.) but rationality can also be employed to further or at least not damage the common good. Rationality is a tool, like a knife. It can be used to cut flowers or to cut throats. That human beings have the faculty to reason does not determine whether they are gardeners or killers. The New Right cannot simply argue that it is rational not to work as soon as benefits are available. Reasoning is the process of decision-making and only if the New Right anthropology of egoistic loners comes into the picture does it make sense to make this claim. If - as was argued in the first section of this chapter (on self-interest and individualism) - this anthropology is biased and built on shaky grounds, it is just as reasonable to maintain that human beings employ their rationality to further the common good as well as their own.

We must therefore conclude that agreement on the faculty of reason does not further the discussion whether *Homo economicus* correctly describes human beings. Rationality is a tool and the conflict lies in its application not its existence.

The overall conclusion which can be drawn from this chapter, is that the three features of *Homo economicus* do not depict humankind adequately. *Homo economicus* is an androcentrically biased concept which ignores experiences of humans outside positions of power, particularly female knowledge. In addition, it contradicts beliefs from earlier philosophers and research findings about the heritage of *Homo sapiens*. Therefore statements by mainstream economists or New-Right thinkers which simply add 'but this is human nature' to political demands must be treated with great caution. Unless individual evidence is brought forward, the mere reference to human nature cannot be accepted as proof for statements on, for example, work incentives. In line with this claim, the next chapter will look at empirical evidence for allegedly widespread work reluctance in welfare states.

Notes

[1] This is what Aristotle says in *Politics*. His best known description of human beings, however, is *zoon logon*, the rational animal.

[2] After the death of Baudelaire's father, his mother remarried and sent him away to boarding school; an event he never came to terms with (Biemel, 1964: 101).

[3] Baudelaire was sent on a two-year maritime journey by his family to prevent him from squandering his inheritance. When he returned early, guardians were assigned to him.

[4] In this book the existentialist view will not be supported. Mary Midgley's (1980: 4) ironic criticism is deemed appropriate: 'According to the Blank Paper view, man ... starts off infinitely plastic ... Forming families, fearing the dark, and jumping at the sight of a spider are just results of our conditioning'.

[5] *Homo economicus* will be referred to as male because feminist economists showed that 'he' has been designed with white, middle-class, privileged males in mind. More later in this chapter.

[6] However, practitioners of the newly established field of 'evolutionary psychology' argue that human nature is universalist and can be derived at scientifically. 'Evolutionary psychology is the search for human universals; adaptations which its supporters claim shape who we are and guide how we behave' (Malone, 1998). Helena Cronin (1998) from the London School of Economics maintains that evolutionary psychology 'is the place where we are going to find out the truth about human nature and that is going to inform every policy, every legal document ... once it gets off the ground'. She thereby takes the same position as Thomas Hobbes nearly 350 years ago, namely that it is possible to arrive at an account of human nature scientifically and that politics should be shaped accordingly.

[7] Adaptiveness and non-adaptiveness are technical terms from the field of evolutionary biology. Edward O. Wilson (1975: 21) defines them as follows: 'A

trait can be said to be adaptive if it is maintained in a population by selection. We can put the matter more precisely by saying that another trait is non-adaptive ... if it reduces the fitness of individuals.'

8   Chromosomal anomaly which leads to sterility, mental deficiencies and eunuch features in human males.

9   Darwin himself did not proceed to approve of eugenics. He believed in the evolutionary success of mutual aid and cooperation and felt that morality had raised human beings above the animal world. Therefore, he thought, it is necessary to accept the disadvantages that are allegedly connected with the reproduction of the weak and ill (Vogel, 1990: 123).

10 A different or supplementary answer is that altruism relies on reciprocity. For the scope of this book, detailed explanations on how altruism could develop under evolutionary pressure are irrelevant. Only its widespread existence is important. A brief discussion of reciprocal altruism can be found in Ruse, Michael (1985) *Sociobiology - Sense or Nonsense*, D. Reidel Publishing Group, Dordrecht, pp.49-51; 69-71. Another discussion can be found in Barash, David (1982) *Sociobiology and Behavior*, Elsevier, New York, pp.134-137. Barash likens the reciprocal theory of altruism to 'notions of enlightened self-interest' as advocated by Machiavelli and Hobbes (ibid. 135).

11 One major critic of sociobiology as a discipline, Marshall Sahlins (1976), argues that it is biased in favour of Western ideology and *laisser-faire* capitalism. Hence, it might be surprising to find that the field is used here to attack *Homo economicus*. However, although sociobiologists concentrate on what Dawkins calls 'the selfish gene' by examining individual selection, their research shows that our ancestors were characterised by sociability and that altruism is widespread, two points that were needed to question *Homo economicus*.

12 Arthur Schopenhauer challenged Kant's categorical imperative as a possible foundation for ethics. He (1979: 41) called it an *a priori* house of cards which lacks in reality and thereby effectiveness. In his opinion, it is just another formulation of egoistic morals (ibid. 54). Under the categorical imperative, people choose justice and charity not because they want to give but because they want to receive. Schopenhauer's alternative is to base ethics on the innate human feelings of sympathy and empathy which do not require abstract reasonings but can be known intuitively (ibid. 143). His metaphysical explanation for the existence of sympathy uses Kant's transcendental aesthetics. Since time and space are only forms of pure intuition and not attributes of things-in-themselves, there is neither side by side nor one after the other. Multitude does only exist in the world of appearances, not in the real world where everything is One (ibid. 166). Hereby he formulates his monistic *Weltanschauung* and calls upon the support of all important monists (Pythagoras, Plotin, Bruno, Spinoza; ibid. 166f). Human beings who are not too deeply entangled in their own egoisms, feel the homogeneousness of the world and develop a deep fellow feeling, a sympathy and empathy for others (ibid. 168f).

13 How Harding defends herself against the challenge of 'anything goes', i.e. relativism, can be read in the cited article (Harding, 1993).

14 That economics is proud of its mathematical credentials has been expressed by Julie Nelson (1993: 26): 'In fact, the less research has to do with actual economies, the higher its status: purely abstract models are commonly referred to as being "highbrow" ... The "acid test" of articles in economic theory, said Nobel Laureate Gerard Debreu in ... 1990 ... comes in "removing all their economic interpretations and letting their mathematical infrastructure stand on its own" '.

15 'Men' in this section is restricted to white, male property owners. Male slaves, for

16   example, do not fit the description of free and autonomous actors.

It must be said that Frank Hahn and Tony Cramp are not coming from the right-wing in mainstream economics and neither are they proponents of *Homo economicus* in the strict sense. Had Hayek or Friedman committed themselves to named benevolence, the inconsistency of neo-classical economics would be more obvious. As it is, Hayek simply ignores the family. It only appears as an 'occasional appendage to the world of production' (Pascall, 1986: 7) in his work.

17   It was explained earlier why the claim to base politics on a scientific concept of human nature cannot be upheld. At the most - and this is the purpose of this chapter - an existing concept can be criticised.

18   At this stage most authors draw attention to the point that Smith published two major books: *The Wealth of Nations* and *The Theory of Moral Sentiments*. The latter book, according to Irving Kristol (1978: 60), proves that Smith 'never believed for a moment that human beings were strictly economic men or women'.

19   The emphasis here will be on the gender divide. Race and class divides will not be included in the discussion, i.e. potential attacks on *Homo economicus* from these angles are not followed up.

20   'Claims to have produced universally valid beliefs - principles of ethics, of human nature, epistemologies, and philosophies of science - are ethnocentric. Only members of the powerful groups in societies stratified by race, ethnicity, class, gender, and sexuality could imagine that their standards for knowledge and the claims resulting from adherence to such standards should be found preferable by all rational creatures, past, present, and future' (Harding, 1993: 60).

21   Bly used to be known as a sixties' peace activist who received the National Book Award for a collection of poems. In the 1980s he turned into a so-called New Age masculinist who tried to re-introduce his fellow men to their buried masculine selves (Faludi, 1992: 340ff).

22   Later, when asked whether he supports violence against women, Bly said that he meant verbal, not physical hits (Faludi, 1992: 345).

23   At the time of publication, the best-selling author was Program Director of the International Center for Economic Policy Studies in Manhattan and Chairman of the Economic Roundtable at the Lehrman Institute.

24   This approach borders on intellectual lunacy considering that Gilder calls himself an economist. He genuinely suggests that employers should forego intelligent, well-qualified staff with good references to employ an aggressive male! In the same line of thought he believes that there is a *problem* with government jobs. This problem is 'that many of them are best suited to women' (Gilder, 1982: 138), whom Gilder obviously does not want in the job market whatever valuable contribution they have to make.

25   Hewlett (1987: 129) indeed found some rather drastic opinions from feminists, such as Ann Dally's belief that the full-time care of a baby is like 'spending all day, every day, in the exclusive company of an incontinent mental defective'.

26   Hewlett does not deplore that only 7 per cent of women are working in top professions neither does she demand increased fatherly participation in child-care.

27   Faludi introduces the so-called Backlash Brain Trust, five men and four women of which Marshner is one. Insights into their personal lives show that all of them are guilty of the same hypocrisy: praising and demanding female home-making while arranging their private lives on the basis of equality in both professional and household duties.

28   Plato's possible reaction to *Homo economicus*' rationality was already detailed earlier in this section, but will be included very briefly again.

29   For a description, see Garrett Hardin (1991) 'The Tragedy of the Commons', in: Dobson, Andrew (ed.); *The Green Reader*, Blackwell, Oxford, pp.37-39.

6 Benefit Fraud, Tax Evasion and the 'Lazy Scrounger'

The work incentives debate is primarily a debate about money and not about work ethics. Lottery winners, wealthy property owners, footballers who retire at 25 or prosperous heirs are not targeted in the discussion. Only those who claim benefits are scrutinised and in many cases found undeserving of provision. Self-reliance and financial independence are promoted as the prime values by libertarians.

This chapter will look for ideological elements in the work incentives debate and see whether the position that non-work is voluntarily chosen by many fraudulent benefit claimants can be upheld. The essential issue is whether the opposition to the welfare state is based on facts or ideology. The chapter is divided into three sections. The first section examines empirical evidence to corroborate or refute claims that voluntary non-work combined with social security fraud are widespread. The second section asks whether tax evasion and benefit fraud are dealt with efficiently so as to maximise available funds for the treasury. The third section considers whether political scapegoating enters the discussion.

Empirical Evidence for Widespread Voluntary Non-Work

When President Clinton signed a new restrictive welfare bill in 1996, the *International Herald Tribune* celebrated this as a 'revival of liberalism' that will create a new 'faith in government' (Kaus, 1996: 6). Voters, states Mickey Kaus, never hated the government, they only hated welfare. With the new bill signed, 'welfare is no longer a free ride' and 'many people will leave the rolls' (ibid.). Kaus's implication is that the American social security system is abused on a grand scale. On the other hand, a German social democrat claimed that the richest country on earth leaves the starving and freezing - rather than the fraudulent and lazy - to fend for themselves

(Kurbjuweit, 1996: 3). A similar conflict of opinion can be observed within Germany. In 1995, the conservative Health Minister, Horst Seehofer (1995: 1063), claimed that *many* work-shy people make themselves a good life at the expense of others. Contradicting this view, a liberal German weekly wrote that benefit abuse is *very small* (Kurbjuweit, 1996: 3).

The issue of benefit fraud and work-shyness seems to reveal different positions held by conservatives on the one hand and social democrats on the other. Conservatives typically argue that social security provision encourages social ills, whilst social democrats tend to refuse any such link. The division has been apparent since the early 19th century. In 1834, Alban de Villeneuve-Bargemont published his three-volume *Economie politique chrétienne* followed in 1835 by Alexis de Toqueville's *Memoir on pauperism*. The former argued that poverty is not a problem of voluntary non-work but rather of lack of employment or insufficient earnings. In contrast, Toqueville believed that pauperism is the inevitable consequence of charity because human beings have a natural passion for idleness (Toqueville, 1997: 28).

In addition to the fundamentally different viewpoints on the underlying *causes* of non-work (laziness versus external reasons), modern politicians often disagree on the *scale* of fraud. In this regard, a role swap between the Tories and Labour could be observed in Britain in early 1997. According to Alistair Burt, the then Tory minister for Social Security and Disabled People, housing benefit fraud amounted to an estimated one billion pounds per year (House of Commons, 1997). New Labour's estimate for housing benefit fraud was twice as high at the same time amounting to two billion pounds (ibid.).

Can empirical evidence bring any light to the discussion as to whether benefit fraud and work-shyness occur on a grand scale in Western welfare states? The next section will present data from the United States and Germany. However, before proceeding, one serious reservation must be made. This book examines the very general and widespread belief that welfare provision in Western states endangers work incentives. No existing scientific study analyses whether work-shyness coupled with benefit fraud is prevalent throughout the West. Typically, studies cover specific areas and restricted time periods. It is, however, considered permissible to infer from time-limited, regional evidence to national patterns since the claim that is being investigated is based on alleged universal statements about human nature. If human nature is extensively characterised by work-shyness, as conservative and libertarian thinkers assume (Minford, 1992: 117; Seldon, 1982: 8), a regional study should be able to detect it. Hence, the next section will introduce empirical evidence which is restricted to certain regions and periods of time and still suppose that it will give useful insights into the discussion on the whole. The findings of two German studies on benefit fraud will be given as evidence as well as data from several US studies. The presentation is intentionally brief, since only research *results* are relevant.

Benefit Fraud in Germany

From 1983 to 1989 the University of Bremen cooperated with the Centre for Social Policy (*Zentrum für Sozialpolitik*) to complete a comprehensive study on benefit abuse and poverty. Researchers examined the case of every tenth new benefit claimant during the seven year period, conducted numerous interviews and analysed around 1,000 old files. They drew the following two conclusions. First, benefit abuse is a rare event as is the phenomenon of work-shyness in claimants, most of whom were either close to pension age, ill or - at the time - without chances in the job market. Second, only a minority of 1.3 per cent of recipients slipped into long-term dependency, i.e. stayed on benefits for more than ten years. Most people were confident and independent enough, according to research findings, to leave the rolls quickly (Leibfried *et al.*, 1995).

In her article *Social Security - Myth and Reality* (1995 - my translation), Petra Buhr describes the provisional conclusions of an on-going study at the Martin-Luther University in East Germany which began in 1994. According to Buhr, who is one of the participating researchers, this study shows that benefit fraud is restricted to a minority of cases. Most recipients are indeed not able to work either because of age, sickness or full-time care obligations. She concludes that 'the reproach of abuse does not carry far: only a minority of benefit recipients is actually able to work ... 'abuse' and 'work-shyness' are not really a subject' (ibid. 1067f - my translation). Rather than being an easy option for work-shy fraudsters, welfare provision does, according to Buhr (ibid. 1068), fulfil its role in society as a temporary aid to self-help.

The findings of these two studies could be interpreted as only partly helpful because of the two-tieredness of the German system. Citizens who are unable to earn a living in Germany can either be supported with basic social security funds (*Sozialhilfe*) or unemployment assistance if they were made redundant recently. Both above studies only examine abuse and fraud in the basic system. It is therefore theoretically possible that wide-spread fraud exists in the unemployment assistance scheme. However, there are two points that can be made against this possibility. First, claimants have to show a work-record to receive unemployment assistance, i.e. eligibility requires past contributions to the unemployment fund. Second, after a limited period, claimants fall back into the basic scheme. Hence, the 'really work-shy' and the long-term unemployed are to be found in the basic scheme, where no significant level of fraud could be detected.

Benefit Fraud in the United States

The North-American welfare state is one of the oldest in the world. It came into being in the 1930s when President Roosevelt introduced the *New Deal*. The United States can therefore look back on a relatively long history of social security policies and possible relations to benefit fraud and work-shyness. In *Incentives to Work* (1970), David Macarov summarises studies on benefit fraud in the 1950s and 1960s. One study from the 1960s found that only 0.1 per cent of benefit recipients refused suitable work. During the same decade 0.27 per cent of recipients were charged with benefit fraud and of these 85 per cent were not sentenced because the courts dismissed the case or refused to prosecute. This leaves 0.04 per cent of benefit recipients being prosecuted for fraud (ibid. 189). Another study cited by Macarov from the 1950s found that at most 2 per cent of recipients abused the benefit system (ibid. 188).

The *New Deal* introduced several big assistance programs which included unemployment compensation, pensions, aid for the disabled or elderly and a program designed to help widows called AFDC.[1] AFDC (Aid to Families with Dependent Children) was the biggest single item in the 1996 US welfare budget and also, by far, the most controversial (Kaus, 1996: 6). This program which mainly supports single mothers attracted most research on benefit fraud in the 1970s. Right-wing critics of the welfare state have been claiming for a long time that AFDC destroys work incentives and undermines family life (Fraser, 1990: 199). Two national investigations carried out in 1963 and 1971, showed that 'recurrent allegations that welfare rolls could be pared by weeding out "cheaters" have not been supported by facts' (Levitan and Rein and Marwick, 1972: 18). Although 15 per cent of AFDC families were shown to have received overpayments in 1971, 10 per cent were underpaid at the same time. The reasons for these errors lay in agency and claimant mistakes, rather than fraud (ibid. 19). The overall conclusion both in 1963 and 1971 was that 'cases involving fraud were reported to be very few' (ibid.).

A third, and more recent analysis of benefit fraud in the United States was presented by Mary Hawkesworth (1992: 390). She analysed the reasons why households were below the poverty line and therefore dependent on state transfers. According to her, 48 per cent of these households were headed by individuals over 65, 12 per cent by disabled citizens and 7 per cent by mothers with pre-school children. 7.5 per cent relied on benefits although the family head worked permanently full-time (the so-called 'working poor'). 5 per cent of claimants were students whose pre-transfer incomes, i.e. funds available before state support, were below the poverty line. Amongst the remaining claimants, 20.4 per cent of households were headed by employees who worked on a part-time basis and 1 per cent of households was unaccounted for. The following figure summarises Hawkesworth's account.

Figure 6.1   Households below the poverty line, United States, 1990s

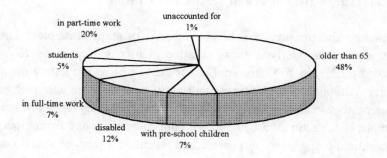

Source: Data from Hawkesworth (1992: 390).

According to Hawkesworth's research, the idea that benefit recipients, especially AFDC householders, refuse to work 'is simply wrong' (ibid.). It is not work-shyness, as the above figure indicates, that throws individuals onto state benefits but reasons such as old age, disability, higher education or care responsibilities.

Based on the above US studies and the two German studies, the existence of extensive benefit fraud cannot be corroborated. On the contrary, fraud was shown to be minimal. These findings stand in marked contrast to statements from politicians about abuse of social security systems in both countries. As was illustrated in the beginning of this section, it is frequently claimed that fraud occurs on a large scale. According to American Peter Germanis (1992: 386), for example, 'fraud and abuse [are] prevalent in our current system'. Or, following former Chancellor Kohl (1995: 2 - my translation), Germany is allegedly a 'collective leisurepark' financed by the state. Could it be that the fraud argument is a right-wing rhetoric, i.e. a well-maintained myth? This conclusion presents itself since statements cannot be squared with empirical data. To affirm this claim, treasury activities by Conservative governments in Britain and Germany will be examined in a first step. The second step will analyse whether ideological elements, particularly scapegoating, can be found by looking at the alleged 'culprits' of fraud and work-shyness.

The Treasury - Benefit Fraud versus Tax Evasion

Defrauding the treasury is a breach of modern state principles. The state relies on income derived from taxation. Citizens pay taxes to achieve specified goals, e.g. to finance police services or provide a safety net against poverty. Although not all citizens will agree with all state activities, elected representatives can be held accountable on how they spend taxes. The principle of taxation as a compulsory collection of money from citizens for democratically approved purposes could be called a form of social contract. This contract is violated if taxes are spent on activities which are not selected by state bodies. Giving state benefits to people who are not entitled to them, is one example for a breach of social contract or as John Kenneth Galbraith (1962: 241) puts it 'a species of fraud upon the community'. According to British Conservative, Nadim Sahawe, (1996) it is important that 'the money spent on welfare, that is yours and my hard earned money and every tax payers' pound is targeted towards those members of our society that are most vulnerable and are justly entitled to benefit from it'.

In Western societies, it is hence seen as a serious wrong-doing to take money from the treasury without democratic consent. Where does this definition of a social contract, which must not be violated by fraud, leave us? The aim of this chapter is to see whether work-shyness coupled with benefit fraud (the 'pathological' explanation of unemployment) is a serious problem in Western welfare states or whether it is pushed up on the political agenda for ideological reasons. So far, it was established that independent studies do not reveal widespread benefit fraud. However, it might be argued that fraud even on a small scale represents a serious problem in the West because it ties up treasury money which is urgently needed in other areas. Social security was the biggest single item in both the British and the German state budget in 1997 (31.7 per cent of the British budget (Jack, 1996: 10) and 31.3 per cent of the German budget (Globus, 1996: 2)). In addition, the British social security budget was the fastest growing of all under the Conservative government (Field, 1996a: 15). It could therefore be argued that benefit fraud deserves resolute attention by politicians, not because it is widespread but because it consumes a huge amount of state resources even if it only occurs on a small scale. 1 per cent social security fraud, for example, would have meant a loss of 1 billion pounds for the British treasury in 1997. Hence, from the point of view of the treasury, benefit fraud committed by a small minority of claimants would still be worth investigating. Strong political focus on benefit fraud could be explained with the loss of resources for worthier causes rather than the quantity of fraudulent claims. This might also explain the previously mentioned high-profile anti-fraud operations from the previous and the current government in Britain. First, the Tories employed MI5 to target benefit cheats, then the Labour government launched the first ever anti-fraud web page with tips on how to report cheats.

Could benefit fraud be so prominent on the political agenda because it loses the treasury important funds? To answer this question, it is necessary to compare benefit fraud with other incidents of fraud which reduce treasury funds; the most important of which is tax evasion. Benefit fraud and tax evasion are very much alike. They can both be described as 'false declarations of personal circumstances to government departments, motivated by the desire to maximize personal gain at the expense of the state' (Cook, 1989: 9). However, tax evaders and benefit fraudsters are treated with enormous differences in the UK as Dee Cook describes in *Rich Law, Poor Law - Differential Response to Tax and Supplementary Benefit Fraud* (1989). Her most important finding, in relation to this chapter, is that it would be far more cost-effective to devote resources to the prevention or detection of tax evasion than to the combat of benefit fraud. She states that tax fraud is 'according to best estimates far more costly and more prevalent than benefit fraud' (ibid. 154).

The situation is very similar in Germany. According to Socialist Gregor Gysi (1996: 7), huge expert committees try to figure out how an overpayment of 10 DM (£3.47^2) to a benefit recipient in Erfurt could be avoided while there are hardly any attempts to prevent tax evasion. If one takes the findings of Dieter Kramer into account, one has to assume that the recovery of revenue is not the overriding reason to devote resources to fraud investigations. Kramer (1994: 146) states that tax evasion causes the German treasury *ten times* as much loss as benefit fraud. Even a high-ranking member of the Conservative party, Heiner Geissler (1995: 5), argues that it would be more worthwhile to act against tax evasion and subsidy fraud than to combat benefit fraud.

The questions which pose themselves are: why are resources to investigate fraud not allocated according to the potential amount of recovered revenue? Why is tax evasion much lower on the political agenda than benefit fraud despite higher losses for the treasury? The reasoning behind resource allocation to combat fraud does not seem to be efficiency in the economic sense (maximum result with fixed input or target result with minimum input). Instead, policies seem to have an ideological component. As Bill Hawkes (1989: 171), Assistant Secretary of the Inland Revenue Staff Federation, puts it: 'When the white middle classes lie [to the Inland Revenue] it is seen as part of the game. If black working-class people lie to the DHSS the morality of it is seen quite differently'.

Since the recovery of funds for the treasury does not seem to be the supreme reason behind fraud control, another motive which can override the efficiency idea must exist. According to Dee Cook, this overriding concern is ideological. In her view (1989: 149), right-wing ideology supports so-called winners and aims to control so-called losers. Tax-payers are regarded as economically successful and principally honest but weighed down by the spiralling, excessive costs of a state bureaucracy (Houghton, 1989: 58). This excessive state bureaucracy, on the other hand, allegedly nannies servile losers, whose work incentives are sapped by welfare systems (Cook, 1989: 172). In Dee Cook's words (ibid. 122): 'The New Right ideology which interprets taxpayers as victims of coercive state regulation views many recipients of state welfare benefits as cosseted by a state which denies them incentives to effort and self-motivation'.

Hence, treasury fraud is seen differently depending on who commits it. This also explains a phenomenon observed by Frank Field and Margaret Grieve. They (1971: 10) were astonished about the very sparse newspaper coverage of widespread tax evasion in comparison with rarer benefit fraud. It seemed that the proportion between coverage and occurrence was reversed. If tax evaders are seen as spirited but highly overburdened citizens (Deakin, 1987: 2) who merely keep their own hard-earned money whilst benefit fraudsters are seen as stealing this money, the issue of fraud becomes less relevant.[3] They both commit the same offence, treasury fraud, but one group is vilified whilst the other is excused of any serious wrong-doing. To demonstrate that tax evasion is seen as 'a gentleman's hobby' whilst benefit fraud is regarded as a serious offence, three prosecution examples from Dee Cook (1989: 1) will be given.

> Two partners in a vegetable wholesalers business admitted falsifying accounts to the tune of 100,000 pounds Sterling. At their trial the judge said he considered they had been 'very wise' in admitting their guilt and they had paid back the tax due (with interest) to the Inland Revenue. They were sentenced to pay fines. ... An unemployed father of three failed to declare his wife's earnings to the Department of Health and Social Security (DHSS). He admitted the offence and started to pay back the 996 pounds Sterling he owed them by weekly deductions from his supplementary benefit. He was prosecuted a year later and sentenced to pay fines totalling 210 pounds Sterling, also to be deducted from his benefit. Magistrates told him that 'this country is fed up to the teeth with people like you scrounging from fellow citizens'. A young woman defrauded the DHSS to the tune of 58 pounds Sterling: she served three months in custody as magistrates said she 'needed to be taught a lesson'.

It must be concluded that benefit fraud is higher on the political agenda than tax evasion because of ideological rather than financial reasons since it would be more economically efficient to try and recover money from tax evaders. That executive forces are mainly trying to recover money for social services and not for the Inland revenue shows that these investigations are led by ideological beliefs namely that tax evaders are clever wealth creators whilst benefits fraudsters are uncreative losers who live at the cost of hard-working tax-payers. Who these losers exactly are, according to right-wing ideology, will be explored in the next section.

The 'Culprits'

A general consensus among all major political groups can usually be brought about to support the 'deserving' poor; those in genuine need. Hermione Parker (1982: 24), for example, argues that the British benefit system attracts large numbers of claimants who are not in genuine need and therefore take resources from the most vulnerable. Peter Germanis (1992: 386) believes that only workfare can reduce widespread fraud in the US welfare system and make 'more money available for those in genuine need'. In contrast to the 'deserving' poor in genuine need, the 'undeserving' poor are said to enjoy a 'pre-paid lifetime vacation plan' (Glazer, 1992: 389) or have slaves in the form of tax-payers working for them (Govier, 1992: 374). John Hospers (1992: 358) even accuses them of moral cannibalism, as was quoted earlier. 'A cannibal in the physical sense is a person who lives off the flesh of other human beings. A *moral* cannibal is one who believes he has a right to live off the "spirit" of other human beings - who believes that he has a moral claim on the productive capacity, time, and effort expended by others'.

What are the distinguishing characteristics of genuine need versus undeservingness? Can a clear line be drawn between them? According to Dee Cook (1989: 169) genuine need in Britain is still understood in terms of the 1834 Poor Law which categorised the elderly, children as well as sick and infirm people as deserving. All other non-working people were, and are still, regarded as undeserving of public help. The next section will examine who today are seen as the 'undeserving' poor in the United States and in Germany. It will be shown that the prototypical welfare cheat image evoked by the Right is being filled with different contents.

The 'Culprits' in Germany

In 1996 and 1997 allegations of wide-spread social security fraud by idle scroungers came to a halt in Germany. While Chancellor Kohl (1995: 2) earlier spoke of 'collective leisure-parks' for the voluntarily unemployed which burdened the economy, he later stopped using the lazy scrounger rhetoric completely. However, unemployment and the resulting spiralling social security budget remained the major domestic problems in Germany. In June 1998, 4.1 million people were registered as unemployed. What changed? Why did the lazy scrounger rhetoric run out of steam?

In August 1995, a bill to target allegedly work-shy individuals was signed by the German parliament. Those who refused suitable work offered by the state-run job centres (*Arbeitsamt*) had their benefits reduced by 25 per cent. It was assumed, that unemployment would fall significantly in the following periods. Estimates brought forward by Conservative politicians suggested that at least 20 per cent of the unemployed could be brought back into work with this measure (ap / dpa, 1995: 1). The following chart shows the development of unemployment figures in Germany in the 1990s.

Figure 6.2   German unemployment, 1991-1997 in %

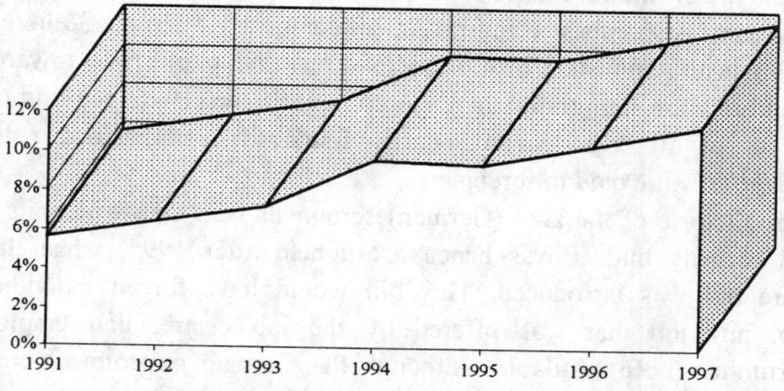

Source: Data from 'Bundesanstalt für Arbeit' (1998).

As can be seen, unemployment figures did not drop. On the contrary, a steady rise could not be halted despite this measure to reduce voluntary unemployment. The assumption that unemployment is motivated by work-shyness in approximately 20 per cent of cases was given up. Figures continued to grow steadily. Nobody argued that unemployment would have grown significantly more without the bill, that the work-shy accepted a reduction in benefits rather than work or that the black economy[4] has grown because of the bill. The rhetoric of the leisure park mentality of voluntarily unemployed Germans simply vanished.

Instead, in a governmental statement in early 1997, Kohl (1997: 3) claimed that the number of full-time jobs has not fallen during the past 20 years. What has changed significantly was not the *demand* but the *supply* of labour. First, women took up employment in huge numbers and second, Germany experienced a large stream of immigrants in recent decades. To elucidate this point, Kohl stated that the traditional immigrant country, the United States of America, allowed entry on a permanent basis to 720,000 individuals in 1995. During the same year, 1.1 million immigrants entered Germany. According to Kohl, the number of individuals of working age who immigrated to Germany over the past eight years amounted to 2.5 million. Due to Germany's history, discussions about immigration are not straightforward.[5] Instead of drawing any conclusions about these numbers, Kohl left the mental arithmetic to the public: 4.6 million unemployed (early 1997) minus 2.5 million working-age immigrants could reduce the unemployment rate to around 5 per cent, a number considered attractive by mainstream economists ('natural unemployment').[6] Horst Seehofer, the German health minister, also tried to direct the public eye towards the expenditures for immigrants. In a speech in 1996, he (1996: 14) said that 32 per cent of all basic social security funds for non-disabled recipients (*Sozialhilfe*) were paid to foreigners.

The rhetoric of the lazy (German) scrounger who causes deficits in the social security budget was hence not upheld after 1995, when the new welfare bill was introduced. This bill would have forced individuals to accept any job that was offered by the job centre, had employment opportunities been available. Although the German government conceded that labour supply exceeded labour demand ('external barrier' argument for unemployment), no new measures to bring supply and demand into balance were proposed. Instead, new scapegoats were found, namely immigrants and women, i.e. those groups who enlarged the labour supply in recent decades. This move by the German government also implied that the work incentives debate disappeared from the political stage since an inflated labour force indicates too high a willingness to work rather than work-shyness.

Two conclusions can be drawn from the above. First, the lazy scrounger rhetoric lacked substance and was not tenable after a new welfare bill was passed. Second, an 'external barrier' explanation for unemployment was adopted, namely that labour supply and labour demand were not balanced. However, rather than initiating policies to adjust supply and demand, immigrants and women were targeted as causing the non-equilibrium.[7] Similar to the lazy scrounger explanation for unemployment, the immigrant / women argument is ideological. Only if one supports the traditional family model of one breadwinner and his dependants is it possible to blame women for an inflated labour force. Equivalently, only if one endorses the belief that natives should have priority over foreigners, is it plausible to argue that the number of immigrants causes unemployment. In a non-ideological setting all individuals of working age would be taken as a fixed constant and labour market policies would have to be designed accordingly. It can therefore be concluded that unemployment explanations by members of the Kohl government were ideologically coloured.

The 'Culprits' in the United States

During the summer of 1996 the American government signed a new welfare bill (as was stated at the beginning of this chapter) which set out to save 55 billion dollars in state expenditure. One part of the bill was called the 'Personal Responsibility and Work Opportunity Act'. After more than 60 years of guaranteed state benefits for needy families, this act legislated that these rights were to be replaced by time-limited support. Since then, US citizens can only rely on the state for a maximum of five years during their lifetime. In addition, eligibility for unemployment benefits was restricted to people who are out of work for less than two years. Before the bill was introduced, 26 million Americans received food stamps and every seventh child was supported by the state (Tenbrock, 1996: 22).

The reasons given to justify the new bill show the main focus in the US welfare debate. President Clinton claims that the most serious of domestic problems is out-of-wedlock birth (Wattenberg, 1996) which is caused by the welfare system itself. This is a startling claim, but the *International Herald Tribune* agree. They write that Clinton's government concede with the new bill that payments to single parents sustain 'a debilitating culture of nonwork and nonmarriage' (Kaus, 1996: 6). By introducing cuts to welfare programs, the government want to free single parents from misery and poverty by forcing them into work or education (Tenbrock, 1996: 22). Once in work, their alleged dependency culture will be broken enabling them to lead a normal self-reliant life.[8]

The welfare debate in the US does not centre around fraud. Instead, the key targets are non-working lone parents who are identified as the biggest domestic problem. Even without any fraud allegations, they are regarded as undeserving recipients of benefits because they are seen as part of a culture of poverty, non-work and dependency. Randy Albelda (1995: 82) writes that for the last decades conservative politicians 'have demonized welfare recipients, arguing that the AFDC program itself causes poverty by breeding dependency and promoting out-of-wedlock births'.

Lawrence Mead (1986) illustrates the ideas that led to the demonisation of welfare recipients, as Albelda puts it. As has already been described briefly, Mead argues that poverty cannot be combated by welfare entitlements without simultaneously imposing obligations, of which working would be the most important (ibid. x). Mead has very strong opinions on people who do not work and rely on benefits. He thinks that non-work is directly related to crime, family break-up and other social ills (ibid. 9). He also claims that serious behavioural problems can more often be found in non-working welfare recipients than working citizens (ibid. 22). To mitigate or remove these problems, it is necessary to break the vicious circle of welfare, which Mead calls a 'devil's bargain' (ibid. 66f). This vicious circle is described by Mead as follows: in order to combat poverty, the federal government distribute benefits to the needy. Recipients do not have to work to support their families, which leads to their moral decline and the formation of an underclass. If instead people were forced to work, poverty and other social problems could be reduced significantly (ibid. 70). Unemployment, seen as the unavailability of jobs, is not a hindrance, says Mead. There are enough jobs for everybody; unemployment has become more and more voluntarily chosen (ibid. 71). Mead cannot understand why 'most welfare mothers avoid jobs when working would usually raise their income' (ibid. 78). What he concludes, together with Senator Carl Curtis, is that welfare recipients do not have the 'moral fibre' to use their opportunities (ibid. 196). By making them work for their welfare payments, they would have to learn their moral lessons (ibid. 67). This would in turn stop the need for hard-working Americans to support a 'large parasitic class' (ibid. 197f). Mead even hints at Malthusianism, in the sense that people would normally limit their number of children in order to be able to support them, but not so in welfare families (ibid.). The new US welfare bill does not follow Mead's recommendations but partly accepts his reasoning, namely that poverty can only be reduced if the dependency circle is broken and people are brought back into work (Tenbrock, 1996: 22).

Traditionally single mothers, i.e. widows, were happily supported by the US state because their role as mothers was seen as overriding their role as potential bread winners. Nowadays, they are expected to work and provide for their families just as their male counterparts. As Mead (1986: 242) puts it: 'Work ... is the clearest social obligation [for] ... adults in the United States ... unless aged or disabled' or not needy. Single mothers who are not financially independent are included in this demand. Ruth Lister (1999: 234) makes the same observation when she writes: 'In both Europe and North America, governments have elevated paid work to the supreme expression of citizenship responsibility'. She argues that the phenomenon can be seen in its extreme form in Wisconsin where lone mothers on state benefits are expected to work as soon as their youngest child is twelve weeks old.

If one compares the present stand on single parents in the US with earlier perceptions and those in other countries, one must draw the conclusion that the vilification of AFDC recipients has an ideological subtext. A look at Australian policies will substantiate the claim that different standpoints towards single mothers reveal different ideologies (the historical position will be explained hereafter). In 1994, the Australian government introduced wide-ranging social security reforms to combat unemployment. It was argued that the existing system created disincentives to work and distorted labour market choices (Saunders, 1995: 49). The arguments against the AFDC program are exactly the same. The answer to these problems as proposed by the Australian government is, however, surprising when viewed from the American perspective. The Australian Social Security Reforms introduced a Parenting Allowance. '[Now] the basis for support has shifted away from dependency (being a spouse) to performing important caring work for children (being a parent) (ibid. 67)'.

Parents who are not gainfully employed are not vilified in the Australian system. Instead, they are actively supported and their contributions to society are acknowledged. That the same problems (unemployment and work disincentives) can lead to two diametrically opposed answers (reduction versus increase of welfare) shows the ideological content of the debate. In Australia the traditional model of full-time caring for children is supported. It is seen as a bonus for society if children are raised by a non-working parent. In the United States, being employed is seen as the all overriding social obligation. Caring responsibilities come second and are not appreciated as a contribution to society on its own. Hence, faced with the same domestic problem, namely unemployment, the Australian and the North-American responses were highly different depending on their appreciation of traditional female work. In the United States, non-working mothers are seen as lazy scroungers who are blamed for a number of social ills, most prominently juvenile delinquency. In Australia they are seen as performing important *work* for which they have to be financially rewarded. (The same is true for Finland where a parenting wage is paid to carers with children under three (Franks, 1999: 228).) This example shows that different ideologies lead to different policies and that the idle scrounger in one setting can be regarded as a valuable contributor to society in another.

A brief look at earlier perceptions of women in paid work (from a British[9] perspective) shall make this point clearer and show that the non-working mother was seen very differently in the recent past. In the 19th century it was considered highly undesirable for women to be gainfully employed. Performing charitable functions was encouraged but working for money was seen as putting oneself 'beyond the pale of polite society' (Wilson, 1977: 24). The situation changed dramatically during both World Wars. Then, working women were - for a few years - regarded as heroines and saviours. After the First World War, however, a formal ban was imposed which regulated against the employment of married women in many fields. Interestingly, the BBC employment ban in 1932 kindly allowed charwomen and lavatory attendants to continue work after marriage (Franks, 1999: 162), although working women were generally perceived as 'parasites, blacklegs and limpets' (Wilson, 1977: 116). After the Second World War, no formal ban was imposed but employers were encouraged to make married women redundant (ibid.). In addition to the parasite reproach, the press accused them of fostering juvenile delinquency by neglecting their children. (The same rhetoric - the causation of social ills - was employed to keep women at home as it is currently used in the United States to get them into work.) Allegedly, the only reason why mothers might want to work was unacceptable greed for material possessions (ibid. 64). This ties in with the well-known statement by William Beveridge (1977: 151) that 'housewives as Mothers have vital work to do in ensuring the adequate continuance of the British Race and of British Ideals in the world'. These perceptions of women's role in society survived well into the second part of the 20th century. As late as 1974, Sir John Newsom (1977: 83) claimed that the main social function of women is to 'make for themselves, their children and their husbands a secure and suitable home and to be mother'.

There is one major difference between these earlier perceptions of women and the current situation of single mothers in the US. Women who were discouraged to work and asked to look after their children on a full-time basis were married, i.e. they were dependants of a male bread-winner. Single mothers do not have an individual provider on whom they can rely for financial support. Hence, it might be argued that single mothers, had they existed in huge numbers earlier in the century, would have been encouraged to earn a living for themselves and their children. However, this does not fit in with the strong insistence on full-time caring responsibilities. The above described role of women puts caring responsibilities before all other duties. It was even argued that women who work harm society as a whole by fostering juvenile delinquency. The perceptional shift regarding the role of women in society from caring for their children to being financially independent must therefore be seen as a real change in ideology.

This chapter showed that the 'pathological' theory of non-work cannot be corroborated by empirical facts about benefit fraud nor can it be justified on the grounds that enormous amounts of treasury funds are lost by fraud. If that was the case, tax evasion would have to be higher on the political agenda. Instead, the 'pathological' theory relies on ideological beliefs which find expression in an ongoing process of scapegoating. US politicians focus on single mothers, whereas German politicians have shifted from the lazy scrounger typology to immigrants and women. In a non-ideological setting, none of this scapegoating could take place. Immigrants and women would be accepted as a natural part of the labour force. Single mothers would not be considered different from married mothers whose non-work is acceptable. Since the 'pathological' theory of unemployment does not withstand scrutiny, the next chapter will look at its counterpart, 'external barrier' theories.

Notes

1   The New Deal also introduced 'minimum-wage legislation, prohibition of child labor, and limitations on hours of work' (Wusfeld, 1994: 102).

2   The exchange rate used in this book is: 2.88 DM (German marks) = £1.

3   Interestingly, Brian Barry attributes this exact frame of mind to Robert Nozick when writing *Anarchy, State and Utopia*. He (1996: 121) argues that Nozick's book articulates 'the prejudices of the average owner of a filling station in a small town in the Midwest who enjoys grousing about paying taxes and having to contribute to "welfare scroungers" '.

4   Estimates about the size of the black economy in Europe showed that Germany was less affected than most other countries in 1995. 4-6 per cent of GDP were calculated for Germany, 6-10 per cent for France, 8-12 per cent for Britain, 12-16 per cent for Belgium and 20-25 per cent for Italy (Willke, 1998: 150).

5   Discussions are not straightforward among mainstream politicians but they are amongst the very Right-wing. The *Deutsche Volksunion* (DVU) demand 'German jobs for German people' and the expulsion of all immigrants who have been convicted of a crime. 1998 was their most successful year to date. On the 27 April 1998 the DVU entered the regional parliament of Sachsen-Anhalt (East Germany) with the support of 13.2 per cent of all voters.

6   Mainstream economists assume that there is a rate of 'natural unemployment' at which inflation is zero. If unemployment falls below this rate, inflation develops (Wusfeld, 1994: 170). In the 1950s, the rate was considered to be 3 per cent but in the 1990s, Wall Street analysts believe it to be 6 per cent (Rifkin, 1995: 10f).

7   A similar instance of opportune scapegoating rather than initiating policy moves was observed by Robert L. Schwartz (1995: 225f) in the American health system. Very high expenditure and widespread lack of access have made the system unacceptable. According to him (ibid. 226f), 'we have reacted to it just as we react to most other scandals ... we have begun our search for scapegoats ... The newest and most original scapegoat upon which we can place the blame for the high cost of health care are those whose life style choices puts their health or lives at risk'. Schwartz's reasonings cannot be repeated here, but he shows convincingly that this claim cannot be upheld (see Schwartz, 1995: 223-250).

8   In contrast, critics of the bill predict that in the medium term several hundred thousand children will be made homeless by this 'reform'(Tenbrock, 1996: 22).

9   The ideology under British Conservatism will not be detailed in a separate section. It combines a resentment of single mothers and immigrants, thus being comparable to the situation in Germany and in the United States. However, the vilification of both groups is less pronounced here. Stephen Bradshaw (1996) claims that single mothers are resented as undeserving in Britain and Dee Cook (1989: 21) writes that they are often blamed for a large number of social ills 'ranging from promiscuity and divorce to crime and delinquency'. Regarding immigrants, the House of Commons under Tory rule signed a bill to abolish welfare payments to immigrants who did not declare on entering the country that they were asylum seekers. The bill was, however, later overturned by the House of Lords.

7 'External Barrier' Theories of Unemployment

Unemployment can be explained in two different ways. On the one hand, it can be interpreted as an individual failure or the consequence of antisocial behaviour, for example, under modern welfare provision (what we called the 'pathological' theory of unemployment). On the other hand it can be attributed to problems which concern economies as a whole and cannot be overcome by single individuals (the 'external barrier' theory of unemployment). If, as the previous chapters have shown, the 'pathological' theory is doubtful, which explanations are left? This chapter will list the most frequently voiced causes of unemployment, categorise them according to the two classifications (pathological or external) and examine the 'external barrier' theories in order to present an alternative to the 'pathological' view.

'External barrier' explanations for unemployment are highly varied ranging from vague charges such as unemployment is 'an inevitable product of chaotic, unplanned capitalist systems' (Barry, 1990: 39) to more technical explanations such as 'when the percentage of growth in productivity surpasses the percentage of growth in the gross national product ... then a loss of jobs occurs (Goudzwaard and de Lange, 1995: 33). Five 'external barrier' explanations of unemployment were identified, namely: economic stagnation, globalisation, productivity boom, minimum wages and the capitalist system itself. With one exception, these explanations will be examined in turn to see whether any of them are tenable. The argument that capitalism inevitably leads to unemployment will be excluded because its verification would only be helpful if realistic alternative systems existed. In agreement with Will Hutton (1997: 2), it will be accepted that capitalism in its various forms is 'now the only game in town'. The aim of this chapter is to show that, in contrast to the 'pathological' theory of unemployment, one 'external barrier' explanation can be solidly corroborated.

Unemployment Causes

The most frequently voiced causes of unemployment in the West are:

- Economic stagnation, i.e. economic growth is too slow and weak to achieve full employment (Dahlmanns, 1997: 35).
- Globalisation and the export of employment opportunities from highly regulated expensive labour markets in the West to cheaper countries in the South and East (Blanpain and Sadowski, 1994: 79f).
- Productivity booms leading to technological unemployment, i.e. the replacement of human labour by machines (Beck, 1996: 3).
- Minimum wages and other constraints on labour supply which impede labour market clearance because the unemployed cannot offer their services at low enough prices (Friedman, 1982: 180).
- Work-shyness coupled with benefit fraud (Parker, 1982: 24).
- Demand inflation amongst the low-skilled and their refusal to accept low-paid jobs (Muhr, 1994: 57).
- Skill shortages or skill mismatch, i.e. a non-equilibrium between labour demand and labour supply (Machan, 1995: 267).
- Inevitable byproduct of capitalism which keeps inflation down (Mishra, 1984: 45).
- Individual hindrances such as full-time care responsibilities (Midgley and Hughes, 1983: 170f).

These nine alleged causes of unemployment can be separated into two strains. One strain assumes that the responsibility for non-work lies with individual citizens. The other strain argues that problems are caused by factors beyond the reach of individuals. Only two of the above arguments see unemployment clearly as personal failure or misbehaviour: first, work-shyness and second demand inflation. In both cases it is argued that welfare provision helps dysfunctioning (Mead, 1986: 68) citizens to rely on benefits either because they are too lazy to work or because they 'don't want to get their hands dirty' (Bäcker, 1995: 19 - my translation). This stance on unemployment is also taken by Jeffrey Archer (1989: 18) who claims: 'I was unemployed with debts of 400,000 pounds Sterling. I know what unemployment is like - and a lot of it is getting off your backside and finding yourself a job'.

The second strain of arguments does not accuse the unemployed individually for their situation. Instead, events beyond the control of individual citizens are used as explanations for unemployment. The most important of these barriers to work in the 1990s are allegedly lack of growth, globalisation and a productivity boom. In addition, libertarians argue that only highly deregulated labour markets can work properly, meaning that minimum wage laws and other constraints cause unemployment. On the other side of the political spectrum, the radical Left argue that capitalism inevitably creates unemployment; a phenomenon which is accepted by mainstream economists because it allegedly keeps inflation down.

This leaves two arguments unclassified: first, skill mismatch or shortage and second, individual hindrances such as full-time care responsibilities. These arguments cannot be grouped easily because they are used by both proponents of the 'pathological' and the 'external barrier' position. On the one hand, it can be argued that skill mismatch is an individual failure or on the other hand, a failure of the education system. Tibor Machan (1995: 267), for example, claims that the unemployed as well as the unskilled have 'placed themselves in a position of weakness' by failing to develop their talents and skills. Contrary to Machan, proponents of positive liberty such as David Held (1986: 30) argue that health, education and resources are not automatically available to everybody and can therefore be inadequate. Lack of social provision is blamed for skill shortages rather than individual failures (Cansfield, 1996: 16). Accordingly, it is not possible to group the problem of skill mismatches with either the 'pathological' or the 'external barrier' theory of unemployment.

The second unclassified argument, individual barriers to employment such as childcare commitments, is also difficult to group. On the one hand, it is argued that 'mothers can work and should be encouraged to do so' (Levitan and Rein and Marwick, 1972: 54). Employment is seen as the social obligation with the highest priority and childcare is regarded as a responsibility which must be subordinated and can be taken care of individually (Mead, 1986: 242, 150, 74). It is claimed that married mothers manage to work in high numbers, whilst 'welfare mothers', in contrast, have a low labour market participation rate, implying that the latter neglect their social duties from choice (Levitan and Rein and Marwick, 1972: 65). This again, is an instantiation of the 'pathological' approach, i.e. putting the blame for unemployment on single individuals. On the other hand, it is argued that the state should provide easy access to affordable childcare (Smith, 1992: xv) or a wage for bringing up children (Midgley and Hughes,

1983: 177) to acknowledge important female work. This position argues that raising children is a form of wealth creation which can either replace employment as a worthwhile social activity or justify state support for childcare (Pahl, 1994: 60). From this point of view, mothers' unemployment[1] is blamed on a lack of childcare facilities which should be provided for by the state, hence it is an 'external barrier' argument. Due to these conflicts of opinion, the 'skill mismatch' and the 'individual hindrances' argument will be listed as not classified in the following table (both arguments will not be analysed in the remainder of the book).

Table 7.1   Alleged causes of unemployment

'Pathological'	'External barrier'	Not classified
Work-shyness	Economic stagnation	Skill shortages / mismatch
Demand inflation	Globalisation	Individual hindrances
	Minimum wages	
	Productivity boom	
	Byproduct of capitalism	

Instead of classifying causes of unemployment according to 'pathological' and 'external barrier' theories, the subdivisions could also have been 'voluntary' and 'involuntary'. It is alleged by proponents of the 'pathological' position that unemployment is voluntarily chosen rather than imposed (Mead, 1986: 71; McLaughlin and Millar and Cooke, 1989: 7). 'External barrier' arguments, on the other hand, support the idea that unemployment is beyond individual control.

It is crucial to know, both for the provision of welfare and the fight against unemployment, whether the 'pathological' or the 'external barrier' position is more tenable. Solutions for technical unemployment, for example, are very different to the imposition of workfare. There is no available conceptual analysis to determine which position is more reasonable. Instead, reasons for unemployment must be examined each on their own merit and in alliance with empirical evidence for a given time. The previous chapters put the work incentives argument into serious question marks. The 'demand inflation' argument will not be examined separately because the underlying welfare state criticism is identical. In both cases, it is maintained that welfare payments provide an 'easy exit' option for either work-shy individuals or people who are not prepared to accept jobs they dislike ('I would like to try stock-broking but I couldn't possibly accept work as a waiter').

Economic Stagnation - Lack of Economic Growth

Lack of economic growth is seen as a major 'external barrier' explanation for unemployment. In 1996, German Finance Minister, Theo Waigel (1996: 2), told parliament that the basis for the preservation of present jobs and the creation of new employment is permanent, sustained economic growth. Wolfgang Schäuble, the Interior Minister agreed. He (1996: 8) claimed that economic growth is indispensable in the fight against unemployment. Amongst academic circles, they received support from Gerhard Voss, head of economic research at the Institute for the German Economy (*Institut der deutschen Wirtschaft*) who claimed that full employment is impossible without high economic growth (Voss, 1995: 55).

Along the same line of reasoning, the then British social security minister Peter Lilley (1996) announced that he would create a virtuous circle of economic growth to generate more jobs and reduce his departmental spending commitments. As Victor Anderson (1991, unnumbered introduction) and David Macarov (1970: 79) rightly observe, most Western governments[2] are bewitched with the simple idea of maximising economic growth to solve all their country's difficulties, especially unemployment.

The following section looks at the phenomenon of economic growth and its effect on employment levels. It will be seen that the 1980s and '90s saw the event of what economists' call 'jobless growth'; a serious impediment to solving unemployment by GDP growth. In addition, it will be shown that the promotion of unrestricted economic growth clashes heavily with environmental concerns and also ignores other limitations such as post-materialist wants.

To see why growth is regarded as a potentially successful weapon against unemployment, it is useful to look at the historic relationship between growth and unemployment figures first. Economic growth will be understood as the increase in gross domestic product compared to the previous year. The example of post-war Germany and its 'economic miracle' was selected for expository purposes. In the 1950s, the German economy experienced a major and sustained boom. Growth rates in the decade averaged at 8 per cent and unemployment fell from 10.3 per cent in 1950 to under 1 per cent in 1960. The then Economic Secretary Ludwig Erhard announced the permanent end of unemployment (1997: 3). The following chart shows German economic growth rates and unemployment figures in the second half of the 20th century.

Figure 7.1   Unemployment and economic growth in %, Germany, 1951-1996

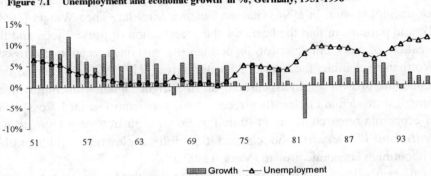

Source: Data from Reuter (1997: 4).

As can be seen, there is initially a strong correlation between these two curves. High growth rates lead to a subsequent fall of unemployment. This also aligns with common logic. If an economy is characterised by high activity and expansion, additional employees will be needed to satisfy growing demand for products or services. However, the correlation becomes blurred in the 1980s and 1990s when the phenomenon of jobless growth first occurred.

Jobless Growth

In the 1980s the percentage of productivity increase surpassed the percentage of GDP increase (Goudzwaard and de Lange, 1995: 33) which led to the event of jobless growth.[3] What exactly does this statement mean? What is jobless growth? To illustrate the phenomenon, an example will be given. The example only deals with one company (micro-economics) although jobless growth is a macro-economic problem. However, for illustration purposes the former is more transparent.

Let us assume that a manufacturer in the 1970s produced 2,100 lamp shades with 70 shop floor workers each day. In the 1980s the company made changes to the production process, e.g. dismissal of middle management, new machines, team work etc. This led to a productivity increase of 10 per cent. Hence, the manufacturer could either produce 2,310 lamp shades with the existing 70 shop floor workers or make 7 workers (10 per cent) redundant and carry on producing 2,100 lamp shades. To keep all 70 employees in work it would have been necessary to sell an additional 10 per cent of lamp shades. If one only takes a single company into consideration, a growth in relative market share of 10 per cent would suffice to avoid redundancies. However, on a macro-economic level the market as a whole would have to grow by 10 per cent. This example shows that for maintaining a certain level of employment, the increase in market share has to be at least as high as the increase in productivity.

Jobless growth occurred when productivity increase surpassed GDP increase. Company profits increased whilst employment decreased. First observed on a massive scale in the 1980s, the productivity revolution gathered speed in the 1990s (Beck, 1996: 3).[4] Fewer workers needed shorter time to produce the same amount of goods as their colleagues in the 1970s. In order to avoid redundancies under conditions of rising productivity, it is necessary to 'pursue vigorous, uninterrupted growth in the gross national product at all costs' (Goudzwaard and de Lange, 1995: 33). Growth is not only needed to create jobs, it is even needed to maintain existing levels of employment.

In a speech to the House of Lords on his *Report on Wealth Creation and Social Cohesion in a Free Society*, Ralf Dahrendorf summed up what jobless growth is and commented on the apparent paradox that production was decoupled from workers' input. He (1996: 195) explained to the Lords that unemployment is 'oddly resistant to growth' because productivity increases have led to fewer people producing ever more goods. Statistical data from the European Union give empirical backing to this observation.

Table 7.2   Jobless growth in the European Union in %, 1984-1996

	1984-92	1993	1994	1995	1996
EU-growth of GDP	+3.0	-0.6	+2.7	+3.0	+2.9
EU-labour force growth	+1.3	-0.8	+0.1	+0.4	+0.4

Source: Data from Hanson (1996: 11).

The table shows that GDP-growth and labour force growth are nearly decoupled in 1990s Europe. GDP-growth of 2.9 per cent was only accompanied by a minor growth in the employment area of 0.4 per cent in 1996 and the situation was slightly worse in 1995. A simplified model can help to identify the amount of growth that would be necessary to solve the unemployment problem in the European Union. Since GDP-growth is higher than labour force growth, it must be assumed that the difference is made up from productivity gains. Hence, productivity gains (p) and labour force increases (lf) make up GDP-growth (g). $(1+g) = (1+p) * (1+lf)$. For 1996 this means: $(1+0.029) = (1+p) * (1+0.004) \Rightarrow p = 2.5$ per cent, i.e. productivity gains were 2.5 per cent. If one wanted to increase the labour force (lf) by 10 per cent (approximate Continental European unemployment in 1998), the equation looks as follows: $(1+g) = (1+0.025) * (lf+0.10) \Rightarrow g = 12.75$ per cent. Hence, it would be necessary to achieve a growth rate of nearly 13 per cent to solve unemployment in 1998.

What can be concluded from this simplified calculation? Economic growth is no longer a straightforward solution to unemployment since it lost its link with job creation in the 1980s and '90s. Rates would have to be extraordinarily high to have any impact on employment. In our example, nearly 13 per cent would have to be achieved to re-establish full employment in Continental Europe. As a comparison, growth rates of around 10 per cent were reached by the Asian Tigers in the mid 1990s but they have since dwindled. The highest post-war growth rate in Germany was 12 per cent (1955) and EU rates in the 1990s fluctuated between -0.6 per cent and 3.0 per cent (Eurostatistics, 1998: 31 and 1997: 31).

The dimension of growth needed to solve unemployment is unlikely to return to Europe in the short or medium term. But, for the sake of argument, let us assume that it was conceivable and examine whether other hindrances can be identified. It is always possible to conjure up circumstances in which unemployment would be significantly reduced. During the Second World War, for example, European economies were characterised by full employment. However, nobody would list 'Absence of war' as a cause for unemployment and herald the immediate onset of fighting as the long awaited solution to the problem. This is the case, because solutions to problems should ideally be practically feasible *and* ethically sound and reasonable. War in Europe might be feasible, but it is not reasonable. Similarly, vigorous, uninterrupted, aggressive double-figured growth in the West would, even if possible, not be ethically sound. It would harm future generations and non-western civilisations. The next section summarises environmentalists' concerns regarding growth as a solution to unemployment. It will be seen that even without double figured growth rates, current economic practices in the West are unsustainable in the long run, threatening the prospects of future generations.[5]

Growth and Environmental Concerns

Economics is the 'science' or field that deals with decisions about alternative uses for limited resources. However, when it comes to *economic growth*, limited resources are suddenly removed from the macro-economic equation. It is worth quoting an extended passage from *Working Harder Isn't Working* by Canadian Bruce O'Hara (1993: 23) in which this is thematised.

> The myth of the permanently expanding economy demands continually expanding consumption, as though the environment had no limits ... The unthinking worship of economic growth has created several environmental crisis:
> - Uncontrolled use and release of CFCs ... threatens the ozone layer;
> - Increasing use of fossil fuels has created a greenhouse effect ... ; ...
> - Current farming and forestry practices wash away topsoil and decrease soil fertility;
> - Rapid consumption is depleting natural resources such as fish stocks and forests ...

It is clear from O'Hara's explanations that unrestricted growth damages the prospects of future generations and hence raises an ethical issue. However, some economists such as Wilfred Beckerman deny that growth represents a worry. He (1995: 1) thinks that long-term malign effects of global warming and damage to the ozone layer are only alleged problems and that it is an 'old myth that we could run out of resources' (ibid.). Calls for sustainable development on the ground of 'phoney disaster scenarios' (ibid. 4) are shrugged off by him claiming that climate change and other 'fashionable issues' are 'grossly exaggerated' (ibid. 8). For him, Greens are alarmists 'bordering on hysteria' (ibid. 4).[6]

If Beckerman was right, economic growth might be a suitable answer to unemployment but his claims clash heavily with research results from environmental scientists. Very prominently, the Brundtland Report[7] entitled *Our Common Future* argued that 'further growth in a conventional sense will not lead to worldwide prosperity. Rather it will ultimately lead to destruction. The very basis of life and prosperity is at stake' (Brundtland report, 1992: 3). The report (Brundtland report, 1994: 12) did acknowledge the need for an increase of employment opportunities in its opening statement, calling employment or a livelihood the most basic of needs. But it still claimed that sustainable development, which is incompatible with traditional economic growth, must be achieved soon so as not to compromise the chances of future generations to meet their needs.

Similarly, *Friends of the Earth* (1994: 7) point out what will happen if the demand for further conventional growth continues to be upheld. They see an Orwellian circularity in the growth argument. Unemployment exists. => Hence, growth is needed to mitigate or solve the problem. => Unfortunately growth creates environmental degradation. => Therefore more growth is needed to pay for the necessary repairs and cures ... and this goes on *ad infinitum* until the spiral of degradation comes to a catastrophic end.

The problem is also acknowledged by high-ranked politicians such as Francois Mitterand (1991: 95), the late President of the French Republic: 'Economic growth has brought us neither greater equity nor greater social harmony and appreciation of life. I believe we have followed the wrong path and must now seek a new course'. If one is sceptical about the affirmations of politicians and environmentalists, one can also approach the question whether continuous high economic growth is feasible and desirable from a common sense point of view. To do that, it is necessary to bear in mind that sustained economic growth equals a constant increase of economic wealth without any stand-still. It means that a country needs to produce more, consume more, save more, invest more and earn more year after year. A good example for exponential progression is population growth: two penguins have two little penguins. If these and their offspring procreate in the same way, the first generation consists of 2 specimen, the second of 4, the fifth of 32 and the seventh of 128 penguins. To see the implications of such growth, it is best to look at the following chart which shows exponential growth set at 10 per cent.

Figure 7.2   Exponential growth, 10%

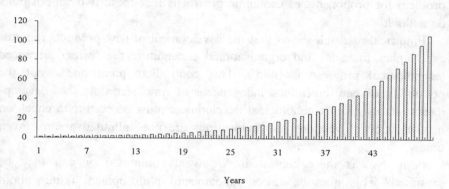

Years

Economic growth is exponential since each year is taken as the basis for the successive one. After 50 years, exponential growth of 10 per cent makes 117 units out of 1. Highly simplified, one could say that one generation needs to consume and produce 117 times more than their grandparents under economic growth conditions of 10 per cent. As the above calculation shows, double-figured growth rates cannot be the solution to unemployment because they are unsustainable in a world of limited resources. Environmental difficulties such as global warming, acid rain, soil erosion and destruction of the ozone layer are present already and will get worse according to research undertaken by the Brundtland Commission if traditional economic growth is not abandoned. If one includes ethical considerations about the life of future generations into the growth debate, conventional economic growth must be rejected as a solution to unemployment. However, to draw the same conclusion even from a non-environmentalist standpoint, the next section will introduce further limits to growth that disregard any ethical issues.

Further Limits to Growth

The possibility of continuous, high economic growth relies on the validity of the following two conditions: 1) the amount of potential inventions and innovations is unlimited, independent of time and 2) wants are unlimited and mainly satisfied with material possessions and personal services in the market, i.e. saturation conditions are non-existent (Reuter, 1997: 10). The problem for proponents of economic growth is that these two suppositions do not hold.

Empirical research shows that the development of new products requires ever higher financial and organisational expenditure the further advanced technological progress is (ibid.). This contradicts point one about the possibility of new inventions independent of time restraints, i.e. developmental status. High technological development must be seen as a check on new products. Inventions and innovations are not unlimited at any given time.

Point two is more contested. Are wants unlimited or can they be saturated? This question raises fundamental philosophical issues about human nature; about wants, needs and desires. In Ancient Greece, the economy was geared towards biologically derived needs rather than wants. Households aimed at sufficient food levels, shelter and adequate sanitation (Bell, 1976: 22). According to Aristotle (1981: 17), the art of organising households was knowing what is useful and essential for life. True wealth, in his opinion, was determined by these essentials which he saw as satiable (ibid.). Research into the differences between Western and Indian economies led Ignacy Sachs to conclude that modern Indian economies have similar priorities. Their 'natural economy', he (1980: 53) writes, is geared towards primary need satisfaction irrespective of the multitude of material possessions. He quotes J. C. Kumarappa (ibid.), a Gandhi contemporary, who wrote the following about the natural Indian economy:

> Our life is something higher than material possessions, and our life is also to be looked at from the possibilities of development of our personality. The personality of an individual does not require for its development the satisfaction of a multiplicity of wants. In fact the simpler the life the more conducive it is for exercising the higher faculties.

In contrast to the natural economy of Ancient Greece and Gandhi's India,

Western economies are based on appetite rather than need, according to Daniel Bell (1976: 22). Ignacy Sachs (1980: 53) describes them as 'artificial economies' based on a multitude of created wants. Distinctions between the natural and the artificial economy led to the differentiation of needs and wants. Needs were described as biologically or physiologically derived, whereas wants were seen as psychologically induced (Bell, 1976: 22). It was argued that wants depend on the mind, whilst needs depend on the body (Wiggins, 1991: 192ff). A popular example to distinguish between needs and wants comes from the field of medicine. A diabetic patient who is ignorant about his condition might *want* chocolate but what he *needs* is insulin. In line with this example, needs were described as objective, empirical and open to expert knowledge whereas wants were seen as subjective (Flew, 1977: 216f). In addition, wants were seen as unsatiable (Macarov, 1970: 68f, 220; Schumacher, 1979: 25), whereas needs were regarded as satiable (Gray, 1992: 38). As Austrian economist Ludwig Edler von Mises (1986: 63) puts it: 'Egoism is the basic law of society ... and as soon as [people's] wishes are satisfied, new wishes spring up'.

This straightforward distinction between needs and wants has been attacked as untenable on the grounds that needs are related to ends which means that pluralistic societies might have varying interpretations of needs (Plant, 1991: 198). A doctor who treats a diabetic patient with insulin might impose his normative conception that life on earth is valuable on somebody who thinks that death will bring nirvana. In addition, the satiability of needs is also restricted by limited resources. Insulin might not be available at any given time and place to maintain the health of diabetes sufferers. For the purpose of this chapter, it is not necessary to find a valid mode of distinction between needs and wants. The simple, though naive distinction between basic needs as potentially satiable and geared towards physiological states and wants as insatiable and going beyond needs, will suffice here and will be used despite being contentious. The question we seek to answer is: are there any limits to growth because material wants might be satiable? Is it reasonable to suppose - at least in theory and disregarding limited resources - that people in the very near future, i.e. 'our' grandchildren, would want to consume a multiplied amount of our goods and services?

This question goes back to issues about human nature. Is 'man' indeed a prisoner bound to hard labour because of a 'perpetual disparity between ... unlimited wants and ... insufficient means'? (Sahlins, 1974: 1). One point that can be made about this contention is that it cannot be universally valid. Not only Ancient Greece and Gandhi's India are exceptions, but studies of hunter and gatherer people showed that their behaviour is not directed at the accumulation of material possessions. As Marshall Sahlins sees it there are two strategies for affluence. First to produce as much as possible and second to desire little, the latter being the 'Zen road to affluence', according to Sahlins (ibid. 2). This Zen road to wealth is taken by hunter and gatherer people who do not cling to their possessions. An example of this way of life from Martin Gusinde (1974: 13):

> Actually, no one clings to his few goods and chattels which, as it is, are often and easily lost, but just as easily replaced ... The Indian does not even exercise care when he could conveniently do so. A European is likely to shake his head at the boundless indifference of these people who drag brand-new objects, precious clothing, fresh provisions, and valuable items through thick mud, or abandon them to their swift destruction by children and dogs ... Expensive things that are given them are treasured for a few hours, out of curiosity; after that they thoughtlessly let everything deteriorate in the mud and wet. The less they own, the more comfortable they can travel, and what is ruined they occasionally replace. Hence, they are completely indifferent to any material possessions.

Hunter and gatherer communities represent humankind for 99 per cent of human history (O'Hara, 1993: 150). Edward Wilson (1978: 34) claims that 'most of the genetic evolution of human social behavior occurred ... when the species consisted of ... populations of hunters-gatherers'. It can therefore not reasonably be argued that the drive to consume and accumulate material possessions on an unlimited basis is a genetic trait. However, insatiable appetite for material possessions does seem to be a very strong and overwhelming feature of humankind in the West; one only has to look at the success of national lotteries. Since the explorations in this book are restricted to Western states, Ancient Greece, Gandhi's India and hunter-gatherer societies cannot be used to establish whether there are any limits to wants. It is therefore possible that no 'appetite barriers' for economic growth exist in the West; that indeed wants for goods and services are insatiable. However, there are also Western authors who doubt this affirmation within their own culture.

Herman Daly and John Cobb (1990: 87) maintain that the existence of aggressive want-stimulating advertising would be unnecessary if the natural human state was characterised by unlimited appetite. Norbert Reuter (1997:

10) supports this view. He argues that modern Western societies experience a change in priorities. Since most Westerners have their needs and wants concerning housing, clothing and mobility satisfied, he sees a shift towards desires for more tranquillity, relaxation and education. These observations are in agreement with ideas advanced in the 1970s and 1980s. It is argued (Gerlach, 1992: 589f) that humans develop a hierarchy of wants beginning with physiological and physical security (material wants) but then progressing to social, cultural and intellectual desires (post-material wants). Those who experience material deprivation in their formative years, will show a life-long commitment to material wants, according to this theory. Those who grow up without significant scarcity, will place a higher premium on post-material wants. Given that most Europeans and North-Americans born after the war did not suffer from material deprivation in their formative years, another limit to unrestrained, high economic growth would present itself. Post-materialist wants do not easily translate into GDP increases. Relaxation might be found by paying a masseur or aromatherapist for their services but it might also be found by fell-walking or lying in a meadow, both of which have no impact on GDPs. It can therefore be argued that massive growth needed to reduce unemployment clashes with people's changing wants and the development of the post-materialist society.

It is not possible to draw a final conclusion about the highly contested question whether wants are satiable or not. The question will therefore be settled in a diplomatic fashion. Whilst it was not possible to disprove the claim that wants are unlimited, reasonable doubt can be brought from two corners. First, new material wants which pop up whenever old ones are satisfied do not seem to be a universally valid feature, i.e. an unchangeable anthropological constant in humans. Non-western cultures were shown to have different perceptions about the number and urgency of wants manifested as material possessions. Second, in the 1990s a shift in the nature of wants was observed in the West and these new non-material wants, such as tranquillity and relaxation, do not contribute to economic growth in the same fashion as old material wants. Besides, it was shown that an impediment for invention and innovation lies in high technological development. Hence, even if wants were unsatiable, a shortage of goods occurred for this reason. This last claim, however, leads to one possible objection that could be brought forward in the debate, which will be looked at to conclude this section.

The potential counter-argument could be phrased as follows: there are still people without cars and even without refrigerators in the West; hence, there is much room for growth in the foreseeable future. If one subscribes to this argument one takes the 'trickle-down' position on wealth and purchasing power. This position has also been called the *echelon advance* theory of economic growth (Plant, 1991: 89). It assumes that inequalities between rich and poor citizens promote innovations since rich people constantly demand and pay for new products. Later, these products trickle down to the remaining population. To achieve the trickle-down effect it is necessary that new, innovative products are only consumed by a minority. The majority will then aspire to own these items which is made possible in the long term by mass production. Plant (ibid.) explains the echelon advance theory of economic growth as follows:

> At one time it was only because the rich were able to provide a market - to take for example, air travel and refrigerators - that these things were developed to any extent, but once developed they trickle down gradually to the rest of the population. Because the rich have an incentive to demand new goods, new goods are produced and find their way into the rest of the economy. So there is an 'echelon' advance in consumption. What the rich consume today will be consumed by more and more people tomorrow.

Although this theory has explanatory powers for post-war years and refrigerators, it is not suitable in our context. Double-figured growth is demanded to counteract mass unemployment. Under conditions of mass unemployment, however, the trickle-down effect is seriously hampered by restraints of purchasing power. The unemployed themselves are not in a position to feed major economic growth from their benefit purses. What about the rest of the population in Western countries? Although it is difficult to measure trickle-down effects, economist Charles Handy (1994: 12) claimed that 'wealth did not trickle down too well in America during ... the Reagan years'. His affirmation can be supported with an observation from the German labour market. During the Kohl-era (1982-1998) real wages for many occupations fell (Lafontaine, 1996: 3). Hence, if it is argued that relative poverty (missing refrigerators) leaves room for economic growth it must be taken into account that the concerned might not be able to afford additional goods. Growth means higher consumption in comparison to the previous year which is impossible with falling real incomes.

The conclusions that can be drawn on growth as an extrinsic explanation and potential solution for unemployment are as follows. Although increased GDP growth used to be intimately connected with falling unemployment rates, the relationship became severed in the 1980s and 1990s. The phenomenon of jobless growth occurred when productivity gains surpassed market growth. To re-establish full employment under conditions of jobless growth, it would be necessary to achieve double-figured GDP growth in 1990s Europe. This would seriously endanger the prospects of future generations as was shown by environmentalists and hence represent an ethical constraint on growth as a solution to unemployment. Irrespective of ethical concerns, it was also shown that economic growth, since it is exponential, would demand that grandchildren consume a hundred times more than their ancestors at double-figured growth rates. Lastly, it was shown that economic growth is restrained by limits to inventions, limits to wants and limits to purchasing power. As a solution to unemployment, conventional GDP growth is therefore not viable. It was argued that causes of problems cannot be called causes unless their reversal would represent a solution (the war-reduces-unemployment example). Accordingly, lack of growth is no acceptable explanation for unemployment.

Globalisation

Swissair booking systems are maintained in India; Siemens information systems are updated on the Philippines; the *Conseil supérieur du notariat francais* uses specialists from the Ivory Coast to write their legal texts; IBM Germany sends software tasks to the USA every night; in Ceylon highly qualified computer specialists can be employed for £100 a month; German 'Lufthansa' employs stewardesses from Thailand and India (Afheldt, 1995: 7 / Lambsdorff, 1996: 6). All the above are instantiations of globalisation and although most people have an idea what the term means, it is mostly used without being defined. Stephan Wackwitz (1997: 25 - my translation) writes:

> Globalisation is the Yeti of ... newspapers. Everybody knows it, but nobody has ever seen it. What does it look like? Tall, monkeyish, hairy? Or rather weasel-like? With glasses? Like a ferret or a marten? At least it is clear that the ubiquitous presence of globalisation contains apocalyptic motives.

The phenomenon of globalisation started in the early eighties, according to Rudolf Welzmüller (1997: 20) and gained speed in the late eighties when communist countries converted to the capitalist system. Trade barriers were removed all over the world and capital started to float freely, undisturbed by national borders. The World Bank called this development a world-wide integration process (Pinzler, 1996: 6), characterised by free movement of persons, goods, services and capital (Mayer, 1997: 33). A definition for the phenomenon was formulated by Manuel Castells (1993: 249 - my translation):

> A globalised economy is an economy which uniformly works in real-time on a world-wide scale. It is an economy in which capital flows, labour markets, information, raw material, management and organisation are internationalised and entirely interdependent.

Harvard professor and former US employment minister Robert Reich (1994: 75) gave an example of globalisation at work. When an American Pontiac Le Mans car is sold for 10,000 dollars, 3,000 dollars go to South Korea for assembly, 1,750 to Japan for electronic fittings, 750 to Germany for body design, 400 to Japan, Singapore and Taiwan for minor components, 250 to Great Britain for marketing, 50 to Ireland and Barbados for data processing and 4,200 dollars remain in Detroit. This example shows that work and thereby employment opportunities in car manufacturing were spread around the globe to whatever country offered the best service and / or the best price.

The impact of globalisation on Western Europe is two-fold. First, globalisation is made responsible for a huge share of redundancies, particularly in Continental Europe (Rexrodt, 1996: 17; Mishan, 1996: 157; Pfaff, 1998: 6). Second, it dramatically increases profits for capital resources and corporate companies because it opens what Sven Steinmo (1994: 10) calls the 'easy exit' option. This means that in a globalised economy, capital and employment can move to whichever country offers the most attractive conditions (e.g. low taxes, low wages for qualified workers, few regulations). In the 1980s and 1990s, capital and job opportunities were moved from the high-wage, high-tax economies of Continental Europe to less regulated countries. In 1995, for example, German companies invested 10.7 billion DM (£3.72 billion) abroad whilst foreign investment within Germany only amounted to a quarter of this sum (BMWI, 1997: 12).

The problem with globalisation as a tenable 'external barrier' explanation for unemployment becomes clear when one analyses who benefited most from the process in the 1980s and 1990s. The beneficiaries were not the so-called 'Asian Tiger' economies (Sommer, 1995: 9; Schumacher, 1997: 40), namely Singapore, Indonesia, Malaysia, Taiwan and South-Korea, as one might assume, but Great Britain and the United States. The following figure shows how much foreign investment and thereby job opportunities went to selected countries from 1985 to 1995.

Figure 7.3   Inward investment in billion dollars, 1985-1995

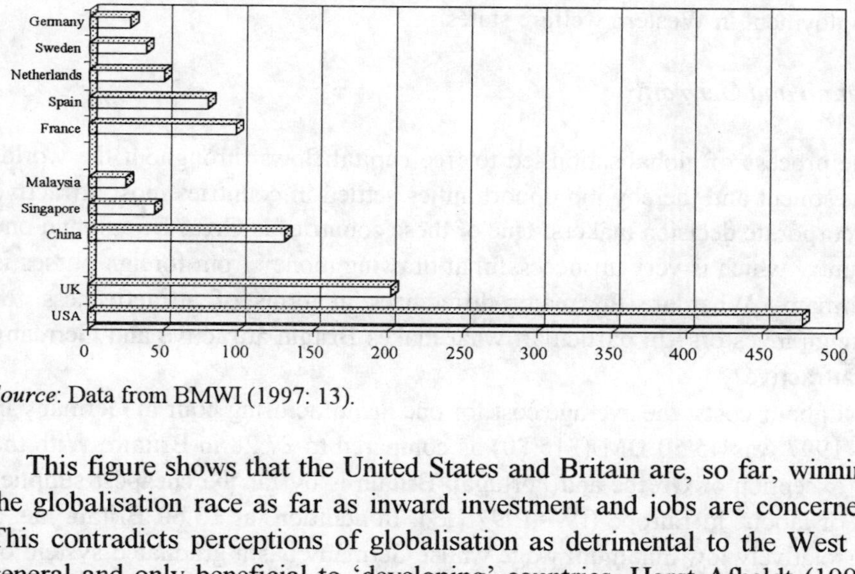

Source: Data from BMWI (1997: 13).

This figure shows that the United States and Britain are, so far, winning the globalisation race as far as inward investment and jobs are concerned. This contradicts perceptions of globalisation as detrimental to the West in general and only beneficial to 'developing' countries. Horst Afheldt (1995: 7), for example, insists that globalisation will make 'work world-wide as cheap as dirt' (my translation) because highly qualified staff can be employed in Asia for a minute salary. Similarly, the French Le Monde diplomatique (1995: 7 - my translation) commented on globalisation: 'when children in the West will voluntarily work chained to a vice, the free market will have won the day'. Oskar Lafontaine (1996a: 2) thinks that globalisation has started a downward spiral of deregulation which no country can win.

The fact that the United States and Britain are profiting most from globalisation whilst Continental Europeans believe that 'their' jobs went to children in India or Thailand is difficult to explain. What can, however, be explained is why globalisation has affected Continental Europe and the Anglo-American block in very different ways. To exemplify the differences, Britain and Germany will be compared in terms of attractiveness for inward investment and the underlying political philosophy. This is necessary to draw a conclusion as to whether globalisation is an acceptable 'external barrier' explanation for unemployment or not. So far, it can only be said that globalisation has a negative effect on employment levels in Continental Europe. However, since Britain has been profiting from the process, it cannot be argued straightforwardly that globalisation is a barrier for employment in Western welfare states.

Britain and Germany

The process of globalisation led to free capital flows throughout the world. Investment and thereby job opportunities settled in countries most attractive to corporate decision makers. One of these countries is Great Britain and one country which is very unsuccessful at drawing money from foreign purses is Germany. What are the major differences in terms of attractiveness for foreign investors? In particular, what makes Britain attractive and Germany unattractive?

- Labour costs: the average cost for one manufacturing hour in Germany in 1997 was 45.50 DM (£15.80) as compared to £7.28 in Britain. With the exception of Greece and Portugal, Britain is by far the cheapest supplier of labour in Europe (IW, 1997: 13). In addition, at £3.60 Britain has a relatively low minimum wage whilst Germany has a graduated system of various minimum wages (building workers, for example, receive at least 18 DM (£6.25) per hour).[8]
- The welfare system: since 1994, German workers and employers have to pay equal shares into a national care insurance to finance care for the elderly, a system which does not exist in England. Similarly, a number of compulsory benefits are paid or granted to German workers which are not available in Britain, unless individually negotiated. These include Christmas money (13th salary), holiday money (on average £300 a year) as well as the longest holidays and shortest working week world-wide (Arendt *et al.*, 1992: 11). In addition, the state-run German pension system which is financed in equal shares by employers and employees is

very expensive because pensions are based on a percentage of salary (graduated system).

- Other:[9] Britain has lower corporate tax rates (Hutton, 1995: 338); a more 'relaxed view on hiring and firing' (*Newsnight*, BBC2, 30/01/1997; *Economist*, 1996: 34) and fewer labour regulations than Germany (Heuser, 1997: 82; Hanson, 1996: 25).

These major differences in labour markets between Britain and Germany are also reflected in political thought. When critics speak about the British model it is seen as a 'low-tax, low-wage, minimal welfare-state variant of capitalism' (Hutton, 1995: 338) which 'seeks competitive advantage by exploiting domestic labour' (Haskins, 1996: 57). The costs of this model are seen as fostering a growing underclass, sustaining the highest income inequalities in Europe (Heuser, 1997: 82), supporting the phenomenon of working poor (Dahrendorf, 1996: 195) and feeding raising crime rates (Kingdom, 1992: 100).[10] In contrast, the German and other Continental European models are regarded as rigid, anti-competitive and over-regulated (Hanson, 1996: 1,3). Countries with high wages, high income tax and high corporate taxes are diagnosed as suffering from the 'German disease' (Rexrodt, 1996a: 9). The costs of this model are seen as creating double-figured unemployment rates which potentially foster racism.[11]

Without going into detail about the Anglo-American and the Continental European models of capitalism,[12] the following can be said to answer the question whether globalisation can be accepted as a persuasive 'external barrier' explanation for unemployment. The majority of Continental European politicians have, so far, resisted labour market 'reforms' to join the low-wage, low-tax, minimal welfare state variant of capitalism which might enable their countries to copy Anglo-American globalisation winners.[13] When resisting change, they refer to the side-effects of the model. Conservative ex-cabinet member Heiner Geissler, for example, does 'not want the hire-and-fire American model, neither the British scene where over half the workforce is casual labour' (*Economist*, 1996: 34). It can therefore be argued, that it is not globalisation which creates unemployment in Europe, otherwise Britain would be affected in the same way as Continental countries. It is the resistance on the continent to accept the conditions and consequences of libertarian capitalism which causes a loss of jobs. Only globalisation *plus* the refusal to give up Continental European standards of life and social cohesion can explain double-figured unemployment levels. It must therefore be concluded that globalisation cannot be made responsible for unemployment on its own.

Minimum Wages

Supporters of libertarian capitalism argue that minimum wage laws cause unemployment. The best known proponent of this claim is Milton Friedman. In *Capitalism and Freedom* (1982: 180f), he argues that although low pay rates are deplorable, it is nevertheless counterproductive to establish a minimum wage. According to him, minimum wages will render exactly those people unemployed who can least afford to lose an income, however small it may be. In more technical terms, the argument is expressed by Norman Barry (1990: 107) who writes that 'minimum wage legislation ... renders unemployed, potential workers whose marginal productivity is lower than the decreed minimum'. Dennis Snower (1994: 40) agrees when he claims that minimum wage laws bar the unemployed 'from offering their services as cheaply as they would like'. The free marketeer reasoning behind these claims is that markets can only reach equilibrium prices required for clearance if they are left unhampered. To understand the concept of equilibrium prices, it is best to look at the following highly simplified figure.

Figure 7.4   Equilibrium price

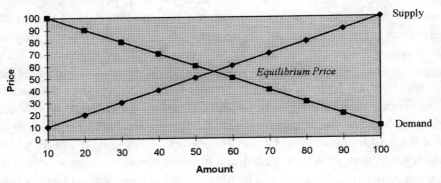

The above figure shows how supply and demand vary with different prices and amounts for a given product. It rests on two assumptions. First, the higher the expected profit, the more suppliers enter the market: see supply curve. If only a price of 10 can be achieved, only 10 items will be produced. However, if the price reaches 100, suppliers would want to offer an amount of 100. Second, the higher the supply of a given good, the lower the price customers are willing to pay, see demand curve. When goods are in short supply, for example 10, customers are willing to pay 100. However, if 100 are offered, the price customers are willing to pay is only 10. Accordingly, expectations of suppliers and customers are highly antagonistic and only meet in one point, the equilibrium price. This price balances the number of suppliers entering the market for a given price with the willingness of customers to pay this exact price.

An example might clarify this further. Let us assume that the products on offer are 'trendy' multicoloured bird-houses. In the beginning, when producers first enter the market, supply is very low. There might only be one supplier and she might produce the first 10 bird-houses in her spare room. For this limited supply, customers are prepared to pay £100 per item. Once successful, the business expands and with more bird-houses being available, the price falls. Let us assume that a huge manufacturer likes the idea and starts mass production. Suddenly there are 100 bird-houses to be sold but demand has not kept up with supply. Although prices were 100 when manufacturing started, they would have to come down to £10 if all items were to be sold. According to free marketeers the equilibrium price, i.e. the price where demand and supply meet, clears a market at its optimum (Woll, 1987: 99).

How does the minimum wage fit into these reflections on equilibrium prices? Minimum wage laws regulate the lowest possible price for the commodity labour. Free marketeers argue that price fixing of any kind can stop a market from balancing at equilibrium (Barry, 1993: 19). Let us take another look at our above figure and let us assume that it represents the supply and demand of qualified librarians. In situations of high demand but low supply, the 10 available librarians would be paid £100 per day for their services. However, in conditions of high supply and low demand, 100 librarians would only be paid £10 per day for their services. What happened if the minimum wage was fixed at £15? According to our figure, only 95 librarians could be employed under this condition, which means that 5 would not be able to sell their services. The labour market cannot clear and - in this case - unemployment occurs.

Is this a reasonable argument: are minimum wages a tenable 'external barrier' explanation for unemployment? To answer this question, it is necessary to look at two points. First, the existence of the so-called 'Iron Law of Wages' and second, the problem that labour markets cannot be put on a par with other commodity markets.

The Iron Law of Wages

David Ricardo (1772-1823) introduced the distinction between the market price for work and its natural price. For him, the natural price reflects the costs of reproduction, i.e. it enables workers to sustain their own and potentially create new life. Ferdinand Lassalle (1825-1864) popularised Ricardo's principle and called it: the iron law of wages. He argued that wages will always average at a level which makes it possible for workers to sustain life and in addition allows for reproduction. The reasoning behind his claim was as follows: if wages were increased above subsistence level, the working population would grow, providing employers with more workers and the option to reduce wages. If wages were to drop under subsistence level, emigration, non-marriage, non-procreation and starvation would lead to a reduction in the available work force, which in turn would be followed by wage increases. Accordingly, average wages always circle around subsistence level (Lassalle, 1994: 21).

Today, the iron law of wages seems outdated. First, the Malthusian inspired hypothesis that workers procreate continuously, as long as they can feed their children, has proved incorrect for modern Western countries. High wages do not automatically lead to an increase of the labour force which in turn would put pressure on wages. Second, welfare state measures prevent average labour prices from adjusting at subsistence level because those who do not receive subsistence wages are not facing starvation or emigration any more because their income is supplemented by benefits.

Given these two phenomena, labour markets under conditions of welfare provision, can never equilibrate at subsistence level. It is the welfare state itself which distorts the free labour market because it prevents starvation and emigration. In modern welfare states without minimum wages, it is possible for employers to hire workers at any price because hardship is prevented by welfare provision. Workers are ready for work even if they could not survive on their wages because the state pays a supplement. It is possible that a Scroogian employer is highly subsidised by the tax-payer.

Welfare state measures therefore distort the market in favour of employers who can disregard the iron law of wages because of the availability of income supplements. If one considers it reasonable - as Lassalle and Ricardo did - that employers should pay a wage which allows for survival and reproduction, the minimum wage is the only way to set a bottom limit for income from work under conditions of welfare provision. Without a minimum wage, employers can benefit from their workers' labour whilst simultaneously pushing off costs to the taxpayer.

Minimum wages, therefore, replace the iron law of wages which cannot work properly within a welfare system. Hence, they are not an 'external barrier' to employment, unless set much beyond subsistence level. If they circle round a level which enables workers to sustain life and reproduce, they merely prevent employers from enjoying the benefits without carrying the full costs of labour.

The Particularity of Labour Markets

It was explained earlier how equilibrium prices are reached when demand and supply curves meet. It will be shown now, that labour markets and other commodity markets differ in one essential point. In most commodity markets, it is usually possible to withhold goods until the market offers a reasonable price. In contrast, it is not normally possible to keep labour from the market beyond short periods (strikes). An example: if people want to sell their houses but realise that current market prices are too low, they will refrain from selling as long as possible, waiting for a recovery of the housing market. This balances the number of available houses with the number of buyers and stabilises prices. In contrast to the housing market, the labour market reacts differently. In *Working Harder Isn't Working* (1993: 64), Bruce O'Hara explains this phenomenon as follows:

> Unfortunately, when wages drop, the demand for employment doesn't shrink. When wages drop, the supply of labour increases as individuals work longer hours in an attempt to maintain their standard of living. The classic example is the former housewife who says, 'I had to go back to work - we couldn't make ends meet on one paycheque any more.' In the past 15 years we've seen the labour force growing faster than the population, as declining wages push more families to add a second breadwinner. While most commodity surpluses are self-correcting, a surplus of labour is self-aggravating.

Although wages at the top end of professional work can be kept up by restricting access (barristers, chartered accountants, etc.), this option is not available at the low-pay end which is the area we are interested in. Since it is not possible to withhold labour from the job market if one depends on low paid employment, the non-professional labour market cannot balance at equilibrium. On the contrary, a drop in demand of labour will increase the supply and aggravate the situation in a downward spiral. Unemployment presses on wages; those in employment work even more to compensate for lower wages; this in turn increases unemployment which again leads to more pressure on wage levels. An equilibrium cannot be established.[14] In the words of Philippe van Parijs (1995: 211): 'There is ... no guarantee that the demand for labour will ever catch up with the supply, short of the point at which the supply dries up through starvation'.

To conclude on minimum wages: in the setting of Western welfare states, minimum wages are no acceptable explanation for unemployment. Their important function is to set minimum pay at subsistence level. Before the arrival of the welfare state, the iron law of wages fulfilled this task. Employers had to pay subsistence wages to have both present and future workers available. If, under welfare provision, non-subsistence wages are topped up with income supplements, employers are subsidised by the taxpayer, i.e. they use labour without fully paying for it. In addition, labour markets are different from other commodity markets. They cannot clear at equilibrium because it is not possible to withhold labour from the market until prices have recovered, a mechanism which achieves equilibrium in other commodity markets.

Productivity Booms

> Now a minority of workers produce the consumer goods for an even larger population at still higher levels of comfort than the richest élites of the past. This leaves the majority free to work in increasingly sophisticated services like health, higher education, scientific research, sport and entertainment - or, if we organise it badly, for low-grade services or unemployment (Perkin, 1996: 199).

The last two decades were characterised by a sweep of activities to reduce costs, particularly personnel costs, in all areas of Western economies.

Catchwords such as business re-engineering, lean management or downsizing whizzed through management circles. Companies were said to be successful, if they were able 'slimmers' and managed to 'prune' jobs (*Economist*, 1995: 83). In 1994, for example, corporate companies in the United States eliminated 516,000 jobs whilst their profits rose by 11 per cent (ibid.). Unemployment analysts describe these forms of job losses as technological displacement, which implies that new technologies replace human labour (Rifkin, 1995: xvi). Although manufacturing was affected most, other economic sectors have also experienced productivity explosions. Wealth created in 1970, is today being generated by half the number of employees in half the time (Willke, 1998: 148). The following section will examine all sectors of the cash-based economy separately to establish how far productivity booms have reduced the need for human labour.

So far, one 'pathological' and three 'external barrier' theories of unemployment were analysed and none of them were found convincing. It will now be seen that unemployment due to productivity booms is indeed an extremely persuasive explanation for job losses in the West. It will be argued with Harold Perkin whose thoughts introduced this section and Jeremy Rifkin (ibid. 292) that the 'near-workerless society' is in sight and that 'the end of work could spell a death sentence for civilization as we have come to know it ... [or] signal the beginning of a great social transformation'.

Classical economics distinguishes three types of economic activities; work in the primary sector is defined as exploiting natural resources (mining, farming etc.); work in the secondary sector as producing goods (manufacturing, construction etc.) and work in the third sector as handling, distributing and maintaining goods and resources as well as offering services. Modern economists subsume paid activities in the above three sectors under the term 'formal economy' in demarcation to the two 'informal' sectors. The fourth sector comprises economic activities which can be partly paid and partly unpaid (charity activities, odd jobs etc.). The fifth sector is wholly unpaid and comprises domestic work (Shankland, 1980: 12-14). The informal economy is irrelevant to the question of unemployment which only deals with remunerated work. We will therefore concentrate on the first three sectors when trying to determine future job prospects.

The following figure shows which sector employed which share of the the working population in the European Union in 1993.

Figure 7.5   The formal economy, EU, 1993

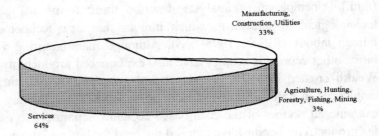

Source: Data from Eurostat (1995: 148).

Jobs in the Primary Sector

In 1993, the primary sector employed (including self-employed) only 3 per cent of the working population. 2.3 per cent in agriculture, hunting, fishing and similar activities and 0.7 per cent in mining.[15] Disregarding mining, how is it possible that 2.3 per cent of the working population (in figures: 2,327,000 people) can provide food for 347,269,700 EU citizens?[16] The answer is: intensive agriculture, i.e. keeping animals in battery farms and multiplying crop yields by using chemical pesticides and fertilisers. Intensive practices led to enormous productivity booms in agriculture in the second half of the 20th century. In the first half of this century, 20 per cent of the French population were engaged in farming to provide food for the country (Sahlins, 1974: 21). This means that one farmer fed five people. Ever since the 1950s, this figure dropped continuously. The following figure shows the data for Germany.

Figure 7.6   One farmer feeds ...

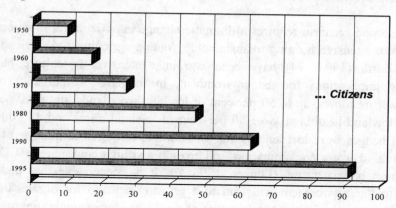

Source: Data from Willke (1998: 45).

What can be said about future employment opportunities in the primary sector? There are two main scenarios. First, intensive farming is maintained and supplemented by methods derived in the field of gene technology. Second, intensive farming is pushed back and in the long run replaced with sustainable, organic agriculture. Let us first consider the gene technology possibility. Gene technology researchers hope to replace cumbersome and time-consuming traditional plant breeding processes with satisfactory solutions from the test tube. Targets for test tube breeding include plants that make better use of sunlight, plants that can tolerate higher stress levels (e.g. more drought, more salty water), plants that are resistant to pests and diseases (Klingholz, 1990: 52) and plants with higher yields (Grefe, 1990: 67) than conventional ones. The so-called 'Green revolution' promises to breed every farmer's dream: plants that need little attention and resources but still give a high yield (Schönherr, 1991: 116). Some of these 'dreams' have already come true. Researchers from the United States, for example, have created a transgenic tomato plant which is resistant to the tobacco hornworm and partly resistant to the tomato fruitworm and the tomato pinworm (British Medical Association, 1992: 92). According to the British Medical Association (ibid. 228f), it is 'probable that food products or ingredients derived from genetic modification of ... plants and animals will become increasingly common'. If this is the case and if there is any truth in 'Green revolution' promises, job opportunities in the primary sector will continue to decrease since higher yields per plant will reduce the labour force further.

The second scenario requires a dramatic change in agricultural practices away from intensive farming to sustainable organic agriculture. As Friends of the Earth (1994: 74) have been warning, intensive agriculture has alarming implications for the environment. In the UK, 95 per cent of wildflower meadows, up to 50 per cent of lowland woodlands, up to 60 per cent of lowland heathland, over 50 per cent of lowland mires and 140,000 miles of hedges were lost since 1945. In addition, intensive farming led to high levels of water contamination, soil erosion and high emissions of CO_2 gases from battery farms (Lünzer, 1996: 6). It is conceivable that these threats to the environment will lead to a growing demand for organically produced food. The British supermarket chain Tesco, for example, reported a 340 per cent rise in sales for organic vegetables and fruits in 1997 (Dibb, 1997: 6). Nevertheless, organic food only represents 1 per cent of the total food market in Britain (*Working Lunch*, BBC2, 02/06/98). Given the slim possibility that organic agriculture might dominate over intensive farming in the medium term, what would be the implications for employment opportunities? Organic farming is more labour intensive than current methods (Friends of the Earth, 1994: 78) since extensive pesticide and fertiliser usage is replaced by technical knowledge and comprehensive supervision of crops. This means that human skills replace material resources. Some estimates suggest that 'organic farming employs twice as many people as conventional farming' (Brown, 1997: 7). Should this second scenario become reality, job opportunities in the primary sector would emerge again. Although nobody can foresee the future, it will be assumed that the first scenario is more likely. The 'Technology Foresight' report (1996) predicts that genetic engineering will increase in the near future and that a 'continuous downward pressure on all costs' will characterise all economic activities, thus favouring cheap products from intensive farming. It will therefore be concluded that the primary sector is unlikely to offer job opportunities for the future.

Jobs in the Secondary Sector

Secondary sector employment comprises jobs in what EU statisticians call 'industry', namely manufacturing, construction and the utilities (provision of electricity, gas and water). We will concentrate on manufacturing, which accounts for nearly 70 per cent of industry jobs (Eurostat, 1995: 148). To understand how booming productivity is achieved in the manufacturing sector, it is necessary to understand what became known as 're-engineering'.

Re-engineering describes a restructuring process within companies to significantly reduce costs. This process normally includes the elimination of management layers, particularly the so-called middle management which mediates between directors and workers (lean management). It often means team work in groups of multiskilled employees who solve problems more quickly and straightforwardly than hierarchically organised groups. Production and distribution processes are shortened and simplified and administration is streamlined, or in other words, cut (Rifkin, 1995: 6f). Typically, re-engineering leads to redundancies for approximately 40 per cent of the original workforce but job losses of as much as 75 per cent have occurred (ibid. 7; Gorz and Kempe, 1994: 593). This phenomenon leads to enormous jumps in productivity. Productivity is commonly defined as the efficiency of economic processes measured by comparing the amount of input required to achieve output (Digel *et al.*, 1987, Vol. 17: 303). If ten people were needed to operate a train signalling system in 1970 and one person plus a computer are needed for the same task in 1990, the productivity gain would consist of nine wages minus the cost of one computer as a percentage of the ten 1970s wages. Today, an ever decreasing work force can produce more goods in less time than ever before and the process is gaining speed (Beck, 1996: 3). The chairman of a pharmaceutical company expressed the trends in the following equation: $\frac{1}{2} * 2 * 3 = P$. 'Half as many people ... , paid twice as well and producing three times as much ... equals productivity and profit' (Handy, 1994: 9).

An example for re-engineering shall clarify how productivity gains are being achieved.[17] Traditionally, manufacturing processes were organised in sequence with a quality control department at the end of all processes. For the production of compact discs this could mean that around 20 different manufacturing steps were undertaken before any quality control system would check the product. Had an error occurred early on in the process, e.g. incorrect aluminium coating on raw disc, all reject discs would nevertheless have gone through the remaining processes and would have ended up on trays and with booklets in the quality control area. A stream-lined, re-engineered manufacturing process includes quality checks at all stages.

Although this can mean additional control equipment or personnel, it nevertheless reduces overall staff levels and material costs significantly because obsolete labour is avoided (printing reject CDs and processing them through the finishing line for trays and booklets, in this case).

One might argue that the process of re-engineering cannot continue over a long period of time. Once automation and rationalisation have taken their toll on the labour market, a tranquil period of stable employment might follow. Even if this were the case, a period of stability cannot be expected for the near future. According to Jeremy Rifkin (1995: 5), only 5 per cent of all companies world-wide have, so far, started 'to make the transition to the new machine culture'. He claims (ibid. 105) that 'corporate re-engineering is only in its infancy'.

Daring employment analysts foresee that by the first quarter of the 21st century only 2 per cent of the world population 'will be needed to produce all the goods necessary for total demand' (ibid. 8). Other predictions anticipate that manufacturing in the 21st century will only require 10 per cent of its current workforce (Bergmann, 1997: 27) or that only 10 per cent of the population will be needed in all employment sectors (Shankland, 1980: 2). Nobel Laureate Wassily Leontief (1983: 3) argues that 'the role of humans as the most important factor of production is bound to diminish in the same way that the role of horses in agricultural production was first diminished and then eliminated by the introduction of tractors'.

Whereas money invested in industry used to *provide* jobs, it nowadays *eliminates* them. According to André Gorz (1983: 50), 100 billion DM (£34.7 billion) of investment in industry created two million jobs between 1955 and 1960. The same amount of money only created 400,000 jobs between 1960 and 1965, when the turning-point was reached and the tractor (automated systems) began to take over from the horse (the worker). From 1965 to 1970, 100 billion DM destroyed rather than created 100,000 jobs and in the period from 1970 to 1975, 500,000 jobs were eliminated with the same amount of investment.

According to Michael Landesmann (1986: 117f), the manufacturing sector cannot be expected to provide jobs for the future if one assesses the trends in Western industrial economies realistically. Ulrich van Suntum shares this view. In his opinion (1995: 11), only the service, i.e. the tertiary, sector will provide job opportunities in the future. Before this sector will be examined, one potential objection must be investigated. In the industrial past, automation boosted productivity which in turn lowered production costs and enabled manufacturers to offer goods at cheaper prices. Thereby, consumers had their purchasing power increased and new goods could enter the market whose production required new employees. Workers who were displaced by machines in the first wave of automation were sucked into the production of completely new products. In a previous section (economic growth), one counterargument against this reasoning was already established. In stages of high industrial development, the rate of new inventions and innovations slows down significantly. Hence, it is more difficult in the 1990s to enter the market with new products than it was in the 1950s. But there is also another argument: empirical evidence shows that, in manufacturing, only highly sophisticated jobs became newly available after the first wave of re-engineering. In the US, new jobs only opened up for a minority of the labour force, namely 'physicists, computer scientists, high-level technicians, molecular biologists, business consultants, lawyers, accountants and the like' (Rifkin, 1995: 36).

It can, therefore, be concluded that the secondary sector does not offer job opportunities in the amount necessary to mitigate unemployment. On the contrary, technological unemployment, i.e. the displacement of workers in favour of machines, is likely to continue unabatedly for the foreseeable future.

Jobs in the Tertiary Sector

In 1993, the European Union published a White Paper on 'Growth, Competitiveness, Employment - Present Challenges and Ways into the 21st Century' (Suntum, 1995: 10 - my translation). The paper argued that, although Europeans have changed to accommodate new economic conditions, e.g. globalisation and productivity booms, the world has changed even faster. According to the Commission, unemployment must be regarded as structural and technological. Job growth for the future is predicted mostly in the personal service sector which, according to the Commission, includes services such as cleaning, child-care and security as well as environmental tasks and work that is necessary to improve public transport (ibid. 11). Before a closer look will be taken at this alleged well for new employment, it needs to be clarified which jobs belong to the tertiary sector.

EU statisticians divide the service sector into the following ten groups.

Figure 7.7   The service sector, EU, 1993

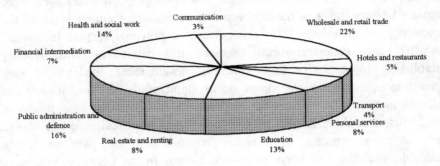

Source: Data from Eurostat (1995: 148).

It would go beyond the scope of this book to examine every group individually and in depth. We will therefore concentrate on the personal service sector which is seen as the most likely source for growing employment opportunities in the future. However, it is possible to make a few general remarks about the remaining areas. Three of the above ten categories rely heavily on state funds, namely health and social work, education as well as public administration and defence. Taken together, these areas provide employment for 43 per cent of third sector workers in the EU. Although it is theoretically possible that employment opportunities in the state sector might grow, the present political climate seems to favour small rather than big government (Wusfeld, 1994: 171; Merkel, 1992: 137; Deppe, 1996: 7). Hence, non-growth appears to be the likelier prospect.[18]

What can be said about the area of financial intermediation which comprises mainly banking? According to Blanpain and Sadowski (1994: 84), staff levels at banks are under significant pressure from automation. Automatic booking systems are being introduced, telephone banking centralises and thereby reduces staff as do cashmachines. In the future, it is expected that voice-recognising computers can take over from telephone banking operators. Another high-technology introduction to the banking sector is Internet banking. In Britain, Internet accounts have been available since autumn 1998 and branch-based business (the 'High Street Bank') is expected to shrink (*Working Lunch*, BBC2, 02/06/98). The German banking sector expects reductions in personnel of up to 60 per cent due to automation (Willke, 1998: 63). Financial intermediation can, therefore, not be regarded as an area with growing job opportunities.

Can any predictions be made about the wholesale and retail trade? Robert Reich (1994a: 201) claims that staff who operate tills will be displaced by machines in the near future. According to him, they belong to the category of routine operators whose labour can be taken over by automated systems. In addition, the success of direct marketing (mail catalogues) reduces overall staff levels in trade because goods are supplied from centralised wholesalers or even manufacturers rather than a high number of single outlets.

In 'real estate and renting' neither increased automation nor growing job opportunities seem to be likely. However, none of the employment analysis' studied, commented particularly on this sector. Therefore no claims will be made as to its development.

In contrast, the communication sector which includes tele-communication, Internet services and the media, is a likely candidate for employment growth in the 1990s, albeit only for particularly high-skilled personnel (Friedrichs, 1997: 5); the majority of which will be university graduates (Willke, 1998: 73).

The personal service sector So far, it was established that only one of ten service sector areas, namely communication, is likely to absorb more workers in the future than it did in the past. However, it was not yet examined whether personal services and hotels and restaurants could be the 'job machines' of the future. Some analysts, including Robert Reich (1994: 202), add hotel and restaurant staff to the personal service sector. Although it is in opposition to EU statistics, this classification will be used here. What exactly are personal services? Which types of jobs are involved?

We have already mentioned some of the jobs which make up the personal service sector. The EU commission on 'Growth, Competitiveness, Employment' listed cleaning, child-care, security, environmental tasks and public transport[19] and, following Robert Reich, hotel and restaurant staff were just added. According to Charles Handy (1985: 7), personal services include all contract domestic work, eating and drinking services, education tourism (tour guides) and health and beauty services. Suzanne Franks has a rather unusual definition for personnel service sector jobs which she describes as work involving 'being nice to people' and therefore considered most suitable for women (Franks, 1999: 18).

As was seen at the beginning of this section, a European White Paper claimed that the personal service sector will provide the majority of new jobs in the future. Support for this claim can be found from institutes such as the Bremen Society for Economic Research (*Bremer Gesellschaft für Wirtschaftsforschung*, 1997: 22) whose studies show that personal services are the only serious contender for employment growth in Western Europe. Former German Chancellor Helmut Kohl is in agreement. He (1997: 3) argued that personnel service employment could lower German unemployment significantly, if terms and conditions were made more attractive to potential employers. Shortly before being voted out of office, he wanted to introduce tax allowances for those who employ domestic helpers.

Where does the West European belief that personal services might significantly reduce unemployment stem from? Both Continental European researchers and politicians point their fingers to the United States where 32 million new jobs were created between 1973 and 1989; most of them in the personal service sector (Handy, 1994: 8). In contrast, Western Europe only created five million new jobs in the same period (ibid.). A comparison of American and German employment structures, showed that seven million personal service jobs could be created in Germany if US employment structures were copied (Klopfleisch *et al.*, 1997: 32). It is this so-called 'American job machine' (Thie, 1997: 9) which fuels Continental European hopes that personal services might provide an employment-boom in the 1990s and into the next century (rtf, 1997: 2).

In addition to this empirical evidence, it is argued that personal services are not affected by globalisation and productivity booms. The jobs of child-minders or security guards cannot be exported to countries where wages or taxes are lower. Hence, globalisation has hardly any impact on this sector (Afheldt, 1995: 10). Similarly, these jobs are not at risk from automatisation to the same extent as jobs in manufacturing are. Although labour-saving devices might reduce hours spent in domestic services, child-minding, environmental work, caring for the elderly and similar jobs are not well suited to rationalisation.

Both empirical evidence from the United States and reflections on the impact of globalisation and productivity booms seem to confirm that the personal service sector is the best hope for future employment opportunities in West Europe. There are, however, moral implications to this solution. It has been shown that the personal service sector can only expand significantly if wage inequalities within a country are very high (Schettkat, 1996: 31). Polarised societies, as Michel Albert (1993: 44) puts it, or nations with 'economic apartheid' or *de facto* segregation (ibid.) are best suited to sustain large personal service sectors. In this section, moral issues in personal service work will be looked at. It will not be denied that the sector can expand significantly in the future. It will, however, be asked whether a major expansion is desirable.

First, let us look at potential evidence that personal service sector work expands in polarised societies. The following figure shows wage inequalities in five different countries: the United States, Britain, France, Germany and Sweden. The figure has been calculated as follows: average wages of the highest earning 10 per cent of the population have been divided by average wages of the lowest earning 10 per cent of the population. In 1980s Sweden, for example, high earners received twice as much income as low earners.

Figure 7.8   Wage inequalities, 1980s and 1990s

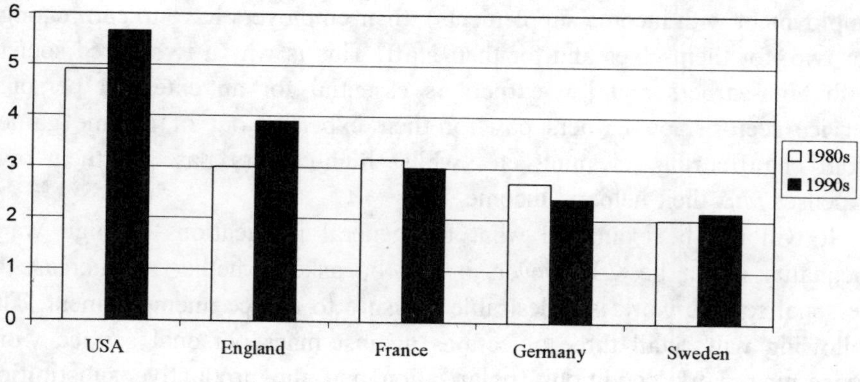

Source: Data from Schettkat (1996: 31).

The above figure illustrates two points. First, the United States, Britain and, to a small degree, Sweden experienced a rise in wage inequalities in the 1990s. In contrast, inequalities were reduced in France and Germany.

Second, in the 1990s, the United States and Britain show much higher absolute wage inequalities than the other three countries. It has been said earlier that the United States created a huge number of new jobs in the personal service sector in the recent past. Similar trends can be observed in Britain where 'servants are back', according to Barrie Clement (1996: 3). He writes that domestic service is the 'latest boom industry' in his country (ibid.). In Germany, on the other hand, a 'shortfall' of seven million personal service workers was calculated given the US employment structure. Gerhard Willke (1998: 61) argues that the expansion of the personal service industry in Germany is hampered by the fact that the country is a 'levelled middle-class society'.[20] A similar 'problem' exists in Sweden, where the number of personal service workers is equally low in comparison with the United States (Schettkat, 1996: 31). This gives credence to the claim that a high number of personal service workers can only be employed in countries where wage inequality is significant.

The relationship between high wage inequality and the number of personal service workers is not surprising. Those people who use personal services, i.e. child-minders, cleaners etc., must earn enough money to settle their bills first and then pay their domestic staff. This is only possible if personal service wages are significantly lower than employers' wages. Since domestic helpers also have to earn a living wage (unless the state subsidises employment with income supplements), their employers have to earn enough for two, for themselves and for their staff. This is why a two-tiered society with high-earners and low-earners is essential for an extended personal service sector. Low-earners pay for their expenses out of income gained from chauffeuring, cleaning etc. whilst high-earners pay for their own expenses *plus* their helpers' income.

It will not be examined what the general implications of high wage inequality might be.[21] However, it will be asked whether an increase in personal service work is a desirable measure to reduce unemployment. The following will detail three objections against mass personal service work concerning work conditions, polarisation and the productive substitution approach to employment.

Work conditions, including pay, are usually open to negotiation between employers and employees (or unions) within current legislation. However, personal services will only be demanded on a scale big enough to reduce unemployment, if pay is very low (see above). Hence, low pay is an unavoidable feature of mass personal service work.[22] This claim is in line with the observation by Frank Deppe (1996: 14) that personal service workers are constantly on the brink of poverty. In addition, he argues that their jobs are characterised by insecurity and the total lack of career prospects. He maintains that work conditions in personal services are so bad that the term 'service proletariat'[23] (ibid. - my translation) is appropriate to describe their situation. Apart from low pay, personal service work is characterised as 'erratic, seasonal, insecure and unprotected' by Charles Handy (1985: 8). Helen Wilkinson (1995: 23) argues that these work conditions make personal service work exploitative and prone to an upstairs-downstairs flavour, which is the second objection voiced against mass personal service work.

André Gorz (1994: 50) coins the phrase of the South-Africanisation of society. He argues that personal service work which is based on large income inequalities between employers and employees applies the 'colonial model' to the 'metropolitan heartlands' to achieve employment growth (ibid.). Similarly, Hans Thie (1997: 9) speaks of a refeudalisation of society and Helen Wilkinson (as was just quoted) and Barrie Clement (1996: 3) criticise the Victorian upstairs-downstairs values which personal service work bring back. Only in a pauperised society is it possible, according to André Gorz (1994: 49), that the high-paid can claim the privilege of unloading their boring and repugnant chores[24] onto the not so lucky. Ian McCartney (1996: 3), the 1996 Labour employment spokesman, expressed his assessment of the rising demand for domestic servants in the following complaint: 'This was the generation of young people who were going to be our engineers, our designers, our scientists ... Instead we've turned them into nursemaids and skivvies for the fat cats'. According to a survey undertaken by Mintel, the domestic service sector in Britain experienced a fourfold growth from 1987 to 1997 (Franks, 1999: 74). In the United States, shoe cleaners will visit offices to polish shoes for those who do not want to get up from their desks and other services include arranging family photo albums or massaging busy executives during conference breaks. In a two-tiered society 'the work-rich buy ... other people's time for themselves' (ibid.).

The last objection against mass personal service work relies on historical observations of waged work. André Gorz (1994: 48) argues that hitherto the growth of employment has always been fuelled by, what he calls, 'productive substitution'. People were drawn into paid employment (rather than staying autark farmers or self-employed shoe-makers) because industrial wage-labourers were able to produce goods quicker, cheaper and often better (ibid. 48). Today, hardly anybody weaves their own fabrics, sews clothes, bakes bread, builds houses etc. because it is possible to buy more services and goods within an industrialised society where labour is divided. 'In other words, industrialisation has saved working time for everyone, throughout society, and the working time saved has been re-employed to a large extent within the economy to produce extra wealth' (ibid.). The personal service industry, on the other hand, has no productive substitution effect. Instead, it just 'dumps' work which one stratum of society finds repugnant onto people who are seen by employers as born to serve; 'in a word, inferiors' (ibid. 49). There is no beneficial overall effect on society in terms of organising work more efficiently and productively. It is just a phenomenon where one privileged group pushes off unpleasant duties to another. A question could be raised in this context: nobody argues that it is unfair on dustmen to perform an arguably unpleasant task. Is this not a similar problem? No, because the employment of dustmen has a significant productive substitution effect. It is much more efficient in terms of working time to employ dustmen rather than requiring every citizen to bring their weekly garbage to landfill sites. A second objection which could be made is as follows: is it not sensible to free the most productive, i.e. the highest earning citizens,[25] from everyday chores so that their undivided full-time effort can be directed towards increasing overall economic performance? Yes, that might be in the interest of society as a whole and it might also have a productive substitution effect. However, it would not serve society if one partner in the contract is paid and treated as an inferior servant. Appropriate wages and regulated working conditions would have to be part of the deal.

The above three objections against increased personal service employment are ethical, rather than based on economic grounds. It is possible to reduce unemployment by promoting and supporting personal service work. However, it requires the acceptance of a two-tiered society in which one group would have to accept bad working conditions merely to act as servants for another group. The worst-case scenario of personal services under conditions of economic apartheid has been captured brilliantly by photographer Paul Almasy in 1950s' Asia.

Figure 7.9 Personal services in Saigon, 1950

The employment society is running out of employment, as Hannah Arendt (1981: 12) foresaw in 1958 and modern analysts confirm today (Mutz, 1997: 31). According to William Bridges (1999: 64f), the hunt after an ever-decreasing number of jobs will be seen as 'a fight over deckchairs on the *Titanic*' in a hundred years time. The present section established that productivity booms in the primary sector and technological displacement in the secondary sector confirm Arendt's predictions. A minority of workers can nowadays produce consumer goods for the population at large. In addition, the tertiary sector did not show major possibilities for employment growth unless one embraced a return to the servant society. What happens to those whose work is not needed any more? 'If we organise it badly', as Harold Perkin puts it (see introductory quote to this section), they will be reduced to unemployment or low-grade services; consigned to the 'scrap-heap of history' (Albert, 1993: 54). This is happening in Continental Europe where all major countries experienced unemployment rates of around 10 per cent in the 1990s (Globus, 1998: 29). Simultaneously, politicians try to promote a two-tiered system where the comfortably employed use those whose work is not needed any more as servants.

If the approach of the near-workerless society is handled constructively, on the other hand, mass unemployment and a booming servants' industry might be avoidable (Rifkin, 1995: 292, 264). The next chapter will describe three different reform approaches each of which has the potential to handle the future of employment constructively.

Notes

[1]   Only mothers who receive state support, such as AFDC, are targeted. Full-time mothers who are married to male breadwinners are not considered unemployed.

[2]   Australia makes an exception. In a *White Paper on Employment and Growth*, the government argued that growth cannot solve the problem of unemployment (Saunders, 1995: 46).

[3]   Some authors claim that jobless growth goes back to the mid-1960s (Espenhorst, 1996: 5). Since the timing is not relevant for the argument, the dispute will be disregarded.

[4]   The phenomenon of increased productivity itself will be examined in the last section of this chapter entitled 'Productivity booms'.

[5]   This section will not include the debate about the North-South divide which claims that even small growth rates in the so-called developed countries rely on the inequity of Southern poverty; a potential second ethical constraint on vigorous GDP growth. Good representations of the discussion can be found in the following two publications: 1) Bob Goudzwaard / Harry de Lange (1995) *Beyond Poverty and Affluence*, Eerdmans Publishing, Michigan. 2) Johan Galtung / Roy Preiswerk / Peter O'Brien (1980) *Self-Reliance - A Strategy for Development*, Bogle-L'Ouverture Publications, London.

[6]   Beckerman claims that the Third World (his choice of words) urgently needs economic growth and that environmentalism can only be afforded by the rich. He (1995: 16) writes: 'The Club of Rome discovered the limits to growth while gathered on the terrace of a villa overlooking the hillside'. In this book, growth is only rejected as a solution to unemployment in Western countries. It is not claimed that it should be avoided under all circumstances. The relationship between growth and falling infant mortality rates (Anderson, 1991: 93) presents a good case in favour of economic growth in conditions of so-called 'under-development'.

7   Named after the Norwegian Prime Minister Gro Harlem Brundtland, the report was published in 1987 whilst she held the chair of the United Nations World Commission on Environment and Development. The report which was produced under her guidance led to the first Earth Summit in 1992. Brundtland has recently (January 1998) been appointed Director General of the World Health Organisation (BBC News Online, 1998).

8   Personnel communication from a German accountant.

9   Advantages and disadvantages which are restricted to either country are not included. One of the major assets of Britain, for example, is the English language (*Newsnight*, BBC2, 30/01/97). A major disadvantage for Germany in the 1990s are the enormous costs of reunification which are partly paid by employers.

10   An international survey undertaken in 1995 found that England and Wales showed the highest level of violent crime amongst eleven analysed countries (including the United States) (Bennetto, 1997: 4).

11   Right-wing politicians can draw votes by mixing together the topics of immigration and unemployment as Christian Hensch and Uli Wismer (1997: 11 - my translation) comment: 'Unemployment – "Foreigners are to blame!! Oh dear! Such threatening peoples, they come in suspect hordes and lie in wait with a greedy taste for the occidental workers' paradise! Alas: bogus asylum seekers! Cheap workers! Hannibal ante Portas!" That immigrants are to be blamed for unemployment is by far the most pretentious rubbish that can be said about the subject. That Pat Buchanan, Jean-Marie Le Pen and Jörg Haider continuously maintain the point, does not make it any more reasonable, only sadder'.

12   For more details on the different models of capitalism see the following three publications: 1) Barry, Norman (1993) 'The Social Market Economy', in: Frankel Paul, Ellen (eds); *Liberalism and the Economic Order*, University Press, Cambridge, pp.1-25. 2) Albert, Michel (1993) *Capitalism against Capitalism*, Whurr Publishers, London. 3) Gray, John (1994) 'From Post-Communism to Civil Society: The Reemergence of History and the Decline of the Western Model', in: Frankel Paul, Ellen *et al.* (eds); *Liberalism and the Economic Order*, University Press, Cambridge, pp. 26-50.

13   The term 'winners' refers to the successful reduction of unemployment rather than economic success in general which is conventionally measured in GDP per head. Given this indicator, Britain is less economically successful than most Western European countries. In 1996 Austria, Belgium, Denmark, Finland, France, Germany, Ireland, Italy, Luxembourg, the Netherlands, Norway, Sweden and Switzerland showed higher GDP figures per head than Britain (Globus, 1997: 6).

14   The only possibility for equilibrium in the labour market is expressed by the 'iron law of wages'. If employees starve or emigrate, labour supply falls and employers have to increase wages but as was argued earlier, this does not happen under welfare conditions.

15   In the same year, exports and imports in the primary sector were balanced. Imports were valued at 36,774,000 ECU, exports at 36,389,000 ECU (Eurostat, 1995: 320, 322) This means that farmers, miners etc. from non-EU countries cannot increase the figure of 3 per cent because this would require a negative trade balance in the primary sector (more imports than exports). It is possible that non-EU primary sector work is more labour intensive, a possibility which would not be reflected in the ECU value of imports. We will nevertheless simplify calculations by assuming that ECU values roughly represent labour input.

16   Population of the European Union on the 1.1.1994 (Eurostat, 1995: 123).

17   Example from my own work at Warner Music Manufacturing Europe (Germany).

[18]   It could be argued that the privatised sector within health and education might grow so significantly that new job opportunities might arise. Although this is a possibility, it is not regarded as very likely, especially not in Continental Europe.

[19]   When the Commission lists the improvement of public transport as a potential candidate for employment growth, it is not bus drivers or train conductors that are expected to find new employment. The example given in the report (Suntum, 1995: 10) are 'catchment taxis' (*Sammeltaxis*), i.e. cars which provide transport after bus hours or in remote areas.

[20]   Willke (1998: 64) sees a second difficulty which is not being encountered in Britain or the United States. German consumers believe that simple personnel services are degrading and consider it arrogant to accept them. Therefore, attempts of German supermarkets to introduce 'buzzboys' or 'buzzgirls' to help consumers packing and carrying their shopping failed.

[21]   Some critics of income inequality insist that it has major side-effects. Will Hutton (1995: 186) lists ghetto housing, racial discrimination, poverty, drug-taking, crime and huge prison populations. Jeremy Rifkin (1995: 208) maintains that a correlation exists between rising wage inequality and increases in violent crime.

[22]   High pay for domestic help is possible (an average of £10.42 per hour (30 DM) are being paid in Germany (rtf, 1997: 2)) but at this rate, personnel services cannot solve the unemployment problem because only the seriously wealthy can or want to afford it.

[23]   Whether Deppe uses the term in its Marxian instantiation or according to its Ancient Greece origin is unclear, but its associations of serious poverty and misery are present in both forms. In Ancient Greece, proletarians were people who owned nothing but their offspring ('proles') (Digel *et al.*, 1987, Vol. 17: 311).

[24]   The great majority (70 per cent) of traditional domestic workers (housewives) dislike housework (Oakley, 1982: 173).

[25]   It is a controversial claim to suggest that pay indicates productivity. In this context, surgeons would be deemed less productive than footballers.

8 Potential Solutions for Unemployment

> Societies which continue to propagate the job ethic and to link basic incomes with jobs, but which leave millions of people jobless, will continue to inflict great damage on those people and themselves. But the practical action must also be visionary (Robertson, 1986: 85).

High unemployment, particularly in Continental Europe, cannot be dismissed as the outcome of antisocial behaviour or individual pathologies. Instead, the previous chapter showed that the employment society is running out of employment. Labour supply seriously outstrips labour demand. One possible solution, namely a return to the Victorian 'upstairs-downstairs' society, is seen as outdated and unfit for the 21st century. However, unemployment must be tackled and this chapter will introduce three different proposals: ecological taxation, measures to ensure a different distribution of employment and basic income. The compilation makes no claim to being exhaustive but preference has been given to proposals which favour fundamental change over piece-meal 'business-as-usual' solutions.

Ecological Taxation

There are few issues on which economists agree. One of them is that scarce resources should be used thriftily and wherever possible be replaced by readily available resources. This leitmotiv underlies the idea of ecological taxation. Finite natural resources are seen as scarce whereas human labour is seen as abundant. Ecological tax reforms are therefore designed to mitigate two major problems in industrialised countries: unemployment and environmental degradation. By imposing a tax on activities that cause environmental damage and simultaneously relieving the tax burden on employment, it is assumed that a 'win-win' situation can be achieved: lower unemployment, less pollution. The following section will briefly describe mainstream eco-tax ideas and illustrate the pros and cons with reference to the discussion in Germany.

The Reasoning Behind Ecological Taxation

Free marketeers claim that the price mechanism in market economies works admirably. However, British economist Arthur Cecil Pigou described the phenomenon of 'externalised costs' as early as 1920. He observed that sparks from steam locomotives set fields alight causing serious damage to farmers that was not paid for by train companies. Costs, in this instance, were externalised. Pigou came to the conclusion that activities which externalise costs impose a burden on society while increasing individual profits. In modern day economics these costs are often referred to as external diseconomies.

The German Ministry of Economics instructed the Prognos-Institute in Basel to calculate the annual external costs of energy production in Germany. They received the results in 1992. Estimated costs externalised during energy production were given as (British equivalent used): £3.5 billion for damages to health; £3.1 billion for damages to forests; £2.6 billion for loss of animal and plant species and £1.3 billion for damages to buildings and bridges (Wille, 1996: 9). Another study showed that the external costs of private vehicle transport lie between 4-7 DM per litre fuel compared to the current price[1] of 1.73 DM per litre (Bode and Werner, 1995: 78).

The problem of externalised costs has been known for a long time but, so far, no solution has been found. Ecological tax reforms are one attempt to redress the balance. If market prices do not speak the 'ecological truth' (kess/vo, 1995: 19), they need to be raised artificially. This could be interpreted as just another trick from the treasury to increase the level of taxation. However, ecological tax reforms are planned to be revenue-neutral. What is taken from the pockets of polluters is put into the pockets of job providers.[2] This is the reasoning behind ecological taxation. But how could it be put into practice?

Proposals

In Germany, two detailed studies have been commissioned and published. In Autumn 1993 *Greenpeace-Deutschland* instructed the German Institute for Economic Research (*Deutsches Institut für Wirtschaftsforschung*, DIW)[3] to carry out research into ecological taxation. They were asked how main economic indicators would change and who would benefit or loose from a tax reform. The DIW proposal looked as follows: tax on electricity, petrol, fuel, diesel and gas is raised gradually starting in 1995. New revenue would be used for two different purposes. First, employers' contributions to state pension systems would be reduced gradually, achieving a reduction of 77 per cent by the year 2005. Second, citizens would receive an 'eco-bonus' to compensate them for higher energy bills. This bonus would be distributed Robin Hood style, giving more to individuals on low incomes and less to well-off citizens. The DIW calculated that individuals earning or receiving under 10,000 DM p.a. (£3,472) would have their incomes raised by 0.89 per cent, individuals on middle incomes would meet no change and individuals on incomes over 120,000 DM (£41,667) would face a reduction of 0.14 per cent. The eco-bonus was implemented to counteract arguments that ecological taxation puts an unproportionate burden on the less well-off (heating in winter only for the rich?). The impact on economic indicators, as investigated by the DIW, has been summarised in Table 8.1. The overall findings of the institute were that ecological reconstruction of the tax system would be 'lawful', 'economically sensible' and 'socially acceptable' (Vorholz, 1995: 17).

Table 8.1   Ecological taxation in Germany, DIW-concept

Year	2000	2005
Energy consumption	-5.3%	-10.4%
CO_2-Emission	-5.3%	-10.3%
Employment	+300,000	+ 610,000
Inflation	+0.6%	+1.5%
National production	+0.1%	-0.2%
National debt	-6.1 bn DM (-£2.1 bn)	-14.3 bn DM (-£5.0 bn)

Source: Data from Vorholz (1995: 17), non-eco-tax related changes excluded.

The second proposal comes from the Support Group for Ecological Tax Reforms (*Förderverein Ökologische Steuerreform*, FÖS), which has the two major eco-tax theorists on board: Ernst Ulrich von Weizsäcker, President of the Institute for Climate, Environment and Energy and Hans Christoph Binswanger, the economist from Switzerland who first published a book on the subject in 1983. The FÖS concept differs from the above introduced proposal in four major points: price increases on energy are lower, but at the same time car-related expenses are higher (petrol, vehicle tax). On the credit side, payments for state-funded unemployment insurances are reduced both for employers and employees. The FÖS concept does not include an eco-bonus, but is also revenue-neutral.

Given these detailed studies, what are the arguments for and against ecological tax reform?

The Pros and Cons of Ecological Taxation

Wilfred Beckerman (1995: 8), a British economist, believes that fashionable global issues, such as climate change or the exhaustion of finite resources, are grossly exaggerated. In his opinion environmentalists in the West paint phoney disaster scenarios (ibid.). On the other hand Herman E. Daly, an American economist, argues that mankind is rushing headlong into destruction by clinging to economic policies that are unsustainable, namely world trade, growth and deregulation (Vorholz, 1995a: 44). If Beckerman represented the Arctic and Daly the Antarctic, proponents of ecological taxation would be situated closer to the Antarctic; incidentally very near to

Rio De Janeiro, the location of the first Earth summit.

Environmental concerns are very real and wide-spread in German-speaking countries not just amongst politicians but also amongst the general public and business leaders. Edzard Reuter (1995: 23), for example, who headed Daimler-Benz from 1987 until 1995 thinks that survival on earth is a question of undreamed-of dimensions requiring sustainable solutions quickly. Ecological taxation which strives to protect the environment might be one of those sustainable solutions. In contrast to conventional policies, such as end-of-pipe controls coupled with fines, ecological taxation is meant to take advantage of market forces. In market systems, prices direct actions and this phenomenon could be turned to good use by increasing the prices of non-renewable and decreasing the prices of renewable resources (including human work). Thereby eco-tax theorists hope to have a significantly higher impact on the reduction of environmental pollution than could be achieved with traditional means.

The second major argument in favour of ecological taxation stems from deliberations on how to implement eco-taxes without putting an undue burden on society and businesses. If a new tax was introduced to protect the environment, citizens and businesses would be worse off than before: less money to spend and less money to invest. In order to avoid this situation revenue-neutrality is being promised. The new income for the treasury would be returned to the public. It was argued that it might be possible to kill two birds with one stone and channel the money into the struggle against unemployment. According to the above DIW-study, unemployment in Germany would fall by 610,000 in ten years.

A third important argument from supporters can be disentangled from the discussion but it is also a necessary prerequisiste to achieve the other two main targets. Theorists think that ecological taxation can and must unleash huge innovation potentials. In the new Club of Rome report *Faktor Vier*, Ernst Ulrich von Weizsäcker and his colleagues B. Amery and L. L. Hunter (1995) argue that it is possible to double prosperity whilst halving resource-input. The authors show the enormous amount of waste in today's economies, of which the following are two examples: 80 per cent of all finished products are thrown away after having been used only once and only 3 per cent of the energy that is put into bulbs comes out as light. After describing the status-quo of wastage, the book explains in great detail and with many case studies how the so-called efficiency revolution would take place once energy prices were increased artificially. Just as business re-engineering makes an enormous number of employees redundant, the efficiency revolution could make an enormous amount of kilowatt-hours redundant, as Weizsäcker (1994: 86) claims. Supporters of the innovation idea also argue that it has worked in the past. Germany has very strict environmental regulations and is at the same time the world's leading exporter of environmental technology (Steenblock, 1996: 2). However, one could argue: is environmental technology not a negligible margin technology for green hysterics? No, a comparison with biotechnology will illustrate the point. Nowadays, this technology is often put forward as *the* field into which every advanced country must venture in order to be competitive and ready for the 21st century. Gerhard Willke (1998: 162) calls it the 'Lead Technology for the next Century'. The world-wide market for biotechnology is estimated to be 150 billion dollars at most. The market for environmental technology is estimated at 1,000 billion dollars (Lafontaine, 1996b: 7).

As there are three major arguments to support ecological tax reforms, there are also three major arguments against it. 1) plant closures or re-location; 2) export of environmental problems to countries with less know-how and technology and 3) unreliable source of revenue for the treasury. In a global market the threat of plant closures and re-locations hangs above all European countries and especially above Germany with its high labour costs. A new tax might be the last straw to induce a plant-closure or a re-location. As the 'Technology Foresight' (1997) predicts, global competition will go on to put a downward pressure on all costs in the foreseeable future. However, the new tax would be revenue-neutral and disadvantages in energy prices should be compensated for by lower labour costs. Critics argue that this might be true for the economy as a whole but there are still clear winners and losers with the latter being likely to re-locate. A cost explosion would have to be faced by the chemical, steel and cellulose industries. Mechanical and electronical engineering as well as most service industries, on the other hand, would benefit from the introduction of ecological taxation (Henkel and Hoffmann, 1995: 29). That re-location has negative impli-cations on employment levels and treasury income must not be stressed here. There is, however, one consequence of re-location that is not so obvious, which leads to point two.

If steel is produced in Brazil, three times as much raw material is used compared to production in Germany (Reuter, 1995: 23). The estimate for coal is less dramatic but still alarming. China uses twice as much raw material to extract energy from coal than Germany (Loske and Vorholz: 1992, 54). Given the possibility of re-location of energy-intensive industries, ecological taxation would lead to a higher amount of overall environmental damage and waste of resources.

The last point that can be made against ecological taxation does not come from business quarters but from the treasury. A tax must be a reliable, steady and calculable income for the state. An ecological tax, however, is purposefully designed to eliminate its own base. Energy usage is planned to decrease after the introduction of ecological taxation thereby removing the basis for taxation at the same time. (The two above described concepts try to solve this problem by implementing a progression. Tax increases yearly by 5 per cent for the FÖS-concept and by 7 per cent for the DIW concept). The pros and cons for ecological taxation are summarised in the following table:

Table 8.2   Pros and cons of ecological taxation

Pros	Cons
Less environmental degradation	Plant closures, re-location
Lower unemployment	Worsening of environmental problems
Efficiency revolution	Unreliable source of tax-revenue

Ecological taxation is a very appealing idea for all those who are concerned about the environment and unemployment levels. By shifting taxation from labour to energy, a 'win-win' situation might be achieved. High energy prices will fuel an energy efficiency revolution which could reduce the usage of nonrenewable resources significantly. On the other hand, labour - a readily available resource in Western Europe - would be partly relieved from the burden of taxation in order to stimulate its demand. Hence, both the problems of unemployment and environmental degradation might be mitigated by the introduction of an ecological tax reform as a medium-term solution.

Overwork and Underemployment - Steps Towards a New Equilibrium

More than one fifth of full-time employees in the European Union would prefer to work part-time according to a survey undertaken in 1989 (Tergeist, 1995: 11). Two million full-time jobs could be created in Germany if all part-time wishes were implemented (Tenhaef, 1997: 2; Klauder, 1997: 28) and an additional 1.4 million if all over-time was converted into new jobs (Schulte, 1996: 17). In Scandinavia, 'young women want the six-hour day, young men want longer vacations, [and] ... men and women want an earlier retirement age' (Hernes, 1987: 102); Norwegians in particular would prefer a quiet, simple life to one with high income and high stress (Wemegah, 1980: 126). At the same time, the majority of unemployed in all European countries want a share in paid employment. Although some of these statistics might oversimplify, it is obvious that the distribution of work is not Pareto optimal. People's preferences could, at least in theory, be optimised without any transgressions by a different distribution of employment.

The phenomenon of overwork on the one hand and underemployment on the other is similar in Western countries outside Continental Europe. In Canada, the 1990s were named the 'era of exhaustion' (O'Hara, 1993: 16) with 'burnout blues' for those in work (ibid. 17) and 'pain and deprivation' for those out of work (ibid. 15). In the United States, Juliet Shor analysed the problem in *The Overworked American* (1991) whilst the American greeting card industry profited by selling cards saying 'Sorry, I can't be there to tuck you in' (Franks, 1999: 74). In Britain, the main development in the 1990s is a rift between the work-rich and the work-poor, i.e. those with two incomes per family and those with none (Heuser, 1997: 84). In contrast, Japan aims to be the lifestyle superpower of the millennium by increasing leisure time for citizens in employment (Rifkin, 1995: 227).

In all these countries, overwork exists alongside unemployment and whilst employment cannot be rationed in a free and liberal society, it might be possible to encourage a more equitable distribution. Three different ways to achieve this goal will be introduced. First, a shortened standard working week; second, voluntary 'downshifting' and third phasing in and out of work; all three of which have the potential to reduce unemployment.

Shortening the Standard Working Week

Since the beginning of the Industrial Age, the standard working week has been reduced continually. To show the extent of this reduction, the following figure summarises the development in Germany from the early 19th century until the mid 1990s.

Figure 8.1   Standard working week in hours, Germany, 1825–1995

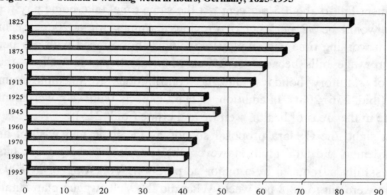

Source: Data from Willke (1998: 95).

Utopian socialists like André Gorz believe that nobody should work more than four hours per day leaving enough time for public duties or useful activities such as gardening, teaching, learning, caring for children or DIY. The ideal he wants to achieve in modern Western societies resembles life in Israeli kibbutzim (Gorz, 1983: 116). A more realistic attempt at advancing a shorter working week has been presented by Canadian Bruce O'Hara in *Working Harder Isn't Working* (1993). His most interesting proposal is the four-day workweek with a two-year preparation program. To lay the groundwork for a four-day workweek, he suggests to introduce the following legislation. Employers have to pay a tax on all overtime wages; all salaried positions must be converted to hourly wage jobs; all benefits available to full-time employees must be available pro-rata for part-timers and pension plans must be altered to allow a phasing-out of work five years before retirement without a reduction in pension payments (ibid. 206f). Once the two preparatory years have passed, more legislation must be brought in. The standard working week must be reduced to four days or 32 hours with the overtime tax applying to this new standard; the minimum wage must be raised to allow subsistence on the new 32-hour full-time job; all statutory holidays must be cancelled as a concession to employers; employers must increase hourly wages on a one-off basis by 15 per cent but at the same time stop to pay unemployment insurance which will be funded from general revenues (ibid. 208). According to O'Hara the impact on unemployment would be powerful. Employment should increase by 14 per cent and unemployment fall to about 3 per cent. At the same time, take-home pay for employees would be 92 per cent of previous earnings for a 20 per cent reduction in working time and employers would only be faced with a 5 per cent rise in wage bills because of increased productivity as well as the abolition of statutory holidays and the contributions to unemployment insurance (ibid. 216, 208f). In addition, O'Hara expects reduced government expenditure in the areas of health, welfare and crime (ibid. 215).

At first sight, the O'Hara proposal sounds as idealistic and wishful as Gorz's gardening and DIY idyll. However, the four-day working week has been successfully introduced by a major corporation, Volkswagen, in 1993 when hours were cut to 28.8 per week. What did the Volkswagen plan entail and how did it come about? In the early 1990s, Volkswagen was able to boost productivity by 23 per cent in a climate of increased global competition. This meant that the corporation faced mass redundancies of around 31,000 (Rifkin, 1995: 224). In November 1993, when Germany was in deep recession, the VW management took an unusual step and started negotiations with union representatives (*IG Metall*). The outcome was hailed as a major success and *the* future model for manufacturing. Working time was reduced by 20 per cent for all 108,000 employees which resulted in a four-day or 28.8 hour week. In return for reduced hours and significantly increased job security, employees accepted a 12 per cent wage cut (Jung, 1997: 253). Although the Volkswagen scheme is the best known example, other German manufacturers introduced the four-day week much earlier. The BMW plant in Regensburg, for example, has been operating the four-day or even three-day week since the mid 1980s. In return for reduced working time, employees agreed to a 9-hour rather than an 8-hour shift and they also agreed to work on Saturdays. Similar agreements were brought about at BMW in Wackersdorf where convertibles are assembled, at Opel (General Motors, Vauxhall) in Rüsselsheim and at the Bosch semi-conductor plant in Reutlingen (Daniels, 1996: 19).

These examples show that the shorter standard working week is feasible. Schemes have passed the experimental stage and turned out to be a valid tool for the safeguarding of jobs. However, unemployment could not be reduced but merely stopped from growing even more vigorously. Still, this is a significant step in coping with mass unemployment; if only, because employers, employees and unions were shown to co-operate in a major success story. Successful co-operation between employers and employees is also the basis for the second possible measure to reduce working time: voluntary 'downshifting'.

Voluntary 'Downshifting'

'Life-style choices' is one of the buzzwords of the 1990s. One of these choices is 'downshifting' or 'voluntary simplicity' which involves the trade-in of income and status for more time and self-control in life. In most cases, the choice is being made because of family responsibilities and earnest attempts at equalising the position of the sexes. Typically, it entails a non-traditional, non-divisional distribution of work in families, with two part-time breadwinners and two part-time carers, aiming to achieve the ideal of an equal, companionate partnership. In addition, this choice is being made by employees who have a major focus in life other than paid work, for example, artists, non-professional athletes etc.

In Britain, 'downshifting' is very much perceived as a middle-class pursuit for the 'fancy that' column of the newspaper or the 'best marketing gimmick since estate agents transformed the humble bedsit into a "studio apartment"' (Franks, 1999: 249, 246). In other words, a variant of the *Good Life*[4] for the 1990s. However, in Continental Europe, particularly in the Netherlands, it is taken more seriously. With 37 per cent of employees working part-time, the Dutch are world leading in redistributing employment across the population. Although no significant amount of new jobs was created in the 1990s, unemployment was reduced from 10 per cent in the 1980s to 5.7 per cent. The prerequisiste for this development was a bill passed in 1996 which gave part-time workers the same rights (*pro rata*) as full-time workers (Heygendorff, 1997: 19). With this important step, the particular insecurities of part-time work, such as no pension rights, no social security rights and no redundancy rights, were abolished. 'Downshifting' was made economically feasible and Dutch employees took the opportunity in great numbers.

But how is it economically feasible for Dutch employers? Judging by the hostile debate about the minimum wage introduced in Britain in 1999, employers cannot be expected to greet additional rights for employees with eagerness. However, studies and surveys support the claim that part-timers are a major asset for employers. Five important advantages for employers can be extracted from studies of part-time work.

- Part-timers and job-sharers have been shown to work more efficiently and productively than their full-time counterparts mainly due to reduced fatigue (McRae, 1989: 30 / Rifkin, 1995: 225).
- Absenteeism can be reduced significantly when employees who want to work part-time have their preferences effectuated (McRae, 1989: 30).
- Employees who work fewer hours are more likely to agree to shift patterns that ensure continuous production, i.e. 24-hour machine running times which are profitable for the company. The above mentioned production of semi-conductors by Bosch, for example, is based on a complicated system of six shifts over seven days, 24 hours a day.
- Employees who work less than the standard working week can sustain a much higher level of tedious work with good humour and cheerfulness in comparison to their full-time colleagues (Handy, 1985: 156).
- Part-timers have, according to studies, more energy and enthusiasm for their work (ibid.).

Given the above advantages for employers, the life-style choice 'downshifting' is a genuine possibility to reduce unemployment once two conditions are fulfilled. Employees must be prepared to accept lower income in return for more time, a choice which has, in the past, only been made by mothers. In addition, the appropriate legal framework has to be in place which ensures that part-timers have the same rights and obligations (*pro rata*) as full-timers. So far, only the Dutch have taken this step.

Phasing In and Out of Work

The last idea to be introduced in this section is the phasing in and out of work, particularly the phasing out before retirement. Mary Midgley and Judith Hughes (1983: 184) believe that the 'today you work, tomorrow you don't' mentality has serious disadvantages. They argue that employees who approach retirement would very often appreciate a gradual reduction of working time (even with the equivalent reduction of income) if their pension rights were not harmed. At the same time, newcomers would frequently welcome a gradual introduction into employment. This approach would facilitate a smooth handover of responsibilities between leaving and starting employees with the older employee acting as a mentor and the younger one acquiring knowledge in a personal way.

Bernhard Borgeest and Udo Perina (1994: 36 – my translation) agree. They believe that the chronological succession of 'swotting, labouring and feeling bored' is out-of-date in today's ageing societies. Why not start a new part-time career at fifty, still work infrequent hours at 78 and take time-out when the children are small or to build a house? In their opinion, it is absurd, that people in the middle of life never seem to have enough time whilst they are utterly bored in later life. In so far, Borgeest and Perina not only propose phasing out for older employees but also sabbaticals or part-time work for younger workers; in other words 'downshifting'.

The reduction of working hours in line with either of the above measures is regarded as a sensible and reliable measure to tackle unemployment in Western welfare states. On the one hand, it does acknowledge the growing wish of employees in Western countries to work a shorter standard week or to work part-time. On the other hand, employers can expect a more energetic, more efficient and more reliable workforce. Experiments, such as the one successfully conducted at Volkswagen, showed that significantly lower working-hours plus reduced pay were acceptable to all sides. However, success depends on negotiated frameworks. Both the Dutch 'part-time bill' and the VW agreement had to be in place before working hours could be reduced significantly. Under current legislation in Britain and Germany, for example, individual reductions in working time (e.g. voluntary 'down-shifting' for carers) are made at individual expense (reduced career prospects, problems with social security). That the reduced working time scenario confers benefits to society, in particular a reduction in unemployment, is not taken into account. One measure that could facilitate the rapid increase of voluntary 'downshifting', phasing in and out of work and a shortened standard working week would be the introduction of basic income.

Basic Income

The concept of 'basic income' entered political debates in the West under various names: state bonus, social credit, social wage, social dividend, guaranteed income, citizen's wage, citizenship income, existence income or universal grant (Parijs, 1992: 3). All terms refer to one idea: a scheme that would pay every citizen a tax-free minimum income irrespective of work commitment[5] or other available income. With its introduction, many state benefits would become obsolete, amongst others: pensions, unemployment assistance and income support. Although the idea can be traced back to the Levellers' movement of the 17th century, it only became known to a wider readership in the 19th century when social reformers such as Charles Fourier (1772-1837) developed their theories of utopian socialism. Fourier argued that modern societies violate people's natural rights to fish, hunt, forage etc. and that the state should therefore pay citizens compensation (ibid. 9f).

At the end of the 20th century, basic income has lost almost all bonds with utopian socialism and instead obtained a modest place in the political mainstream. According to Samuel Brittan (1998), all major political parties in Ireland 'are prepared to look at it seriously'. According to Philippe van Parijs (1992: 6) it has advanced from an '*idée fixe* of a handful of cranks' into an 'essential ingredient in any serious discussion of the future of advanced capitalist countries'. In order to evaluate this proposal and its implications for unemployment levels, it is necessary to look at advantages and disadvantages separately.

The Pros of Basic Income

The introduction of basic income schemes is often proposed because of their potential to reduce unemployment (Rifkin, 1995; 262; Standing, 1992: 58; Robertson, 1989: 114). But how can a citizen wage reduce unemployment, unless 'many people would relax into irresponsible idleness' (Robertson, 1989: 115)?

In a first step, the status 'unemployed' would be abolished, since almost all Western governments calculate unemployment rates as the percentage of citizens claiming benefits. But this is just a statistical effect which would not lessen the supply-side pressure on the labour market, i.e. it would not reduce the number of citizens unable to find paid employment. There are, however, developments likely to happen under a basic income scheme, which would change labour supply, namely the full or part withdrawal of individual groups from the formal economy and the entrance of others. First, let us look at those groups that presumably want to reduce their participation in the formal economy, i.e. that might consider 'downshifting' given the right circumstances.

- Citizens with an occupation who are only in paid employment to ensure a minimum income. The most obvious group to illustrate this point are students, but there are others: painters, writers and other artists who cannot live from their commissions or contracts and hence undertake additional *paid* work; sportspeople or musicians on the verge of becoming professionals; citizens who would like to become self-employed but cannot yet afford to, possibly inventors, craftspeople, fashion designers etc. These groups are characterised by the fact that they have a serious occupation which, however, does not provide a livelihood. Asked what they do, they might well say: 'I am a guitarist', and not 'I stock shelves at Kwiksave', although the latter might describe what they do 'for a living'.

- A second group of citizens that might retreat in parts from the formal economy is the so-called 'sandwich generation' (O'Hara, 1993: 95); the generation of people between 25 and 50 who carry a triple burden in modern Western societies. They bear almost the complete employment load and at the same time raise children and possibly care for ageing parents. It is likely that some members of this group would opt for a reduction in working time, for example, to spend more time with their children.

- In addition, a general increase of part-time work might be expected if basic income was granted to individual citizens. Surveys undertaken in 1994 found that employees in the European Union wished to work slightly fewer hours than they did, with the Dutch and the English opting for the lowest working week (29 hours and 32 hours) and the Spanish and Portuguese wanting to work longest (both 35 hours per week) (Willke, 1998: 110).

- Last and numerically minute (given the findings from this book), some citizens might welcome the introduction of basic income as a convenient way to finance a life of idleness.

Accordingly, the introduction of basic income should remove strain from the formal economy by reducing the available labour force. However, there are other groups that might re-enter the formal economy if a basic income scheme was introduced.

- Retirement is increasingly seen as enforced idleness or 'social banishment' (Shankland, 1980: 48) rather than a well-earned rest. In most European countries, early retirement programs have 'cleared' the workforce of employees over the age of 60. In France, only 13 per cent of men aged between 60 to 65 are still in employment. The figures for other countries are similarly low: Belgium 18 per cent, Austria 19 per cent, the Netherlands 22 per cent, Germany 28 per cent, Italy 30 per cent and only Great Britain, Portugal and Sweden show figures of just over 50 per cent (Globus, 1996a: 19). Once an early retirement package has been accepted, particularly if state funds were involved, the return to the formal economy is blocked. The introduction of basic income could change this because work and welfare would become untangled. The status 'pensioner', i.e. not working but receiving a state or private pension for subsistence, would be abolished and with it many restrictions of becoming involved in the formal economy.[6] The previously examined 'phasing in and out of work' would also become more attractive. It can therefore be expected that some pensioners, particularly those who retired very early, might re-enter the job market and that some employees might opt for phasing out of work rather than early retirement.

- Other groups that are driven into non-work by state regulations might also re-enter the job market. British research, for example, showed that most women of unemployed men will cease to work once their partners cannot claim national insurance pay anymore (Franks, 1999: 83f). According to Frank Field (1996: 16) 'means tests operate like a vice locking both partners into long-term unemployment'. Similarly, the so-called poverty trap can enforce idleness. If means-tested benefit payments exceed potential income from work, claimants might not be able to afford going to work. Since basic income schemes are designed to replace all means-tested benefits, the poverty trap would be abolished and former recipients can - at least in theory - return to the formal economy.

It is difficult to predict exact numbers for each group and quantify the correct impact basic income policies might have on unemployment levels, particularly since it will vary significantly between individual Western countries.[7] However, it is reasonable to anticipate that the numbers of citizens who might reduce their participation in the formal economy will outnumber pensioners who might re-enter. This leaves a vacuum to be filled by citizens who are involuntarily unemployed, be it because they are trapped in the welfare system or because labour supply is higher than labour demand. It can therefore be assumed that basic income schemes will reduce the number of citizens unable to find paid employment. Although this is the most important result, there are more reasons to support basic income schemes.

A major concern of welfare theorists has always been the inability of services to reach everybody in need. The picture of an old lady in bed with her assortment of hot water bottles, unable to pay her heating bill, springs to mind. According to British research, 1.2 million UK citizens, mostly pensioners, are entitled to income support but fail to claim it (Baird, 1998: 16). The introduction of basic income would provide all those with non-stigmatised income who are too frightened or too ashamed to claim means-tested benefits. This is seen as a major advantage of basic income schemes. Citizens for whom welfare services were created would finally receive what is rightly theirs. However, this point is controversial. The Institute of Directors, for example, argue that although some theorists present

> low take-up rates [as] a weakness of the present system, we think them a strength. First, a low take-up saves large amounts of Government spending. Second, it is in substantial measure the result of self-selection amongst potential users of the welfare system ... some people are reluctant to accept such payments ... for reasons of self-respect. We see nothing wrong in this sentiment and many would consider it admirable (Cook, 1989: 123).

This statement can only be described as contemptuous of government decisions. If a democratically elected parliament establishes a minimum threshold under which no citizen should fall, the implementation of this regulation should be carried out as comprehensively as possible. Otherwise one would have to determine which parliament decision should be executed with vigour and which should not. Should rapists, for example, be pursued? In the above frame of mind, one could argue that a self-respecting victim might prefer silence to the stigma of a police investigation and that tax payers could look forward to reduced government spending. If - as the IoD assert - no self-respecting citizen can accept benefits without loss of dignity, there is an urgent need for improvement and basic income schemes might be the solution. In a lawful society, it is not justifiable to offer welfare services and hope that shame might result in low take-up rates, even if some theorists advocate financial benefits of a demeaning welfare system (Gilder, 1982: 120). This point will therefore be included unreservedly in the list of positive outcomes of unconditional basic income provision.

Feminists and other theorists who focus on equality of opportunity and fairness in society have contributed a further argument in favour of basic income. As early as 1953, J. Rhys-Williams (1989: 117) promoted a so-called social dividend scheme to help women

> who are still living as slaves in the midst of our free society - the wives of mean or broken men who give them no money to spend at their own discretion and little enough upon which to provide food and clothing for the family, but from whose tyranny they cannot escape without abandoning their children.

Contemporary thinkers agree and argue that it permits 'greater sexual equality' (Standing, 1992: 59) and a fairer deal for carers (Robertson, 1989: 114). Standing and Robertson start from the same position, namely that women's unpaid domestic work is performed with high opportunity costs, i.e. at the expense of a career and own income. However, they proceed to different conclusions. Standing believes that basic income will enable men to accept part-time positions and subsequently take over more responsibilities in the domestic sphere ('downshifting'). Robertson, on the other hand, does not expect a new distribution of domestic labour but argues that the unpaid work of carers and voluntary workers will finally be financially rewarded. Basic income schemes have the potential to challenge the gender divide by making part-time work more acceptable for both sexes and by providing an income to those who stay at home caring for children or elderly relatives.

Another argument in favour of basic income schemes rests on deliberations about fairness. Well-paid professionals might wonder: 'Why am I earning thousands of pounds per month, whilst an assembly-line worker who sorts my litter into recyclable and non-recyclable refuse (German system) in a loud and smelly environment only receives the minimum wage?' Should financial incentives not rise with mental and physical unpleasantness? A basic income would reduce the dependency of poorer workers on menial work and thereby drive up wages to compensate for a retreating work force. As James Robertson (1989: 115) puts it: 'It might then be possible to reverse the present paradoxical situation in which well-off people get highly paid for doing pleasant, interesting work and badly-off people get poorly paid for doing disagreeable but essential work'. This argument is mainly based on a sense of fairness: if, in a community of equals, a minority of citizens is burdened with the most unpleasant chores, they should be compensated.[8]

Apart from the fairness argument, there are other potential benefits, of which Claus Offe offers two. He believes that the stigma of deficiency and failure which is attached to unemployment and low-grade jobs will be removed by a basic income scheme and that consequently the 'symptoms and social pathologies of marginalization would ... disappear' (Offe, 1992: 76). Unfortunately, Offe does not give any details on the social pathologies that will vanish but other authors have linked the stigma of failure and unemployment with a rise in violent crime (Rifkin, 1995: 208), poor mental health (Pascall, 1986: 57), and declining physical health (Grint, 1991: 41). The second benefit Offe sees is again connected with expected wage rises for unpleasant jobs. He argues that this development will provide an incentive for employers to eliminate such tasks by investigating technical and organisational solutions (Offe, 1992: 76).

Finally, one could argue that the polarisation of society into professionals and their servants might be reversed if higher wages compensated for unpleasant work. Under a basic income scheme, it is unlikely that personnel service jobs such as cleaning private houses would be in high demand unless working conditions, particularly pay, would improve significantly. It is therefore conceivable that what has been called the 'service proletariat' (Deppe, 1996: 14 - my translation) would vanish.[9] This argument will be revisited in the following section on objections against basic income schemes, where potential wage rises are seen as a negative development.

The Cons of Basic Income

Two major objections dominate the basic income debate against which all other criticism fades into insignificance: the question of money and the question of morals. First, critics assume that basic income schemes must be enormously expensive and therefore unaffordable under present economic conditions. Second, they believe that basic income is just an outlandish formula to increase the number of already existing free-riders and lazy scroungers. Let us begin with the first objection.

Based on straightforward reasoning, it seems evident that paying a basic sum to all citizens must be more expensive than focusing resources on those in need. Under these premises, it could be expected that tax levels must rise significantly in order to accommodate additional spending. However, this simple inference ignores one problem of current welfare provision: the enormous bureaucracy required to sustain a system of means-testing. To find out what the financial implications of basic income schemes really are, the German Ministry of Finance commissioned a study on the topic. In 1996, the DIW (German Institute for Economic Research) published its findings in Volker Meinhardt *et al.* (1996): *Fiskalische Auswirkungen der Einführung eines Bürgergeldes* (Fiscal Implications of Basic Income Schemes).

The authors examined two forms of basic income schemes, a moderate negative income tax version and a more ambitious social dividend version. The main difference between the two schemes is the timing of tax assessments. Under negative income tax conditions, the assessment is *ex ante*, i.e. before transfer. If somebody's income reaches the defined threshold without a transfer, he or she will not receive any payments. In this respect, negative income tax is not an unconditional arrangement but has an element of means-testing. However, it differs significantly from current practices because it only requires extended inland revenue services to administer the scheme. Recipients would not be categorised as pensioners, unemployed, incapacitated, single parents etc. and their reasons for not being able or not willing to earn a living would not be investigated. If a personal tax account did not show sufficient income, payments would be made unconditionally. The tax assessment in the more ambitious social dividend scheme is *ex post*, i.e. every citizen would receive a transfer payment first which would then be subject to taxation together with other incomes.[10]

The results of the DIW study were as follows: given certain technical parameters which will not be repeated here, the negative income tax scheme could be introduced without tax rises. It was calculated that an additional 44.3 billion DM would be needed to finance the scheme and to compensate for a reduced tax base. In the areas of income support, housing benefit and student grants, savings of 30 billion DM could be expected and 14 to 18 billion DM could be released from unemployment assistance (sums include savings in administrative costs). This means that the scheme would be revenue neutral. The more expensive social dividend scheme could also be introduced without tax rises, according to the DIW, but only if all tax relief on income from work and pension investments would be abolished. The overall conclusion of the study is that basic income schemes are a realistic fiscal option (Opielka, 1997: 25).

If one accepts that basic income provision is feasible in fiscal terms, the question remains whether its introduction is desirable. Critics argue that it would encourage idleness and that 'a great many people - even some with relatively pleasant jobs - might simply cease to work if they could receive non-stigmatized government money to live on' (Govier, 1992: 379). This contention is almost identical to the work incentives argument that was examined throughout this book. Without repeating our findings, it can be said that charges of idleness could not be substantiated for the work incentives debate. Hence, it could be claimed that idleness would not pose a major threat to the introduction of basic income schemes. There are, however, two connected areas which would have to be investigated in more detail, a potential paradigm shift in the evaluation of work and disagreements about the meaning of 'idleness'.

If employment ceased to be the major source of income for many citizens, a value shift might occur. Currently, employment provides everything 'that is important in life: freedom, independence, security, recognition, [and] self-respect' (Offe, 1994: 28 - my translation). This might not be the case after the introduction of basic income, when a certain degree of freedom, independence and security would become available without work. Shifts in emphasis on what is important in life cannot easily be predicted. For Plato it was a sign of superiority *not* to work for a living; in our current societies it is mostly regarded as a sign of inferiority. It is impossible to foresee the long-term future but it is conceivable that the introduction of basic income would initiate a major paradigm shift and that the current importance of work would decline. For those who strongly believe in the work ethic, the condemnation of basic income schemes is therefore paramount. However, not everybody would agree. This leads us to the second point, the definition and evaluation of 'idleness'.

Aside from work ethic proponents, two further groups have an interest in the current discussion. Those who do not regard the state of idleness as objectionable and those who disapprove of idleness but define a very small range of activities as idle. The philosopher Bertrand Russell belongs to the first group as his essay 'In Praise of Idleness' (written in 1932) clearly shows. Although he was brought up on the saying 'Satan finds some mischief still for idle hands to do', he believes that 'far too much work [is] done in the world [and] that immense harm is caused by the belief that work is virtuous' (Russell, 1958: 9). He claims that the root of civilisation is leisure and that only meddlesome busybodies promote the work ethic (ibid. 15, 17). In his opinion, four hours of work a day should suffice and people should be able to spend the rest of their time as they wished (ibid. 25). The result will be happiness and joy rather than 'frayed nerves, weariness and dyspepsia' (ibid. 28). Transferred from the 1930s to the 1990s, it can be assumed that Russell would be an emphatic champion of basic income schemes and the accompanying freedoms.

The middle ground between proponents of the work ethic and defenders of idleness is taken by those who argue that any socially useful activity should entitle citizens to the basic comforts of life. Two approaches are possible. On the one hand there are thinkers like André Gorz who principally share the uneasiness of work ethic hard-liners that basic income would make people stay at home and watch TV (Gorz and Kempe, 1994: 599f). He embraces the 'necessary evil' position of work and argues that only conditional basic income schemes which demand work for payments will be successful. On the other hand, it is argued that most citizens already engage in socially useful labour without being paid for it. According to this opinion, a basic income scheme will not increase the number of feckless idlers but rather reward selfless carers and others for their contributions to society (Robertson, 1989: 114). As Robert Goodin (1992: 207) puts it: 'The "undeserving" might look a lot more deserving if we took into account alternative forms of socially useful activity'.

The linchpin of this discussion is the definition and evaluation of idleness. Hard-liners will maintain that anybody who fails to earn a living without good reason is idle. This group would principally object to basic income schemes. Supporters of conditional schemes hold that idleness is characterised by the lack of social usefulness and that it would occur on a grand scale under an unconditional scheme. The third group agrees with the definition of idleness as non-usefulness but supports an unconditional scheme on the grounds that the majority of citizens are already involved in valuable labour of some kind but are not compensated for it. Finally, the fourth group maintains that an accurate definition of idleness is superfluous since work is not superior to idleness. Consequently, they would not object to basic income schemes on the grounds of idleness. Which group will win the battle of public opinion will decide about the future acceptability of basic income schemes.

Before this section will be closed, one last argument against basic income schemes will be introduced. Earlier it was argued that physically and mentally demanding work is not always compensated for by adequate pay. The example of an assembly-line worker who sorts waste for recycling was given. Other examples would be cleaning public lavatories or maintaining huge underground sewage tunnels. If financial pressures would abate under a basic income scheme, 'Who would do the nasty and boring jobs then? Many of them are not eliminable and they have to be done somehow, by someone' (Govier, 1992: 379). Above, it was spelled out that salaries would have to rise significantly to counterbalance the unpleasantness of certain jobs. This was seen as an advantage of basic income schemes because it aligns with a sense of fairness. *Laisser-faire* market economists, however, do not accept these and similar reasonings about fairness. They argue that the market will provide the best solution to any distribution problem including the distribution of toil. Interference on the grounds of social justice or social fairness 'risks damaging the working of the whole' and should therefore be avoided (Hayek, 1988: 84). The 'invisible hand' of the *laisser-faire* market economy is the only reliable means to bring about welfare for citizens. The introduction of basic income would be a major manipulation of free market proceedings and as a result the labour market might not settle at equilibrium. In this particular case, employers might not find employees at rates they can afford. Nobody would do nasty jobs and the public would be stuck with uncleaned toilets, sewage leaks and similar predicaments.

Two points can be made to answer this argument. First, even if one accepted that *laisser-faire* markets worked more efficiently than social market economies, fairness might be valued higher than efficiency. Second, high wages for unpleasant labour might be considered a price worth paying to achieve the above listed positive outcomes of basic income schemes, particularly a reduction of mass unemployment.

To summarise, the pros and cons of basic income schemes will now be listed in a table.

Table 8.3   Pros and cons of basic income schemes

Pros
>   Lower unemployment
>   Improved targeting efficiency of welfare services
>   Greater sexual equality
>   Greater fairness and less polarisation

Cons
>   Perceived high costs and high taxation
>   Moral hazard and the encouragement of idleness
>   Distortion of *laisser-faire* market procedures

The idea behind basic income schemes is straightforward and simple and its advantages are manifold, including the reduction of unemployment. However, challenges are grave and difficult to overcome, particularly the notion that the lazy will exploit the hard-working. Although the concept has entered academic circles on a grand scale and the political arena on a smaller scale, its introduction in any European country seems unlikely in the next decade. One major step towards its acceptance has not been taken, namely to understand that the 'lazy scrounger' does not pose a significant threat to Western welfare states. If it is assumed that malingering fraudsters pervade even the current system which relies heavily on stigmatised and inconvenient means-testing, a more permissive system has no chance of acceptance. This book has taken a first step towards reversing this misapprehension but more work is needed before basic income schemes might become acceptable.

This chapter summarised three visionary proposals to reduce unemployment: ecological taxation, measures to reduce working time per head and basic income. It was shown that all suggestions are feasible. Studies showed that ecological taxation and basic income schemes are financially viable, and a look at the Dutch labour market and the working patterns at Volkswagen revealed that employment distribution can be optimised. However, apart from isolated successes such as the VW scheme or the described Dutch achievements, very few developments can be reported from the European political scene. The idea of ecological taxation evolved in the early 1980s and found its way into European politics with extraordinary speed. Speed of reception could, however, not be matched with speed of implementation.

Despite widespread national support, EU member countries failed to agree on joint policies. The idea reached its peak in 1992 shortly before the Earth Summit in Rio. Seven years after the summit, only Denmark[11] has an ecological tax reform that deserves the name. Simultaneously, the optimisation of employment distribution has begun on a small scale. Shorter working weeks for reduced pay could, however, be negotiated in more corporations to safeguard jobs or even create new employment opportunities. Voluntary downshifting might become more acceptable as more citizens are attracted to it or as more countries follow the Dutch example and remove discrimination against part-time work. The idea of basic income, on the other hand, has only just started to enter the political mainstream. Widespread public acknowledgement and genuine political debate are required before any assessments can be made as to its potential acceptance and success. The major difficulty will be to counter the 'idleness' argument. None of the above are instant, easy, success-guaranteed solutions to unemployment, but they are certainly preferable to the 'pathological' theory which offers no action apart from scapegoating.

Notes

[1]   June 1999.

[2]   There are numerous suggestions where the new incoming tax money should go to. The mathematician and economist Franz Josef Radermacher (1995: 62), for example, wants to finance pension systems in the so-called 'underdeveloped' world to tackle the problem of overpopulation. Pensions should replace the present system of having huge families to guarantee survival in old age. We will deal with the mainstream idea of imposing a tax on energy and reducing employment costs.

[3]   The DIW is one of the five major think-tanks (*Die Fünf Weisen*) that are consulted twice yearly by the German government on current economic questions.

[4]   A 1970s' British sitcom with a 'green' couple attempting to achieve self-sufficiency within middle-class suburbia.

[5]   André Gorz (1994: 600) and others reject the unconditionality of most basic income proposals and suggest schemes which would require recipients to perform a limited amount of socially useful work.

[6]   Restrictions of certain professions with definite dates of retirement would be unaffected. It, for example, makes sense to restrict the working lives of fire-fighters.

[7]   In Germany, for example, hardly anybody is locked into a poverty trap because of a combination of high minimum wages within a high-wage society. Only families without earnings and three children between the age of fourteen and seventeen could obtain more income from social services than in the labour market in 1994

(Brower-Rabinowitsch, 1994: 19).

[8]   For an in-depth discussion on unpleasant work and fairness, see Walzer, Michael (1985) 'Hard Work' in: *Spheres of Justice - A Defence of Pluralism and Equality*, Basil Blackwell, Oxford, pp.165-183.

[9]   A vanishing 'service proletariat' would, however, put new pressure on the labour market.

[10]   Both schemes do not meet our narrow definition of basic income as tax-free. However, the social dividend scheme comes very close to the definition and the negative income tax scheme could be used in a transitional stage.

[11]   The Danish government introduced a tax reform in October 1994 that changed the structure of the tax system profoundly. Tax is now due on CO_2-emissions, fertilisers, pesticides, packing material and industrially-used poisons. In return, income taxes were reduced.

9 Résumé

After the collapse of communism, the Western welfare state came under sustained attack. It was represented as a reformist version of its Eastern cousin and accused of suffering from guilt by association. Political analysts demanded that social democrats stopped clinging to the welfare state as a disguised version of the failed Soviet experiment. One of the favoured explanations for Soviet failure was the system's inability to provide work incentives. It was argued that human beings have a natural desire for repose and an aversion to work. This disposition was suppressed during most of human history when work was accepted as an unpleasant but unavoidable evil; a necessity to ensure survival. The emergence of communism and the Western welfare state, however, untangled the age-old relationship between work and subsistence making it possible for an ever increasing number of 'lazy scroungers' to live off other people's efforts. This book set out to refute or validate the claim that Western-style welfare provision seriously undermines work incentives.

The historical section examined human attitudes towards work in the past to see whether an anthropological constant could be revealed. If an unchanging aversion to work was dominant throughout history, the work incentives argument would gain in strength considerably. However, no human universal could be identified. Two polarised understandings of work and its significance for human beings were revealed; the 'necessary evil' position and what we called the *'Homo Faber'* position. Whilst no conclusive statement could be made about humans in the Stone Age, it was seen that important thinkers from Ancient Greece (Plato, Aristotle) and the Middle Ages (Aquinas) as well as utopian writers (More, Campanella) and utilitarians (Bentham, James Mill) supported the 'necessary evil' view. They argued that work to sustain life was an unavoidable curse whilst paradise was characterised as a place of eternal leisure. Attitudes, however, changed at the onset of the Modern Age. The Protestant movement endowed work with religious significance and branded able-bodied non-workers as sinners. Martin Luther characterised work as an ennobling, moral and religious duty. The glorification of work went even further following Thomas Carlyle who claimed that any type of work, however unpleasant, blesses the worker with eternal nobility. Ambiguous positions in the debate were expressed by Marx and Hannah Arendt both of whom distinguish between two contrasting understandings of work. For Marx, labour to sustain life under capitalism is an alienated, compulsory activity which is avoided like the plague. On the other hand, humans can realise their true potentials through productive activity, i.e. uncoerced, self-determined work. Similarly, Arendt differentiates between labour and work. The first summarises activities to sustain life, the second implies the production of durable goods by transforming natural processes and materials. However, according to Arendt human happiness requires both labour and work. Hence, she does not see labour as evil. It was concluded that no anthropological constant can be found in human attitudes towards work. Neither the 'necessary evil' position nor the '*Homo Faber*' view was dominant throughout history. Accordingly, the work incentives argument cannot be based on the claim that humans have continually rejected work in the past.

The conceptual section of this book clarified the terms 'action', 'intention' and 'incentives' and arrived at the following definition: incentives are the only external stimulant to trigger consciously and willingly performed acts of human agents with preconceived plans directed at specific goals. It was seen that two different positions can be distinguished in the work incentives debate. Those who support the 'necessary evil' view on work allege that only pecuniary incentives will motivate people to work. This view was called the 'narrow view' on work incentives. By consulting research from psychology, it was contrasted with the 'broad view'. The field of occupational psychology identifies a number of non-pecuniary incentives that were categorised into three groups: extrinsic incentives, intrinsic incentives and general characteristics of work. Whilst extrinsic motivators such as prestige, respect, power (and income) only apply to a restricted number of highly regarded professions, intrinsic incentives such as identity, self-respect, pride of accomplishment and happiness are applicable to a wider range of jobs. Research showed that happiness, for example, is created by euphoric streams of productive activity whether undertaken by an obsessed scientist or a focused welder is irrelevant. Studies on the psychological effects of unemployment supported claims that although monotonous labouring does not offer the above extrinsic or intrinsic rewards, it is still preferable to nonwork because it facilitates social contact, gives purpose and provides time-structure (general characteristics of work). Medical studies revealed that long-term unemployed can show 'signs of dying' or symptoms normally correlated with the loss of a friend or a relative (ill health, chronic lethargy and despair). It was therefore concluded that the narrow view on work incentives is too restrictive and does not explain comprehensively why humans work (1990s, West). Non-pecuniary work incentives were shown to be numerous and significant and they cannot easily be compensated for by welfare payments. It was concluded that the work incentives argument is based on too limited a concept of what motivates humans to work.

The foundation of the 'necessary evil' position on work and the 'narrow view' on work incentives is the depiction of humans as isolated, autonomous, self-interested beings without social ties who use rationality to achieve personal utility maximisation, namely: *Homo economicus*. Although the claim that human beings have an innate aversion to work does not belong to the canonical assumptions of mainstream economics (the creators of *Homo economicus*), it is an important secondary feature. Analysts of mainstream labour supply theory claim that rational individuals will choose leisure over work unless the loss of spare time is being compensated for by an increase in income. The three core characteristics of *Homo economicus*, individuality, self-interest and rationality, were examined to see whether the foundational pillars of the work incentives argument could be corroborated. It was argued that in contrast to the alleged atomistic individualism, sociability is a very old innate drive in human beings. Of the two major groups of hominids which are distinguished by anthropologists, the individualist species (*Australopithecus*) is now extinct, whilst the socially inclined species (*Homo*) has survived. In addition, it was shown that altruism is a widespread phenomenon in human and animal communities which could not be explained if self-interest was as dominant a characteristic as the depiction of *Homo economicus* suggests. According to research from sociobiology, sociability and altruism are part of the biological heritage of the human species.

Feminists also claim that *Homo economicus* does not give an adequate account of humankind, rather it expresses the androcentric biases of a small group of white, privileged, educated males who completely disregard the fact that autonomy is only a transient and ephemeral period between childhood and senility. Only because of traditionally self-sacrificing women can most men feel autonomous and atomistic in certain stages of their lives. Feminists also argue that self-interest is no dominant feature in humankind. As sociobiologists, they point to the widespread phenomenon of altruism and ask mainstream economists how they can explain it. 'Named benevolence' or 'family greed' was the answer they were given, i.e. altruism occurs within the family but not in the market place. In answer to this assertion, Paula England convincingly argued that an emotionally connective self which is necessary to act altruistically within the family cannot suddenly march into the market as a selfish maximiser, unable to empathise with others. Human beings cannot be described as predominantly selfish and individualist. The only potential explanation for widespread altruism and sociability which could be brought forward in defence of *Homo economicus* would rely on a fundamental difference between the sexes; presupposing egoistic, individualist males and altruistic, connected females; an approach taken by so-called 'backlash' strategists trying to preserve the traditional family model. However, psychological studies revealed that women's nature is not other-oriented and that women and men want the same things in life. It was, for example, demonstrated that employment showed the strongest and most consistent connection to female good health when compared with marriage and children. Hence, research from sociobiology and feminist studies contradicts the claim that human beings are predominantly self-interested and individualist.

The third core feature of *Homo economicus* is rationality, the faculty to reflect, understand, come to decisions and act meaningfully in given situations. It was seen that rationality is indeed a major characteristic of human beings. However, it was argued that it is only a tool and that no predictions about human behaviour can be made unless human goals are known. Mainstream economists predict that human rationality is used to further self-interested behaviour. In contrast, Plato argued that rationality is applied to problems of the common good. For the former, insurance fraud can be rational, for the latter it would be despicable and certainly not the product of rational ponderings. It was therefore concluded that although rationality is an important human feature, it is its application not its existence which is crucial to human nature studies. Hence, the mere knowledge that humans are rational does not allow for statements such as the ones made by labour supply theorists (rational individuals are expected to prefer leisure to work unless compensated for by additional income). Simplified statements such as these include a judgement, namely that the 'necessary evil' view on work and the 'narrow view' on work incentives are true. Based on this judgement, it is argued that the tool of rationality is directed towards work-avoidance. However, if - as Plato claims - rationality is used to further the common good or if the 'broad view' on work incentives is more tenable as was suggested, the same faculty could be applied to the opposite effect. The knowledge that human beings are rational does therefore not make any contribution to the study of human behaviour; as a tool it can support a wide range of contradicting human ends. Overall it was concluded that *Homo economicus* does not represent a fair depiction of human nature and that proponents of the work incentives argument cannot base their reasonings on this picture of humankind.

One major factor which fuelled the work incentives debate in the 1990s was the resurgence of mass unemployment in Continental Europe. To see how exactly this impacted on the debate, alleged causes of unemployment were classified into two categories: 'pathological' and 'external barrier' explanations. The 'pathological' theory of unemployment explains the phenomenon as individual failure or the consequence of antisocial behaviour. Hence, alleged work-shyness coupled with benefit fraud and demand inflation amongst the low-skilled and their alleged refusal to accept low-paid jobs, were classified in this category. The 'pathological' theory of unemployment was then examined from different angles. It was shown that empirical research in Germany and the United States could not reveal widespread benefit fraud. Claims of benefit abuse did not carry far because only a small minority of recipients were actually able to work, according to surveys. Since these findings stand in marked contrast to the strong presence of the work incentives argument in political debates, it was examined whether ideological elements had entered the discussion. This hypothesis was strengthened by the analysis of treasury activities. Studies estimate that tax evasion causes the German treasury ten times as much loss as benefit fraud. Nevertheless treasury resources are predominantly spent to detect or prevent benefit fraud. The same incongruity was shown for Britain, where fraud investigations were also focused on benefit recipients. The former Tory government employed MI5 to target benefit cheats and the current Labour government introduced a website with tips on how to report benefit fraudsters. However, estimates revealed that tax evasion is far more costly than benefit fraud. The reason why resources were not allocated according to the potential amount of recovered revenue is, it was claimed, ideological. Dee Cook showed that tax evaders are regarded as spirited but highly overburdened citizens who merely keep their hard-earned money whilst benefit fraudsters are seen as stealing other people's money; an ideological judgement. Similar evidence of ideological elements was found when analysing the prototypical welfare cheat image. In Germany, widespread criticism of idle scroungers who enjoyed leisurely lives came to an abrupt halt after a new welfare bill was introduced in 1995. The bill recorded that benefits were to be reduced by 25 per cent for those who refused suitable work. Predictions estimated that at least 20 per cent of unemployed could be brought back into work with this measure. However, unemployment figures continued to rise steadily and the idle scrounger rhetoric was given up. Its place was taken by the claim that women and immigrants had inflated labour supply in recent decades. Two conclusions were drawn from this analysis of 'culprits'. First, the 'lazy scrounger' rhetoric was kept up as long as possible even though empirical research could not corroborate widespread benefit fraud. Only when a newly introduced 'malingerer' bill had no effect on unemployment levels, the scrounger rhetoric was finally given up as untenable. Second, the new inflated labour supply explanation was just as ideological. Only if one supports the traditional family model within closed national borders was it possible to argue that women and immigrants caused a non-equilibrium between labour supply and demand. In a non-ideological setting, all individuals of working ability would be taken as a fixed constant and labour market policies designed accordingly. The 'culprits' in the United States were identified as single mothers who were accused of living within a culture of nonwork and nonmarriage which allegedly presents the most serious of domestic problems. It was shown on two accounts that the vilification of single mothers is ideological. First, the Australian government faced with the same problem of spiralling social security bills and high unemployment introduced a parenting allowance in 1994. Mothers or fathers were paid to stay at home and do important caring work for children. Hence, caring for children is seen as *work* within the Australian system and as *nonwork* within the American system. Second, mothers have only in recent times been accused of wrong-doing for not being financially independent.

Only three decades ago, Western women were accused of causing a number of social ills if they went out to work. This perceptional shift regarding the role of women in society must be seen as a significant change in ideology. Overall, it was concluded that the 'pathological' theory of unemployment contains strong ideological elements and could not be corroborated with empirical data.

To present an alternative to the 'pathological' theory, four 'external barrier' explanations for unemployment were analysed, namely lack of economic growth, globalisation, minimum wages and productivity booms. In contrast to 'pathological' explanations, 'external barrier' theories identify events or circumstances beyond the control of individual citizens as causes for unemployment. One of these explanations is 'lack of economic growth'. It is argued that low unemployment can best be achieved with high economic growth rates; a formula successfully applied in the recent past. However, the correlation was decoupled in the 1980s when the percentage of productivity increases surpassed the percentage of GDP growth; a phenomenon called 'jobless growth'. It was calculated that double-figured growth rates would be necessary to solve current unemployment problems in Continental Europe; an undertaking which - even if possible - would raise serious environmental concerns and collide with other constraints on growth (limits to inventions and innovations, post-materialist consumer behaviour). It was concluded that lack of economic growth does not represent a satisfactory alternative to the 'pathological' theory because it does not offer realistic perspectives for change. (It was argued that only explanations which offer viable solutions to unemployment could present an alternative, otherwise 'lack of war' would be a tenable explanation, since unemployment figures usually drop during wars.)

The second 'external barrier' explanation we analysed was globalisation, i.e. the process of removing world-wide trade barriers to allow free flow of capital, labour, information and goods. Since globalisation opens the 'easy exit' option for investors, capital and jobs move to countries which offer the most attractive conditions. Although employment opportunities have been exported from Europe, globalisation on its own cannot be made responsible for unemployment because Britain - one of the countries focused on throughout this book - is a clear globalisation winner together with the United States. It was concluded that unemployment in Continental Europe is indeed caused by globalisation but only in conjunction with the refusal to give up attained standards of life and social cohesion. On its own it cannot be accepted as a viable 'external barrier' explanation, otherwise Britain would have to be affected.

The third explanation we examined was the claim that minimum wages cause unemployment. The argument maintains that interferences with market mechanisms prevent supply and demand from balancing at equilibrium leaving uncleared labour supply at too high prices. Two objections were brought forward against this claim. In the past, the iron law of wages ensured that employers paid sufficient wages to enable employees to sustain life and allow for reproduction. Under conditions of welfare provision, no bottom line for wages exists since starvation or emigration are precluded by state measures. Employers can pay as little as they want since potential shortfalls are being made up from the social security budget. Hence, the first objection holds that minimum wages replace the iron law of wages in welfare states to ensure that employers are not unjustly subsidised by the treasury. The second objection argues that labour markets react differently from commodity markets and that they can never balance at equilibrium. The reasoning behind this claim is that sellers usually refrain from offering their commodities if prices are very low, e.g. houses are withheld from sale when prices seem unreasonable to sellers. As a consequence, fewer houses are on the market and prices rise. Sellers who refrained from selling can now achieve a higher price. Labour markets are a special case because labour cannot normally be withheld from the market. To the contrary, if prices for labour fall, labour supply paradoxically increases because employees work overtime or add a second wage to maintain their standard of living. Hence, it was concluded that the labour market cannot balance at equilibrium because of principal differences with commodity markets rather than minimum wages. Given these two objections, minimum wages cannot be considered as a viable alternative to the 'pathological' theory of unemployment.

Finally it was examined whether productivity booms or technological displacement is the principal reason for Western unemployment. Fifty years ago, Hannah Arendt predicted that the employment society will run out of work and our analysis confirmed her prognosis. Modern technology and organisational advances have achieved a unique reduction in working hours with a simultaneous increase in output. We looked at all three economic sectors and came to the following conclusions. New employment opportunities cannot be expected in the primary sector (mainly agriculture) unless intensive farming is replaced by organic practices on a massive scale. In the secondary sector (mainly manufacturing), productivity booms are most noticeable and employment analysts predict a steady decline of job prospects for the future. The tertiary sector (services) is less homogeneous and predictions can only be made for individual subsectors. Nearly half of all service jobs are financed directly through the treasury (health, education, social work etc.). Since the 1980s and 1990s could be called the era of 'small' rather than 'big' government it was claimed that increasing employment opportunities in this subsector are unlikely. In financial intermediation (mostly banking) and trade, analysts predict a fall of staff levels due to technological advances similar to the ones experienced in manufacturing (Internet banking, direct marketing, computers with voice-recognition etc.). The subsector which could potentially absorb growing numbers of jobless are personnel services (mostly contract domestic work); an assumption expressed in a European White Paper on employment. Although we share this assumption, it was argued that the moral implications of this scenario would be undesirable. Personnel service sector work can only flourish in societies with high wage inequality since employers must earn enough for themselves and their staff. This situation leads to what André Gorz calls the 'South-Africanisation' of society. It was concluded that productivity booms impact on most economic sectors with the exception of the personnel service industry whose enlargement is, however, not deemed desirable. The approach of the near workerless society through technological displacement is therefore regarded as the most convincing of all unemployment explanations and a persuasive alternative to the 'pathological' theory.

As this book showed, unemployment cannot be dismissed as the outcome of individual pathologies. We therefore looked at three visionary but realistic proposals to reverse the reduction of employment opportunities: ecological taxation, measures to ensure a more Pareto optimal distribution of employment and basic income. Ecological taxation has the potential to achieve a 'win-win' situation. By imposing a tax on polluters whilst relieving the tax burden on employment, it is assumed that environmental damage and unemployment can be reduced simultaneously. External diseconomies would finally be addressed by applying the price mechanism to previously underpriced finite resources such as clean air and clean water. At the same time, the price of abundantly available labour would fall without the drawbacks of a two-tiered servants' society. Salaries would not drop but employers' contributions to social security schemes would. Shortly before the 1992 Earth Summit in Rio, the European Union came very close to reaching a unilateral agreement on ecological taxation. In the end, however, it was decided that individual member countries must legislate on their own. So far, only Denmark has introduced a far-reaching revenue-neutral ecological tax scheme. Realistically, it must be said that the idea of ecological taxation might have passed its zenith without being implemented on a major scale. However, the mastermind behind ecological taxation, Swiss economics professor Hans Christoph Binswanger, believes that new ideas need fifty years to be accepted. Since he only launched his idea in 1983 with the book *Arbeit ohne Umweltzerstörung* (Work without environmental destruction), there are still thirty-four years left.

The second proposal for the reduction of unemployment we introduced was seen as the most realistic one. Empirical data showed that employment is not distributed in a Pareto optimal fashion. A notable and unwanted gulf exists between those who are overworked and those who are underemployed. It would therefore be possible to optimise people's work preferences without any transgressions by a different distribution of employment. Various examples were given on how to achieve such a new distribution, the most significant of which were the Dutch approach to part-time work and the Volkswagen 4-day week. With 37 per cent of employees working part-time, the Dutch are world leading in distributing employment across the population. This was made possible by legislation passed in 1996 which gave full-time and part-time workers the same rights (*pro rata*). Employers benefited from the new deal because part-timers were shown to work more efficiently and more enthusiastically and also to agree more easily to shift patterns that ensure continuous production. In addition, absenteeism could be reduced significantly. The Dutch approach is based on individual part-time preferences with citizens deciding for themselves how much they want to work. In contrast, the Volkswagen scheme was agreed between employers, employees and union representatives and led to a 20 per cent reduction in working time (28.8-hour week) accompanied by a 12 per cent wage cut. The model saved 31,000 jobs. Both approaches tackled unemployment whilst acknowledging the growing wish of employees in Western countries to work slightly less.

The idea of basic income has only just entered the political mainstream.

To provide every citizen with a tax-free income irrespective of work commitment or other available means was previously seen as an *idée fixe* of a group of imbeciles. At the turn of the millennium, however, it has entered political debate on a medium scale. In Ireland, for example, all political parties are prepared to look at it seriously. Its supporters claim that it will reduce unemployment, will finally reach those in genuine need and thereby improve targeting efficiency of welfare services, will achieve greater sexual equality and greater fairness with less polarisation. Its opponents argue that it is hugely expensive, that it fosters moral hazard and malingering and that it distorts *laisser-faire* market procedures. We analysed its potential to reduce unemployment and came to the conclusion that small individual movements within the labour market following the introduction of basic income would indeed provide room for non-working citizens to enter. But it was also acknowledged that challenges to the idea are grave and difficult to overcome, particularly the notion that the lazy will exploit the hard-working. However, a major German study commissioned by the Ministry of Finance established that basic income would be financially feasible, mainly because hugely expensive bureaucratic systems of means-testing could be abolished. The step towards the acceptance of basic income schemes is therefore smaller than expected and rests mainly on the reversal of ideological ideas about malingering. (This book made a first move in the right direction by seriously questioning the validity of the 'lazy scrounger' argument within the context of current welfare provision.) The conclusion reached was that all three above proposals to combat unemployment (ecological taxation, measures to achieve a more equitable distribution of employment and basic income) are reasonable suggestions which are certainly preferable to the 'pathological' approach that does not offer anything apart from scapegoating.

To conclude: The work incentives argument holds a dominant but unjustified position in the welfare state debate. In addition, it obscures the realisation that technological displacement is the most worrying and weighty of all unemployment causes. This means that three scenarios for the employment society are conceivable. First, the 'pathological' theory of unemployment remains in place. Ever growing numbers of unemployed will be accused of malingering whilst welfare provision will decrease to compensate for growing financial pressure. Alternatively, within this scenario, scapegoats such as immigrants might be held responsible for the shortage of jobs. Societies will be split into two groups: those with and those without work. This scenario is most likely in comprehensive Continental European welfare states. Second, the personnel service sector absorbs high numbers of unemployed, thereby reintroducing the Victorian servant system. A different type of two-tiered society ensues distinguishing between those within permanent, highly paid work and their menials. This scenario is most likely in the United States and Britain. Both scenarios partially describe the status-quo which could, however, worsen. Jeremy Rifkin (1995: 293) speaks of a 'death sentence for civilization' in this context because he foresees that worldwide unemployment and increasing polarisation will lead to 'social upheaval ... on a scale never before experienced in the modern age' (ibid. 290).[1] In contrast to the first two scenarios, the third requires a major rethink of current positions on unemployment. Only if the 'pathological' theory is given up and only if the extent of technological displacement is acknowledged can an alternative path open and possibly one of the three described solutions to unemployment be implemented.

Note

[1]   Rifkin's prediction applies to the 'servant' scenario. The equivalent prediction for the Continental European scenario would, in my opinion, be racism on a massive scale, as is already foreshadowed by the rise of the extreme Right in France, Germany, Austria and Sweden.

Bibliography

Acton, H. B. (1971) *The Morals of Markets - An Ethical Exploration*, Longman, London.

Afheldt, H. (1995) 'Ausstieg aus dem Sozialstaat? Gefährdungen der Gesellschaft durch weltweite Umbrüche', in: *Aus Politik und Zeitgeschichte*, 16/06/95, No.B25-26, pp.3-12.

Albelda, R. (1995) 'The Welfare Reform Debate You Wish Would Happen', in: Strassmann, D. (ed.); *Feminist Economics*, Vol.1, No.2, pp.81-83.

Albert, M. (1993) *Capitalism against Capitalism*, Whurr Publishers, London.

Alcoff, L. / Potter, E. (1993) 'Introduction: When Feminisms Intersect Epistemology', in: Alcoff, L. / Potter, E. (eds); *Feminist Epistemologies*, Routledge, New York, pp.1-14.

Anderson, V. (1991) *Alternative Economic Indicators*, Routledge, London.

ap, dpa (1995) 'Sozialhilfe sinkt bei Arbeitsverweigerung', in: *Kölner Stadt Anzeiger*, 19/07/95, p.1.

Archer, J. (1989) cf. Cook, D., *Rich Law, Poor Law - Differential Response to Tax and Supplementary Benefit Fraud*, Open University Press, Milton Keynes, p.18.

Arendt, H. (1981) *Vita Activa oder Vom tätigen Leben*, Piper, München.

Arendt, W. *et al.* (1992) *Soziale Marktwirtschaft; Große Tradition - Gefährdete Zukunft*, Deutscher Institutsverlag, Köln.

Aristotle (1981) *Aristoteles - Politik* , Felix Meiner Verlag, Hamburg.

Arthur, C. J. (1986) *Dialectics of Labour - Marx and his Relation to Hegel*, Basil Blackwell, Oxford.

Ash, T. G. (1990) *We The People - The Revolution of '89 witnessed in Warsaw, Budapest, Berlin & Prague*, Granta Books, Cambridge.

Ashdown, P. / Rogers, S. (1997) 'A Liberal Dose of Common Sense', in: *The Big Issue in the North*, 03/03/97, No.144, pp.14-17.

Bäcker, G. (1995) 'Sind die Grenzen des Sozialstaates überschritten? Zur Diskussion über die Reformperspektiven der Sozialpolitik', in: *Aus Politik und Zeitgeschichte*, 16/06/95, No.B25-26, pp.13-25.

Baird, R. (1998) 'Why not enough people are feeling the benefit', in: *The Guardian*, Money Supplement, 17/01/98, pp.16-17.

Baratta, M. von *et al.* (1993) *Der Fischer Weltalmanach 1994*, Fischer Taschenbuch Verlag, Frankfurt.

Barry, B. (1996) cf. Lund, B., 'Robert Nozick and the Politics of Social Welfare', in: *Political Studies*, Vol.XLIV, No.1, p.121.

Barry, N. (1986) *On Classical Liberalism and Libertarianism*, Macmillan Press, London.

Barry, N. (1990) *Concepts in the Social Sciences - Welfare*, Open University Press, Buckingham.

Barry, N. (1993) 'The Social Market Economy', in: Frankel Paul, E. (ed.); *Liberalism and the Economic Order*, University Press, Cambridge, pp.1-25.

Baumol, J. W. / Blackman, S. A. B. (1991) *Perfect Markets and Easy Virtue - Business Ethics and the Invisible Hand*, Blackwell, Cambridge, Massachusetts.

BBC News Online (1998) *Profile: Gro Harlem Brundtland, the New WHO Head*, on the Internet, 13/05/98, http://news.bbc.co.uk/low/english/world/newsid_51000/51080.stm.

Beck, M. (1996) 'Krise des Sozialstaats steht bevor', in: *Das Parlament*, Vol.46, No.7, p.3-4.

Beckerman, W. (1995) *Small is Stupid - Blowing the Whistle on the Greens*, Duckworth, London.

Beenstock, M. (1996) 'Unemployment Insurance Without the State', in: Seldon, A. (ed.); *Re-Privatising Welfare: After the Lost Century*, Institute of Economic Affairs, London, pp.51-61.

Bell, D. (1976) *The Cultural Contradictions of Capitalism*, Heinemann Educational Books, London.

Bennetto, J. (1997) 'Violent Crime puts Britons in Fear of Dark', in: *The Independent*, 30/07/97, p.4.

Bentham, J. (1962) *The Works of Jeremy Bentham - Volume I*, Russell & Russell, New York.

Bentham, J. (1970) *The Principles of Morals and Legislation*, Hafner Publishing Company, New York.

Bergmann, F. (1997) 'Das Gold in den Köpfen heben', in: *Die Zeit*, Vol.52, No.11, p.27.

Berlin, I. (1986) c.f. Berry, C. J., *Human Nature*, Macmillan Education, Houndmills, p.39.

Berry, C. J. (1986) *Human Nature*, Macmillan Education, Houndmills.

Beveridge, W. (1977) cf. Wilson, E., *Women and the Welfare State*, Tavistock Publications, London, p.151.

Biemel, W. (1964) *Sartre*, Rowohlt, Reinbek.

Blanpain, R. / Sadowski, D. (1994) *Habe ich morgen noch einen Job? Die Zukunft der Arbeit in Europa*, Verlag C.H. Beck, München.

Blüm, N. (1997) 'Teilzeit mit Teilrente verbinden', in: *Das Parlament*, Vol.47, No.42, p.14.

Bly, R. (1993) *Iron John - A Book About Men*, Element, Shaftesbury, Dorset.

BMWI (1997) 'Auslandsinvestitionen', in: *Zeit-Punkte - Die mageren Jahre*, No.1, pp.12-13.

Bode, T. / Werner, H. (1995) 'Visionen gegen Infarkt', in: *Zeitpunkte: Wie teuer ist uns die Natur?*, No.6, pp.76-78.

Borgeest, B. / Perina, U. (1994) 'Die graue Revolution', in: *Zeitpunkte: Weltbevölkerung*, No.4, pp.35-37.

Bradshaw, S. (1996) 'From Cradle to Grave: Broken Promises', in: Hewlett, S. (producer); *Panorama*, BBC1, 23/01/96.

Brandenstein, B. von (1973) 'Handlung', in: Krings, H. *et al.*, *Handbuch philosophischer Grundbegriffe*, Band 3, Kösel-Verlag, München, pp.677-685.

Bremer Gesellschaft für Wirtschaftsforschung (1997) cf. Czada, R., 'Uneinigkeit über Ursachen und Lösungen', in: *Das Parlament*, Vol.47, No.44-45, p.22.

Bridges, William (1999) cf. Franks, Suzanne, *Having None of It: Women, Men and the Future of Work*, Granta Books, London, p.64f.

British Medical Association (1992) *Our Genetic Future - The Science and Ethics of Genetic Technology*, Oxford University Press, Oxford.

Brittan, S. (1998) on: *Counterblast*, BBC2, 15/04/98, 19:30-20:00.

Brower-Rabinowitsch, A. (1994) 'Abstand gewahrt', in: *Die Zeit*, Vol.49, No.35, p.19.

Brown, P. (1997) 'Boom in Organic Food Prompts Farm Aid Rethink', in: *The Guardian*, 30/07/97, p.7.

Brundtland Report (1992) cf. Weizsäcker, E. U. von / Jesinghaus, J., *Ecological Tax Reform - A Policy Proposal for Sustainable Development*, Zed Books, London, p.3.

Brundtland Report (1994) cf. Friends of the Earth, *Working Future? Jobs and the Environment*, Friends of the Earth Trust Ltd, London, p.12.

Buhr, P. (1995) 'Sozialhilfe - Mythos und Realität, Klarstellungen zur aktuellen Reformdebatte', in: *Blätter für deutsche und internationale Politik*, Blätter Verlagsgesellschaft, Bonn, Vol.40, No.9, pp.1060-70.

Bullinger, H.-J. (1995) 'Arbeit der Zukunft und Zukunft der Arbeit', in: *Wirtschaft und Wissenschaft*, Stifterverband für die deutsche Wissenschaft; No.4, pp.34-38.

Bundesanstalt für Arbeit (1998), Inquiry by telephone, 30/04/98, 0049-911-1790.

Campanella, T. (1960) 'Civitas Solis - Sonnenstaat', in Heinisch, K. J. (ed.); *Der utopische Staat*, Rowohlt, Hamburg, pp.111-170.

Cansfield, A. (1996) *Your Business Matters - Executive Summary*, Institute of Directors, London.

Carlyle, T. (1965) *Past and Present*, Oxford University Press, London.

Castells, M. (1993) 'European Cities, the Informational Society, and the Global Economy', in: *Tijdschrift voor Economische en Sociale Geografie*, No.84, p.249.

Clement, B. (1996) 'Servants Back in Below-Stairs Britain', in: *The Independent*, 01/07/96, No.3027, p.3.

Code, L. (1993) 'Taking Subjectivity into Account', in: Alcoff, L. / Potter, E. (eds); *Feminist Epistemologies*, Routledge, New York, pp.15-48.

Collard, D. (1991) 'Love is not enough', in: Meeks, G. (ed.); *Thoughtful Economic Man - Essays on Rationality, Moral Rules and Benevolence*, Cambridge University Press, Cambridge, pp.17-28.

Cook, D. (1989) *Rich Law, Poor Law - Differential Response to Tax and Supplementary Benefit Fraud*, Open University Press, Milton Keynes.

Cooper, G. (1997) 'Housing Benefit Fraud Hits 1bn Pounds', in: *The Independent*, 29/07/97, p.7.

Cramp, T. (1991) 'Pleasures, Prices and Principles', in: Meeks, G. (ed.); *Thoughtful Economic Man - Essays on Rationality, Moral Rules and Benevolence*, Cambridge University Press, Cambridge, pp.50-73.

Cronin, H. (1998) interviewed on: *Darwin: The Legacy*, 29/03/98, BBC2, 22:05-23:00.

Crouch, C. / Marquand, D. (1993) 'Introduction', in: Crouch C. / Marquand D. (eds); *Ethics and Markets - Co-operation and Competition within Capitalist Economies*, Blackwell Publishers, Oxford.

Csikszentmihalyi, M. (1996) cf. Sesin, C. P., 'Süsse Lust der Arbeit', in: *Die Woche Extra*, 20/12/96, No.52, p.14.

Dahlmanns, G. (1997) 'Mehr Markt für den Arbeitsmarkt', in: *Aus Politik und Zeitgeschichte*, 22/08/97, No.B35/97, pp.33-38.

Dahrendorf, R. (1992) cf. Merkel, W., 'After the Golden Age - Is Social Democracy Doomed to Decline?', in: Lemke, C. / Marks, G. (eds); *The Crisis of Socialism in Europe*, Duke University Press, Durham, United States, p.136.

Dahrendorf, R. (1996) 'On the Dahrendorf Report', in: *The Political Quarterly*, Vol.67, No.3, pp.194-197.

Daly, H. (1995) *The Irrationality of Homo Economicus*, on the Internet: http://iisd1.iisd.ca/didigest/special /daly.htm, 22/05/97.

Daly, H. / Cobb Jr, J. B. (1990) *For the Common Good*, Green Print, London.

Daniels, A. (1996) 'Atmende Fabriken - atemlose Belegschaften', in: *Die Zeit*, Vol.51, No.33, p.19.

Darwin, C. (1990) cf. Vogel, C., 'Ethische Überlegungen zur Anthropologie und Ethologie', in: Herbig, J. / Hohlfeld, R. (eds); *Die zweite Schöpfung - Geist und Ungeist in der Biologie des 20. Jahrhunderts*, Carl Hanser Verlag, München, p.123.

Dawkins, R. (1989) *The Selfish Gene - New Edition*, Oxford University Press, Oxford.

Deacon, A. (1996) 'Welfare and Character', in: Deacon, A. (ed); *Stakeholder Welfare*, IEA Health and Welfare Unit, London, pp.60-74.

Deakin, N. (1987) *The Politics of Welfare*, Methuen & Co., London.

Deppe, F. (1996) 'Arbeitslosigkeit, Wohlfahrtsstaat und Gewerkschaften in der Europäischen Union', in: *Sozialismus Supplement*, Vol.23, No.2, pp.1-21.

Deutsche Bundesbank (1996) 'Arbeit muß sich lohnen', in: *Das Parlament*, Vol.46, No.11, p.13.

Dex, S. (1989) cf. McLaughlin, E. / Millar, J. / Cooke, K., *Work and Welfare Benefits*, Avebury, Aldershot, p.15.

Dibb, S. (1997) 'Organic Revolution', in: *Vegetarian Good Food*, November 1997, p.6.

Dietz, M. (1991) 'Hannah Arendt and Feminist Politics', in: Shanley, M. / Pateman, C. (eds); *Feminist Interpretations and Political Theory*, Polity Press, Cambridge, pp.232-252.

Digel, W. *et al.* (1987) *Meyers grosses Taschenlexikon*, Vol. 1-24, B.I.-Taschenbuchverlag, Mannheim.

Economist (1995) 'Trust in Me', Vol.337, No.7945, p.83.

Economist (1996) 'Redesigning the German Model', Vol.338, No.7950, p.33-34.

Ehrenfeld, D. (1991) 'The Arrogance of Humanism', in: Dobson, A. (ed.); *The Green Reader*, André Deutsch, London, pp.45-47.

Eibl-Eibesfeldt, J. (1984) *Liebe und Hass - Zur Naturgeschichte elementarer Verhaltensweisen*, Piper Verlag, München.

Eley, G. (1992) 'Reviewing the Socialist Tradition', in: Lemke, C. / Marks, G. (eds); *The Crisis of Socialism in Europe*, Duke University Press, Durham, United States, pp.21-60.

Elser, M. *et al.* (1992) *Enzyklopädie der Philosophie*, Weltbild Verlag, Augsburg.

England, P. (1993) 'The Separative Self: Androcentric Bias in Neoclassical Assumptions', in: Ferber, M. A. / Nelson, J. A. (eds); *Beyond Economic Man - Feminist Theory and Economics*, The University of Chicago Press, Chicago, pp.37-53.

Erhard, L. (1997) cf. Reuter, N., 'Arbeitslosigkeit bei ausbleibendem Wachstum - das Ende der Arbeitsmarktpolitik?', in: *Aus Politik und Zeitgeschichte*, 22/08/97, No.B35, p.3.

Espenhorst, J. (1996) 'Zeit der Wohlstandswende?', in: *Aus Politik und Zeitgeschichte*, 12/01/96, No.B3, pp.3-16.

Eurostat (1995) *Basic Statistics of the European Union*, Office for Official Publications of the European Communities, Luxembourg.

Eurostatistics (1997) *European Community Statistics*, Office des publications officielles des Communautés européennes, Luxembourg, No.02/1997.

Eurostatistics (1998) *European Community Statistics*, Office des publications officielles des Communautés européennes, Luxembourg, No.12/1998.

Faludi, S. (1992) *Backlash - The Undeclared War Against Women*, Vintage, London.

Ferber, M. A. / Nelson, J. A. (1993) 'Introduction: The Social Construction of Economics and the Social Construction of Gender', in: Ferber M. A. / Nelson J. A. (eds); *Beyond Economic Man - Feminist Theory and Economics*, The University of Chicago Press, Chicago, pp.1-22.

Field, F. (1996) 'Making Welfare Work: The Underlying Principles', in: Deacon, A. (ed.); *Stakeholder Welfare*, IEA Health and Welfare Unit, London, pp.7-44.

Field, F. (1996a) 'How to Open the Benefit Trap', in: *The Independent*, 01/07/96, No.3027, p.15.

Field, F. / Grieve, M. (1971) *Abuse and the Abused - Poverty Pamphlet 10*, Child Poverty Action Group, London.

Fisher, M. (1995) *After the Wall - Germany, the Germans and the Burdens of History*, Simon & Schuster, New York.

Flew, A. (1977) 'Wants or Needs, Choices or Commands', in: Fitzgerald, R. (ed.); *Human Needs and Politics*, Pergamon Press, Oxford, pp.213-228.

Franks, Suzanne (1999) *Having None of It: Women, Men and the Future of Work*, Granta Books, London.

Fraser, N. (1990) 'Struggle Over Needs: Outline of a Socialist-Feminist Critical Theory of Late-Capitalist Political Culture', in: Gordon, L. (ed.); *Women, the State, and Welfare*, University of Wisconsin Press, Madison, Wisconsin, pp.199-225.

Freud, S. (1970) cf. Macarov, D., *Incentives to Work*, Jossey-Bass Inc. Publishers, San Francisco, p.89.

Friedman, M. (1982) *Capitalism and Freedom*, University of Chicago Press, Chicago.

Friedrichs, J. (1997) 'Globalisierung - Begriff und grundlegende Annahmen', in: *Aus Politik und Zeitgeschichte*, 08/08/97, No.B33-34/97, pp.3-11.

Friends of the Earth, (1994) *Working Future? Jobs and the Environment*, Friends of the Earth Trust Ltd., London.

Fukuyama, F. (1992) *The End of History and the Last Man*, Penguin Books, London.

Galbraith, J. K. (1962) *The Affluent Society*, Penguin Books, Harmondsworth.

Gellner, E. (1996) 'Return of a Native', in: *The Political Quarterly*, Vol.67, No.1, pp.4-13.

Gerlach, I. (1992) 'Wertewandel', in: Anderson, U. / Woyke, W. (eds); *Handwörterbuch des politischen Systems der Bundesrepublik Deutschland*, Leske Verlag, Opladen, pp.589-592.

Germanis, P. G. (1992) 'Workfare: Breaking the Poverty Cycle', in: Mappes, T. A. / Zembaty, J. S. (eds); *Social Ethics - Morality and Social Policy*, McGraw-Hill, New York, pp.384-387.

Gilder, G. (1982) *Wealth & Poverty*, Buchan & Enright, London.

Glazer, N. (1992) cf. Hawkesworth, M., 'Workfare and the Imposition of Discipline', in: Mappes, T. A. / Zembaty, J. S. (eds); *Social Ethics - Morality and Social Policy*, McGraw-Hill, New York, pp.387-394.

Globus (1996) 'Bundeshaushalt 1991 bis 1997', in: *Das Parlament*, Vol.46, No.48-49, p.2.

Globus (1996a) 'Arbeiten im Alter?', in: *Süddeutsche Zeitung*, 08/10/96, p.19.

Globus (1997) 'Rangfolge der Wirtschaftsstärke 1996', in: *Das Parlament*, Vol.47, No.17, p.6.

Globus (1997a) 'EU-Karte der Arbeitslosigkeit', in: *Das Parlament*, Vol.47, No.47, p.17.

Globus (1998) 'Lohnquote und Arbeitslosigkeit', in: *Die Zeit*, Vol.53, No.53, p.29.

Goodin, R. (1992) 'Towards a Minimally Presumptuous Social Welfare Policy', in: Parijs, P. van (ed.); *Arguing for Basic Income - Ethical Foundations for a Radical Reform*, London, Verso, pp.195-214.

Gorz, A. (1983) *Wege ins Paradies - Thesen zur Krise, Automation und Zukunft der Arbeit*, Rotbuch Verlag, Berlin.

Gorz, A. (1994) *Capitalism, Socialism, Ecology*, Verso, London, pp.44-52.

Gorz, A. / Kempe, M. (1994) 'Thema: Arbeit, Arbeit, Arbeit? Gespräch mit André Gorz', in: *Die Neue Gesellschaft Frankfurter Hefte*, Vol.41, No.7, pp.592-602.

Goudzwaard, B. / de Lange, H. (1995) *Beyond Poverty and Affluence - Toward an Economy of Care*, Eerdmans Publishing, Michigan.

Gould, S. J. (1990) 'Biologische Potentialität contra biologischer Determinismus', in: Herbig, J. / Hohlfeld, R. (eds); *Die zweite Schöpfung - Geist und Ungeist in der Biologie des 20. Jahrhunderts*, Carl Hanser Verlag, München, pp.132-142.

Govier, T. (1992) 'The Right to Eat and the Duty to Work', in: Mappes, T. A. / Zembaty, J. S. (eds); *Social Ethics - Morality and Social Policy*, McGraw-Hill, New York, pp.372-383.

Grapard, U. (1995) 'Robinson Crusoe: The Quintessential Economic Man?', in: Strassmann, D. (ed.); *Feminist Economics*, Vol.1, No.1, pp.33-52.

Gray, J. (1992) *The Moral Foundations of Market Institutions*, IEA Health and Welfare Unit, London.

Grefe, C. (1990) 'Kein Brot für die Welt', in: Klingholz, R. (ed.); *Die Welt nach Maß*, Reinbek, Rowohlt Taschenbuch Verlag, pp.61-77.

Grint, K. (1991) *The Sociology of Work - An Introduction*, Polity Press, Cambridge.

Gusinde, M. (1974) cf. Sahlins, M., *Stone Age Economics*, Tavistock Publications, London, p.13.

Gysi, G. (1996) '"Den sozialen Krieg erklärt"', in: *Das Parlament*, Vol.46, No.19, pp.6-7.

Hahn, F. (1991) 'Benevolence', in: Meeks, G. (ed.); *Thoughtful Economic Man - Essays on Rationality, Moral Rules and Benevolence*, Cambridge University Press, Cambridge, pp.7-11.

Handy, C. (1985) *The Future of Work*, Basil Blackwell, Oxford.

Handy, C. (1994) *The Empty Raincoat - Making Sense of the Future*, Hutchinson, London.

Hanson, C. (1996) *Social Europe - The economic implications of current European social policy*, Institute of Directors, London.

Harding, S. (1993) 'Rethinking Standpoint Epistemology: What Is "Strong Objectivity"?', in: Alcoff, L. / Potter, E. (eds); *Feminist Epistemologies*, Routledge, New York, pp.49-82.

Harris, R. (1995) cf. Hutton, W., *The State We're In*, Vintage, London, p.174.

Hartmann, H. (1993) cf. Strassmann, D., 'Not a Free Market: The Rhetoric of Disciplinary Authority in Economics', in: Ferber, M. A. / Nelson, J. A. (eds); *Beyond Economic Man - Feminist Theory and Economics*, The University of Chicago Press, Chicago, p.62.

Haskins, C. (1996) 'Debate Two - Against', in: *Director, Special Supplement*, The 1996 IoD Annual Convention, pp.55-58.

Hawkes, B. (1989) cf. Cook, D., *Rich Law, Poor Law - Differential Response to Tax and Supplementary Benefit Fraud*, Open University Press, Milton Keynes, p.171.

Hawkesworth, M. (1992) 'Workfare and the Imposition of Discipline', in: Mappes, T. A. / Zembaty, J. S. (eds); *Social Ethics - Morality and Social Policy*, McGraw-Hill, New York, pp.387-394.

Hayek, F. A. (1966) *Dr. Bernard Mandeville*, Proceedings of the British Academy, Volume LII, Oxford University Press, London, pp.125-141.

Hayek, F. A. (1988) *The Fatal Conceit - The Errors of Socialism*, Routledge, London.

Held, D. (1986) 'Liberalism, Marxism and the future direction of public policy', in: Nolan, P. / Paine, S. (eds); *Rethinking Socialist Economics - A New Agenda for Britain*, Polity Press, Cambridge, pp.13-34.

Heneman, H. G. (1973) 'Work and Nonwork: Historical Perspectives', in: Dunnette, M. D. (ed.); *Work and Nonwork in the Year 2001*, Wadsworth Publishing Company, Monterey, pp.12-28.

Henkel, H.-O. / Hoffmann, L. (1995) 'Mehr Verlierer als Gewinner?' in: *Zeitpunkte: Wie teuer ist uns die Natur?*, No.6, pp.27-30.

Hensch, C. / Wismer, U. (1997) 'Bad Acid - Editorial', in: Hensch, C. / Wismer, U. (eds); *Zukunft der Arbeit*, pp.8-14.

Hernes, H.M. (1987) *Welfare State and Woman Power - Essays in State Feminism*, Oxford University Press, Oxford.

Hesiod (1978) cf. Rogers, D. T., *The Work Ethic in Industrial America 1850-1920*, The University of Chicago Press, Chicago, p.2.

Heuser, U. J. (1997) 'Oase für das Kapital', in: *Zeit-Punkte - Die mageren Jahre*, No.1, pp.80-85.

Hewlett, S. A. (1987) *A Lesser Life - The Myth of Women's Liberation*, Michael Joseph, London.

Heygendorff, P. von (1997) 'Das Cappuccino-Prinzip wird adoptiert', in: *Das Parlament*, Vol.47, No.47, p.19.

Hickey, T. (1993) '"They are not Tigers" - Myth and Myopia in the Quest for a Liberal Economic Order', in: Brecher, B. / Fleischmann, O. (eds); *Liberalism and the New Europe*, Avebury, Aldershot, pp.59-88.

Himmelfarb, G. (1997) 'Introduction', in: *Memoir on Pauperism*, by A. de Toqueville, IEA Health and Welfare Unit, London, pp.1-16.

Hollands, J. (1996) *Conservative Party Conference*, Bournemouth, 09/10/96, BBC2, 14:10-16:00.

Homann, K. (1997) 'Individualisierung: Verfall der Moral? Zum ökonomischen Fundament aller Moral', in: *Aus Politik und Zeitgeschichte*, 16/05/97, No.B21/97, pp.12-21.

Hospers, J. (1992) 'What Libertarianism is', in: Mappes, T. A. / Zembaty, J. S. (eds); *Social Ethics - Morality and Social Policy*, McGraw-Hill, New York, pp.352-359.

Houghton, Lord (1989) cf. Cook, D., *Rich Law, Poor Law - Differential Response to Tax and Supplementary Benefit Fraud*, Open University Press, Milton Keynes, p.58.

House of Commons, (1997) *Oral Answers to Questions: Social Security*, on the Internet: http://www.parliament.the-statione...nsrd/cm970128/debtext/7012 8 -01.htm, 28/01/97.

Hügli, A. *et al.* (1991) *Philosophielexikon*, Rowohlt Verlag, Hamburg.

Hume, D. (1978) *A Treatise of Human Nature*, Clarendon Press, Oxford.

Hutton, W. (1995) *The State We're In*, Vintage, London.

Hutton, W. (1997) 'The Stakeholder Society', in: Green, D. G. (ed.); *Stakeholding and its Critics*, IEA Health and Welfare Unit, London, pp.1-16; 86-93.

Immisch, J. (1966) *Zeiten und Menschen - Europa und die Welt*, Schöningh, Paderborn.

IW (1997) 'Arbeitskosten in der verarbeitenden Industrie', in: *Zeit-Punkte - Die mageren Jahre*, No.1, p.13.

Jack, M. (1996) *Financial Statement and Budget Report 1997-1998*, Treasury Chambers, London.

Jackson, P. R. (1994) 'Influences on Commitment to Employment and Commitment to Work', in: Bryson, A. / McKay, S. (eds); *Is It Worth Working? Factors affecting labour supply*, Policy Studies Institute, London, pp.110-121.

Jahoda, M. *et al.* (1975) *Die Arbeitslosen von Marienthal - Ein soziographischer Versuch*, Suhrkamp Verlag, Frankfurt.

Jennings, A. L. (1993) 'Public or Private? Institutional Economics and Feminism', in: Ferber, M. A. / Nelson, J. A. (eds); *Beyond Economic Man - Feminist Theory and Economics*, The University of Chicago Press, Chicago, pp.111-129.

Johnson, N. (1991) 'Farewell to the Red Flag: Some Lessons of Eastern Europe's Revolution for the West', in: *The Political Quarterly*, Vol.62, No.1, pp.24-34.

Jung, A. (1997) *Die Jobkiller - Wie deutsche Unternehmen Millionen Arbeitsplätze vernichten*, Econ, Düsseldorf.

Kaus, M. (1996) 'How the New Welfare Law Will Save Liberalism and the Poor', in: *International Herald Tribune*, No.35286, p.6.

kess/vo (1995) 'Die ökologische Wahrheit', in: *Zeitpunkte: Wie teuer ist uns die Natur?*, No.6, p.19.

Kingdom, J. (1992) *No Such Thing As Society? Individualism and Community*, Open University Press, Buckingham.

Kirkpatrick, B. (1987) *Roget's Thesaurus of English Words and Phrases*, Longman, Harlow.

Klauder, W. (1997) 'Arbeit ist genug vorhanden', in: *Der Spiegel*, No.2, 1997, pp.27-29.

Klingholz, R. (1990) 'Neues Leben für Stall und Acker', in: Klingholz, R. (ed.); *Die Welt nach Maß*, Reinbek, Rowohlt Taschenbuch Verlag, pp.48-60.

Klopfleisch, R. *et al.* (1997) 'Wirksame Instrumente einer Arbeitsmarkt- und Beschäftigungspolitik', in: *Aus Politik und Zeitgeschichte*, 22/08/97, No.B35/97, pp.23-32.

Kohl, H. (1995) cf. Sussenburger, J., 'Es geht ans Eingemachte', in: *Kölner Stadt Anzeiger*, Dumont, Köln, 19/07/95, p.2.

Kohl, H. (1996) 'Soziale und wirtschaftliche Anpassungen', in: *Das Parlament*, Vol.46, No.19, pp.2-3.

Kohl, H. (1997) 'Eine gute Zukunft für Deutschland', in: *Das Parlament*, Vol.47, No.7/8, pp.3-4.

Kramer, D. (1994) 'Suchbewegungen in der Krise der Arbeitsgesellschaft', in: Hoffmann, H. / Kramer, K. (eds); *Arbeit ohne Sinn? Sinn ohne Arbeit? Über die Zukunft der Arbeitsgesellschaft*, Beltz athenäum, Weinheim, pp.133-172.

Kristol, I. (1978) 'A Capitalist Conception of Justice', in: de George, R. T./ Pichler, J. A. (eds); *Ethics, Free Enterprise, & Public Policy - Original Essays on Moral Issues in Business*, Oxford University Press, New York, pp.57-69.

Kühl, J. (1996) 'Warum schaffen zwei Millionen Betriebe und Verwaltungen nicht genügend gute Arbeitsplätze für alle?', in: *Aus Politik und Zeitgeschichte*, 12/01/96, No.B3, pp.26-39.

Kukathas, C. (1992) 'Freedom versus Autonomy', in: Gray, J., *The Moral Foundations of Market Institutions*, IEA Health and Welfare Unit, London, pp.101-114.

Kurbjuweit, D. (1996) 'Der Sozialstaat ist sein Geld wert', in: *Die Zeit*, Vol.51, No.33, p.3.

Kwiatkowski, G. *et al.* (1985) *Schülerduden - Philosophie*, Dudenverlag, Mannheim.

Lafontaine, O. (1996) 'Regierungsvorschläge sind unausgewogen', in: *Das Parlament*, Vol.46, No.19, p.3-4.

Lafontaine, O. (1996a) 'Schaden von den Bürgern abwenden', in: *Das Parlament*, Vol.46, No.32, pp.2-3.

Lafontaine, O. (1996b) ' "Ihr Angebot ist unzureichend" ', in: *Das Parlament*, Vol.46, No.8, p.7-8.

Lambsdorff, O. (1996) 'Produktionskosten sind zu hoch', in: *Das Parlament*, Vol.46, No.7, p.6.

Landesmann, M. (1986) 'UK Policy and the International Economy: An Internationalist Perspective', in: Nolan, P. / Paine, S. (eds); *Rethinking Socialist Economics - A New Agenda for Britain*, Polity Press, Cambridge, pp.115-134.

Lassalle, F. (1994) 'Gründung von Produktivgenossenschaften', in: Beywl, W. (ed.); *Soziale Sicherung*, Bundeszentrale für politische Bildung, Bonn, pp.21-22.

Le monde diplomatique (1995) cf. Afheldt, H., 'Ausstieg aus dem Sozialstaat? Gefährdungen der Gesellschaft durch weltweite Umbrüche', in: *Aus Politik und Zeitgeschichte*, 16/06/95, No. B25-26, p.13.

Leibfried, S. *et al.* (1995) *Zeit der Armut - Lebensläufe im Sozialstaat*, edition suhrkamp, Frankfurt.

Lemke, C. / Marks, G. (1992) 'Preface', in: Lemke, C. / Marks, G. (eds); *The Crisis of Socialism in Europe*, Duke University Press, Durham, US, pp.ix-x.

Leontief, W. (1983) 'National Perspective: The Definition of Problems and Opportunities', Paper presented at the *National Academy of Engineering Symposium*, 30/06/83, p.3, cf. Rifkin, 1995, 5f.

Levitan, S. A. / Rein, M. / Marwick, D. (1972) *Work and Welfare Go Together*, John Hopkins University Press, Baltimore.

Lilley, P. (1996) *Conservative Party Conference*, Bournemouth, 09/10/96, BBC2, 14:10-16:00.

Lillie, W. (1955) *An Introduction to Ethics*, Methuen & Co. Ltd, London.

Lister, R. (1999) '"Reforming Welfare Around the Work Ethic": New Gendered and Ethical Perspectives on Work and Care', in: *Policy and Politics*, Vol.27, No.2, pp.233-246.

Lohmann, K. R. (1997) 'Was ist eigentlich Wirtschaftsethik? Eine systematische Einführung', in: *Aus Politik und Zeitgeschichte*, 16/05/97, No.B21/97, pp.31-38.

Loske, R. / Vorholz, F. (1992) 'In der Energiefalle', in: *Zeit-Schriften: Ein Gipfel für die Welt*, No.1, pp.52-56.

Lünzer, I. (1996) 'Gesunde Nahrungsmittel sind das Ziel', in: *Das Parlament*, Vol.46, No.30, p.6.

Macarov, D. (1970) *Incentives to Work*, Jossey-Bass Inc. Publishers, San Francisco.

Macarov, D. (1980) *Work and Welfare - The Unholy Alliance*, Sage Publications, Beverly Hills.

Macarov, D. (1982) *Worker Productivity - Myths and Reality*, Sage Publications, Beverly Hills.

Machan, T. R. (1995) 'A Defence of Property Rights and Capitalism', in: Almond, B. (ed.); *Introducing Applied Ethics*, Blackwell Publishers, Oxford, pp.260-271.

Malone, D. (1998) narrator and producer of: *Darwin: The Legacy*, 29/03/98, BBC2, 22:05-23:00.

Marshall, A. (1987) cf. Woll, A., *Allgemeine Volkswirtschaftslehre*, Verlag Franz Vahlen, München, p.3.

Marx, K. (1984) cf. Oakley, A., *Marx's Critique of Political Economy*, Routledge & Kegan Paul, London.

Marx, K. (1986) cf. Berry, C. J., *Human Nature*, Macmillan Education, Houndmills, p.73.

Marx, K. / Engels, F. (1981) *Manifest der Kommunistischen Partei*, Dietz Verlag, Berlin.

Mayer, O. G. (1997) 'Globalisierung und wohlfahrtsstaatliche Aufgaben', in: *Aus Politik und Zeitgeschichte*, 08/08/97, No.B33-34/97, pp.29-38.

Mazlish, B. (1975) *James and John Stuart Mill*, Hutchinson, London.

McCartney, I. (1996) cf. Clement, B., 'Servants Back in Below-Stairs Britain', in: *The Independent*, 01/07/96, No.3027, p.3.

McLaughlin, E. / Millar, J. / Cooke, K. (1989) *Work and Welfare Benefits*, Avebury, Aldershot.

McRae, S. (1989) *Flexible Working Time and Family Life*, Policy Studies Institute, London.

Mead, L. (1986) *Beyond Entitlement*, Free Press; Macmillan, New York.

Mead, L. (1997) 'From Welfare to Work - Lessons from America', in: Deacon, A. (ed.); *From Welfare to Work*, IEA Health and Welfare Unit, London, pp.1-55.

Merkel, W. (1992) 'After the Golden Age - Is Social Democracy Doomed to Decline?', in: Lemke, C. / Marks, G. (eds); *The Crisis of Socialism in Europe*, Duke University Press, Durham, US, pp.136-170.

Meyer, D. (1996) 'Die Wohlfahrtsverbände: Intermediär und Dienstleister', in: Dierkes, M. / Zimmermann, K. (eds); *Sozialstaat in der Krise*, Gabler, Wiesbaden, pp.211-237.

Midgley, M. (1980) *Beast & Man - The Roots of Human Nature*, Methuen, London.

Midgley, M. / Hughes, J. (1983) *Women's Choices - Philosophical Problems Facing Feminism*, Weidenfeld and Nicolson, London.

Miegel, M. (1991) 'After the Tremor from the East', in: *The Political Quarterly*, Vol.62, No.1, pp.16-23.

Mill, J. (1975) cf. Mazlish, B., *James and John Stuart Mill*, Hutchinson, London, pp.101-125.

Millar, J. (1994) 'Understanding Labour Supply in Context: Households and Incomes', in: Bryson, A. / McKay, S. (eds); *Is It Worth Working? Factors Affecting Labour Supply*, Policy Studies Institute, London, pp.77-92.

Minford, P. (1992) 'Gray on the Market', in: Gray, J.; *The Moral Foundations of Market Institutions*, IEA Health and Welfare Unit, London, pp.115-118.

Mises, L. (1986) cf. Barry, N.,' *On Classical Liberalism and Libertarianism*, Macmillan Press, London, p.63.

Mishan, E. J. (1996) 'Technological Unemployment: Why There are Hard Times Ahead', in: *The Political Quarterly*, Vol.67, No.2, pp.151-157.

Mishra, R. (1984) *The Welfare State in Crisis - Social Thought and Social Change*, Harvester Press Group, Brighton.

Mitterand, F. (1991) cf. Gorz, A., 'A Possible Utopia', in: Dobson, A. (ed.); *The Green Reader*, André Deutsch, London, p.95.

Monk, R. (1998) 'Thinkers Never Die' in: *The Times Higher*, 20/11/98.

Moody-Adams, M. M. (1995) 'Race, Class, and the Social Construction of Self-Respect', in: Dillon, R. S. (ed.); *Dignity, Character and Self-Respect*, Routledge, London, pp.271-289.

More, T. (1981) *Utopia*, Diogenes, Zürich.

Morris, W. (1993) *News from Nowhere and Other Writings*, Penguin Classics, London.

Muhr, G. (1994) 'Bekämpfung der neuen Armut erfordert Gegenmacht', in: Beywl, W. (ed.); *Soziale Sicherung*, Bundeszentrale für politische Bildung, Bonn, pp.57-58.

Murdock, G. (1978) cf. Wilson, E., *On Human Nature*, Harvard University Press, Cambridge, Massachusetts, p.22.

Murray, C. (1996) 'The Emerging British Underclass', in: Lister, R. (ed.); *Charles Murray and the Underclass - The Developing Debate*, IEA Health and Welfare Unit, London.

Mutz, G. (1997) 'Zukunft der Arbeit - Chancen für eine Tätigkeitsgesellschaft?', in: *Aus Politik und Zeitgeschichte*, 21/11/97, B48-49/97, pp.31-40.

Myrdal, G. (1960) *Beyond the Welfare State - Economic Planning in the Welfare States and its International Implications*, Yale University Press, Yale.

Negt, O. (1995) 'Die Krise der Arbeitsgesellschaft: Machtpolitischer Kampfplatz zweier "Ökonomien"', in: *Aus Politik und Zeitgeschichte*, 07/04/95, No. B15, pp.3-9.

Nelson, J. A. (1993) 'The Study of Choice or the Study of Provisioning? Gender and the Definition of Economics', in: Ferber, M. A. / Nelson, J. A. (eds); *Beyond Economic Man - Feminist Theory and Economics*, The University of Chicago Press, Chicago, pp.23-36.

Newsom, J. (1977) cf. Wilson, E., *Women and the Welfare State*, Tavistock Publications, London, p.83.

Norton-Taylor, R. / Hencke, D. (1997) 'MI5 Fights Benefit Cheats', in: *The Guardian*, 22/09/97, p.1.

Nosow, S. / Form, W.H. (1970) cf. Macarov, D., *Incentives to Work*, Jossey-Bass Inc. Publishers, San Francisco, p.145.

Novak, M. (1996) on: *Tales from the Wasteland I*, Channel 4, 05/06/96, 21:00.

Nozick, R. (1974) *Anarchy, State and Utopia*, Basil Blackwell, Oxford.

Oakley, A. (1982) *Subject Women*, Fontana, London.

Oakley, A. (1984) *Marx's Critique of Political Economy*, Routledge & Kegan Paul, London.

Offe, C. (1992) 'A Non-Productivist Design for Social Policies', in: Parijs, P. van (ed.); *Arguing for Basic Income - Ethical Foundations for a Radical Reform*, London, Verso, pp.61-78.

Offe, C. (1994) 'Prämien für Aussteiger', in: *Die Zeit*, Vol.49, No.11, p.28, 11/03/1994.

O'Hara, B. (1993) *Working Harder Isn't Working*, New Star Books, Vancouver.

Opielka, M. (1997) 'Leitlinien einer sozialpolitischen Reform', in: *Aus Politik und Zeitgeschichte*, 21/11/97, No.B48-49, pp.21-30.

Pahl, R. (1994) 'Balancing All Forms of Work', in: Bryson, A. / McKay, S. (eds); *Is It Worth Working? Factors Affecting Labour Supply*, Policy Studies Institute, London, pp.60-76.

Parijs, P. van (1992) 'Competing Justifications of Basic Income', in: Parijs, P. van (ed.); *Arguing for Basic Income - Ethical Foundations for a Radical Reform*, London, Verso, pp.3-43.

Parijs, P. van (1995) *Real Freedom For All - What (if Anything) Can Justify Capitalism?*, Clarendon Press, Oxford.

Park, Y. C. (1997) 'Die Krise des Kapitalismus ist ein schauriger Erfolg des Sozialismus', in: *Welt am Sonntag*, 15/06/97, p.41.

Parker, H. (1982) *The Moral Hazard of Social Benefits - A Study of the Impact of Social Benefits and Income Tax on Incentives to Work*, Institute of Economic Affairs, London.

Pascall, G. (1986) *Social Policy - A Feminist Analysis*, Tavistock Publications, London.

Perkin, H. (1996) 'The Third Revolution and Stakeholder Capitalism: Convergence or Collapse', in: *The Political Quarterly*, Vol.67, No.3, pp.198-208.

Pfaff, W. (1998) 'Das Diktat des Westens', in: *Die Zeit*, Vol.53, No.2, p.6, 02/01/98.

Pinzler, P. (1996) 'Offener Handel statt begrenzter Hilfe hat weltweit größten Effekt', in: *Das Parlament*, Vol.46, No.46, p.6.

Plant, R. (1991) *Modern Political Thought*, Basil Blackwell, Oxford.

Plato (1993) *Der Staat*, Felix Meiner Verlag, Hamburg.

Radcliffe Richard, J. (1983) cf. Midgley, M. / Hughes, J., *Women's Choices - Philosophical Problems Facing Feminism*, Weidenfeld and Nicolson, London, p.21.

Radermacher, F. J. (1995) '"Tanz auf dem Vulkan"', in: *Zeitpunkte: Wie teuer ist uns die Natur?*, No.6, pp.61-63.

Rawls, J. (1972) *A Theory of Justice*, Clarendon Press, Oxford.

Rawls, J. (1995) 'Self-Respect, Excellences and Shame', in: Dillon, R. S. (ed.); *Dignity, Character and Self-Respect*, Routledge, London, pp.125-132.

Reich, R. (1994) cf. Blanpain, R. / Sadowski, D., *Habe ich morgen noch einen Job? Die Zukunft der Arbeit in Europa*, Verlag C.H. Beck, München, p.75.

Reich, R. (1994a) cf. Handy, C., *The Empty Raincoat - Making Sense of the Future*, Hutchinson, London, p.201.

Reuter, E. (1995) 'Wider das Schweigekartell der Oberingenieure', in: *Zeitpunkte: Wie teuer ist uns die Natur?*, No.6, pp.20-23.

Reuter, N. (1997) 'Arbeitslosigkeit bei ausbleibendem Wachstum - das Ende der Arbeitsmarktpolitik?', in: *Aus Politik und Zeitgeschichte*, 22/08/97, No. B35, pp.3-13.

Rexrodt, G. (1996) 'Gegen Konjunkturpessimismus', in: *Das Parlament*, Vol.46, No.15, p.17.

Rexrodt, G. (1996a) 'Opposition folgt alten Strickmustern', in: *Das Parlament*, Vol.46, No.19, pp.8-9.

Rhys-Williams, J. (1989) cf. Walter, T., *Basic Income - Freedom from Poverty, Freedom to Work*, Marion Boyars, London, p.117.

Riedel, M. (1973) 'Arbeit', in: Krings, H. *et al.*; *Handbuch philosophischer Grundbegriffe*, Kösel-Verlag, München, pp.125-141.

Rifkin, J. (1995) *The End of Work - The Decline of the Global Labor Force and the Dawn of the Post-Market Era*, Jeremy P. Tarcher / Putnam Books, New York.

Robbins, L. (1993) cf. Nelson, J. A., 'The Study of Choice or the Study of Provisioning? Gender and the Definition of Economics', in: Ferber, M. A. / Nelson, J. A. (eds); *Beyond Economic Man - Feminist Theory and Economics*, The University of Chicago Press, Chicago, p.25.

Robertson, J. (1986) 'What comes after full employment?', in: Ekins, P. (ed.); *The Living Economy*, Routledge, London, pp.85-96.

Robertson, J. (1989) *Future Wealth - A New Economics for the 21st Century*, Mansell Publishing, London.

Robson, W. A. (1977) *Welfare State and Welfare Society*, George Allen & Unwin, London.

Rogers, D. T. (1978) *The Work Ethic in Industrial America 1850-1920*, The University of Chicago Press, Chicago.

Rose, M. (1985) *Re-Working the Work Ethic - Economic Values and Socio-Cultural Politics*, Batsford Academic and Educational, London.

Rosenstiel, L. von (1996) *Motivation im Betrieb - Mit Fallstudien aus der Praxis*, Rosenberger Fachverlag, Leonberg.

Rousseau, J.-J. (1983) *Schriften zur Kulturkritik - Die zwei Diskurse von 1750 und 1755*, Felix Meiner Verlag, Hamburg.

Rowse, A. L. (1973) *The England of Elizabeth - The Structure of Society*, Cardinal, London.

rtf (1997) 'Unbezahlbare "Hausperlen"?', in: *Das Parlament*, Vol.47, No.19/20, p.2.

Ruse, M. (1985) *Sociobiology: Sense or Nonsense?*, Reidel Publishing Company, Dordrecht.

Russell, Bertrand (1958) 'In Praise of Idleness', in: *In Praise of Idleness and Other Essays*, George Allen & Unwin Ltd, London, pp.9-29.

Sachs, I. (1980) 'Gandhi and Development: A European View', in: J. Galtung / P. O'Brien / R. Preiswerk (eds); *Self-Reliance - A Strategy For Development*, Bogle-L'Ouverture Publications, London, pp.45-57.

Sahawe, N. (1996) *Conservative Party Conference Speech*, Bournemouth, 09/10/96, BBC2.

Sahlins, M. (1974) *Stone Age Economics*, Tavistock Publications, London.

Sahlins, M. (1976) *The Use and Abuse of Biology*, University of Michigan Press, Ann Arbor.

Samuelson, P. A. (1987) cf. Woll, A., *Allgemeine Volkswirtschaftslehre*, Verlag Franz Vahlen, München, p.3.

Sartre, J.-P. (1978) *Baudelaire*, Rowohlt, Reinbek.

Sartre, J.-P. (1985) '"Wir müssen unsere eigenen Werte schaffen"', in: *Sartre über Sartre*, Rowohlt, Reinbek, pp.129-143.

Sartre, J.-P. (1991) cf. Plant, R., *Modern Political Thought*, Basil Blackwell, Oxford, p.34.

Saunders, P. (1995) 'Improving Work Incentives in a Means-Tested Welfare System: The 1994 Australian Social Security Reform', in: *Fiscal Studies*, Vol.16, No.2, pp.45-70.

Schäuble, W. (1996) 'Steuererhöhungen ausgeschlossen', in: *Das Parlament*, Vol.46, No.8, p.8.

Schettkat, R. (1996) 'Das Beschäftigungsproblem der Industriegesellschaften', in: *Aus Politik und Zeitgeschichte*, 21/06/96, No.B26, pp.25-35.

Schönherr, J. (1991) 'Chancenlos? Gentechnik und die ökologische Krise', in: Wobus, A. / Wobus, U. (eds); *Genetik zwischen Furcht und Hoffnung*, Urania-Verlag, Leipzig, pp.109-123.

Schopenhauer, A. (1979) *Preisschrift über das Fundament der Moral*, Felix Meiner Verlag, Hamburg.

Schulte, D. (1996) 'So kann man nicht mit uns umgehen', in: *Die Zeit*, Vol.51, No.11, p.17.

Schumacher, E. F. (1979) *Good Work*, Jonathan Cape, London.

Schumacher, O. (1997) 'Blase geplatzt', in: *Die Zeit*, Vol.52, No.37, p.40.

Schwartz, R. L. (1995) 'Life Style, Health Status, and Distributive Justice', in: Grubb, A. / Mehlman, M. (eds); *Justice and Health Care: Comparative Perspectives*, John Wiley, Chichester, pp.225-250.

Seehofer, H. (1995) cf. Buhr, P., 'Sozialhilfe - Mythos und Realität, Klarstellungen zur aktuellen Reformdebatte', in: *Blätter für deutsche und internationale Politik*, Vol.40, No.9, p.1063.

Seehofer, H. (1996) 'Mehr soziale Gerechtigkeit', in: *Das Parlament*, Vol.46, No.11, p.14.

Seibt, F. (1990) 'Probleme der Wirtschaftsorganisation im Mittelalter', in: Engels, W. (ed.); *Arbeit und Einkommensverteilung in der Informationsgesellschaft der Zukunft*, Heidelberg, pp.79-95.

Seldon, A. (ed.) (1982) 'Preface', in: Parker, H., *The Moral Hazard of Social Benefits - A Study of the Impact of Social Benefits and Income Tax on Incentives to Work*, Institute of Economic Affairs, London, pp.7-8.

Sevenhuijsen, S. (1998) *Citizenship and the Ethics of Care*, Routledge, London.

Shankland, G. (1980) *Our Secret Economy - The Response of the Informal Economy to the Rise of Mass Unemployment*, Anglo-German Foundation, London and Bonn.

Sharpe, S. (1986) cf. Pascall, G., *Social Policy - A Feminist Analysis*, Tavistock Publications, London, p.57.

Showstack Sassoon, A. (1987) 'Women's New Social Role: Contradictions of the Welfare State', in: Showstack Sassoon, A. (ed.); *Women and the State - The Shifting Boundaries of Public and Private*, Hutchinson, London, pp.158-190.

Skillen, A. (1995) cf. Almond, B., 'Introduction: Ethical Theory and Ethical Practice', in: Almond, B. (ed); *Introducing Applied Ethics*, Blackwell Publishers, Oxford, p.1.

Smith, A. (1986) *The Wealth of Nations Books I-III*, Penguin Books, London.

Smith, J. (1992) 'Preface', in: Faludi, S.; *Backlash - The Undeclared War Against Women*, Vintage, London, pp.xiii-xv.

Snower, D. J. (1994) 'Why People Don't Find Work', in: Bryson, A. / McKay, S. (eds); *Is It Worth Working? Factors Affecting Labour Supply*, Policy Studies Institute, London, pp.39-59.

Solow, R. M. (1993) 'Feminist Theory, Women's Experience, and Economics', in: Ferber, M. A. / Nelson, J. A. (eds); *Beyond Economic Man - Feminist Theory and Economics*, The University of Chicago Press, Chicago, pp.153-158.

Sommer, T. (1995) 'Asien - Partner oder Widerpart?' in: *Zeitpunkte: Nach uns die Asiaten?*, No.4, pp.5-11.

Speakman, A. J. (1951) *Work Study and Incentives - An Introduction*, Emmott & Co., Manchester.

Standing, G. (1992) 'The Need for a New Social Consensus', in: Parijs, P. van (ed.); *Arguing for Basic Income - Ethical Foundations for a Radical Reform*, Verso, London, pp.47-60.

Steenblock, R. (1996) 'Signale für die Volkswirtschaft', in: *Das Parlament*, Vol.46, No.6, p.2.

Steinmo, S. (1994) 'The End of Redistribution? International Pressures and Domestic Tax Policy Choices', in: Bartel, R. D. (ed.); *Challenge - The Magazine of Economic Affairs*, M. E. Sharpe, New York, Vol.37, No.6, pp.9-17.

Stiglitz, J. E. (1994) *Whither Socialism?*, MIT Press, Cambridge, Massachusetts.

Tawney, R. H. (1990) cf. Furnham, A., *The Protestant Work Ethic - The Psychology of Work-Related Beliefs and Behaviours*, Routledge, London, p.1.

Taylor-Gooby, P. (1996) 'Paying for Welfare: The View from Europe', in: *The Political Quarterly*, Vol.67, No.2, pp.116-126.

Technology Foresight (1996) *Technology Foresight 3* on the Internet, www.open.gov.uk/ost/foresigh/p3. htm#3_01), 17/10/96.

Technology Foresight (1997) *Technology Foresight*, on the Internet, http://www.dti.gov.uk/ost/foresigh/driver. htm, 15/08/97.

Telfer, E. (1995) 'Self-Respect', in: Dillon, R. S. (ed.); *Dignity, Character and Self-Respect*, Routledge, London, pp.107-116.

Tenbrock, C. (1996) 'Das Ende einer Epoche', in: *Die Zeit*, Vol.51, No.33, p.19.

Tenbrock, R. H. / Goerlitz, E. (1966) *Die Zeit der abendländischen Christenheit*, Schöningh, Paderborn.

Tenhaef, R. (1997) 'Eine Halbierung ist nicht unmöglich', in: *Das Parlament*, Vol.47, No.13, p.2.

Tergeist, P. (1995) 'Introduction', in: *Flexible Working Time - Collective Bargaining and Government Intervention*, OECD, Paris, pp.9-16.

Thie, H. (1997) 'Die Schatten eines gepriesenen Vorbilds', in: *Das Parlament*, Vol.47, No.36, p.9, 29/08/97.

Tong, R. (1989) *Feminist Thought - A Comprehensive Introduction*, Unwin Hyman, London.

Toqueville, A. de (1997) *Memoir on Pauperism*, IEA Health and Welfare Unit, London.

Trivers, R. L. (1985) cf. Ruse, M., *Sociobiology - Sense or Nonsense*, D. Reidel Publishing Company, Dordrecht, p.69.

Trumbore, S. (1995) "*Homo Economicus*", on the Internet: http://www.cyberstreet .com/trumbore/sermons/ S5b1.htm, 22/05/97.

van Suntum, U. (1995) 'Hohe Arbeitslosigkeit in den Industrieländern - Was sagen die Ökonomen?', in: *Aus Politik und Zeitgeschichte*, 07/04/95, No. B15, pp.10-15.

Voelske, A. / Tenbrock, R. H. (1970) *Urzeit - Mittelmeerkulturen und werdendes Abendland*, Schöningh, Paderborn.

Vogel, C. (1990) 'Ethische Überlegungen zur Anthropologie und Ethologie', in: Herbig, J. / Hohlfeld, R. (eds); *Die zweite Schöpfung - Geist und Ungeist in der Biologie des 20. Jahrhunderts*, Carl Hanser Verlag, München, pp.122-131.

Vorholz, F. (1995) 'Ohrfeige für die Bremser', in: *Zeitpunkte: Wie teuer ist uns die Natur?*, No.6, pp.17-18.

Vorholz, F. (1995a) 'Die letzte Party', in: *Zeitpunkte: Wie teuer ist uns die Natur?*, No.6, pp.41-45.

Voss, G. (1995) 'Der Irrtum des Verzichts', in: *Zeitpunkte: Wie teuer ist uns die Natur?*, No.6, pp.54-55.

Wackwitz, S. (1997) 'Und ewig fiept das Tamagotchi', in: *Die Woche Extra*, 19/12/97, p.25.

Waigel, T. (1996) 'Neuer gesellschaftspolitischer Konsens', in: *Das Parlament*, Vol.46, No.7, p.2-3.

Walther, R. (1990) 'Arbeit - Ein begriffsgeschichtlicher Überblick von Aristoteles bis Ricardo', in: König, H. *et al.* (eds); *Sozialphilosophie der industriellen Arbeit*, Westdeutscher Verlag, Opladen, pp.3-25.

Waring, M. (1990) *If Women Counted - A New Feminist Economics*, HarperCollins, San Francisco.

Warr, P. (1985) cf. Handy, C., *The Future of Work*, Basil Blackwell, Oxford, p.165.

Wattenberg, B. J. (1996) *Welfare as Seen by Those Who Know*, on the Internet: http://www.aei.org:80/oti6829. htm, 08/96.

Weizsäcker, E. U. von (1994) 'Arbeit und Umwelt - Perspektiven für das 21. Jahrhundert', in: Hoffmann, H. / Kramer, D. (eds); *Arbeit ohne Sinn? Sinn ohne Arbeit? Über die Zukunft der Arbeitsgesellschaft*, Beltz athenäum, Weinheim, pp.69-86.

Weizsäcker, E. U. / Amery, B. / Hunter, L. L. (1995) *Faktor vier; Doppelter Wohlstand, halbierter Naturverbrauch*, Droemer Knaur, München.

Welzmüller, R. (1997) 'Zu den Folgen der Globalisierung für die nationalen Güter-, Finanz- und Arbeitsmärkte', in: *Aus Politik und Zeitgeschichte*, 08/08/97, No. B33-34/97, pp.20-28.

Wemegah, M. (1980) 'Self-Reliance and the Search for an Alternative Life-Style in Industrial Countries', in: Galtung, J. / O'Brien, P. / Preiswerk, R. (eds);

Self-Reliance - A Strategy For Development, Bogle-L'Ouverture Publications, London, pp.115-135.

Whalen, C. / Whalen, L. (1994) 'Institutionalism: A Useful Foundation For Feminist Economics?', in: Peterson, J. / Brown, D. (eds); *The Economic Status of Women Under Capitalism - Institutional Economics and Feminist Theory*, Edward Elgar, Aldershot, pp.19-34.

Wickler, W. (1990) 'Von der Ethologie zur Soziobiologie', in: Herbig, J. / Hohlfeld, R. (eds); *Die zweite Schöpfung - Geist und Ungeist in der Biologie des 20. Jahrhunderts*, Carl Hanser Verlag, München, pp.173-186.

Wiggins, D. (1991) cf. Plant, R., *Modern Political Thought*, Basil Blackwell, Oxford, pp.192-194.

Wilkinson, H. (1995) 'One Woman's Equality is Another's Poverty', in: *The Independent*, 10/03/95, p.23.

Wille, J. (1996) 'Neue Ideen brauchen 50 Jahre zur Durchsetzung', in: *Das Parlament*, Vol.46, No.30, p.9.

Willke, G. (1998) *Die Zukunft unserer Arbeit*, Bundeszentrale für politische Bildung, Bonn.

Wilson, E. (1975) *Sociobiology - The New Synthesis*, Harvard University Press, Cambridge, Massachusetts.

Wilson, E. (1978) *On Human Nature*, Harvard University Press, Cambridge, Massachusetts.

Wilson, Elisabeth (1977) *Women & the Welfare State*, Tavistock Publications, London.

Woll, A. (1987) *Allgemeine Volkswirtschaftslehre*, Verlag Franz Vahlen, München.

Wuketits, F. M. (1984) *Evolution, Erkenntnis, Ethik - Folgerungen aus der modernen Biologie*, Wissenschaftliche Buchgesellschaft, Darmstadt.

Wusfeld, D. R. (1994) *The Age of the Economist*, HarperCollins, New York.

Index